D0914253

# Continental Divides ∾

## Revisioning American Literature

*Anne E. Goldman*

palgrave

813.309978
G61c

CONTINENTAL DIVIDES
Copyright © Anne E. Goldman, 2000.
All rights reserved. No part of this book may be used or reproduced in any
manner whatsoever without written permission except in the case of brief
quotations embodied in critical articles or reviews.

First published 2000 by
PALGRAVE™
175 Fifth Avenue, New York, N.Y. 10010 and
Houndmills, Basingstoke, Hampshire, England RG21 6XS
Companies and representatives throughout the world.

PALGRAVE™ is the new global publishing imprint of St. Martin's
Press LLC Scholarly and Reference Division and Palgrave Publishers
Ltd (formerly Macmillan Press Ltd).

**Library of Congress Cataloging-in-Publication Data**
Goldman, Anne E., 1960-
    Continental Divides : revisioning American literature / Anne E.
Goldman.
        p.   cm.
    Includes bibliographical references and index.
    ISBN 0-312-23280-2
    1. American fiction—West (U.S.)—History and criticism. 2. American
fiction—19th century—History and criticism.   3. Frontier and pioneer life
in literature.   4. Regionalism in literature.   5. West (U.S.)—In literature.
I. Title.
PS271 G65   2000
813'.309978—dc21
                                                                00–038241

A catalogue record for this book is available from the British Library.

Design by Letra Libre, Inc.

First edition: October, 2000
10   9   8   7   6   5   4   3   2   1

*For my beautiful Zoë:*
*formidable artist,*
*sweetest of daughters*

University Libraries
Carnegie Mellon University
Pittsburgh, PA 15213-3890

# Contents

# Acknowledgments

Book projects are difficult to sustain without the faith, encouragement, support, and good humor of many people. This one is no exception. First of all, thanks to my family, for enriching my life with their collectively lively conversation, animated argument, and gifted storytelling: Zoë Pollak, Susan and David Faust, Julia Wada, Michael, Charles, Barbara, Julie, and Claire Goldman, and my brother David, without whose remembered presence this group is not complete. My parents have always supported and believed in my work; indeed, their unceasing care and confidence in me has made this project possible. My father Michael's generous help enabled me to continue working on this project during the year I moved back to California from Colorado. My mother Barbara spent hours snarled in Bay Area traffic and many more playing with Zoë when I was teaching late in Rohnert Park. My brother Charles's sense of humor helped me maintain my own. My sister Susie never failed to ask how the book was going; her thoughtful affirmations of my work have meant a great deal to me. My daughter Zoë put up with my constant return to the keyboard after hours with a kind of understanding people three times her age would find difficult to maintain. Her affectionate companionship enriches and sustains my life.

I would also like to thank my friends and colleagues for their personal support and professional help: Cynthia Franklin, whose entertaining and gracefully written E-mails could sell a lot more copies than any scholarly book and whose critical comments have clarified this book in countless ways; Sandra Gunning, whose unfailing encouragement and support have many times kept me from discouragement, and who has listened patiently across the miles to my protracted discussions of diverse academic difficulties; Amelia María de la Luz Montes, whose energy and enthusiasm makes me look forward to scholarly collaboration; Genaro Padilla, whose incomparable conversation never fails to make me laugh, and who always has faith in my work but never lets me get away with intellectual laziness; Eric Peterson, whose generous commentary on the Cather chapter has improved it immensely; Katheryn Rios, who made sure I wore a coat during Boulder winters and whose professional grace and integrity is a model for me; Terry Rowden, whose conversation enlivens even the tackiest of MLA convention rooms; and Jacqueline Shea-Murphy, whose expertise on regionalism has helped my own thinking and whose assurances that "small planes are the safest" work almost as well as wine.

At Sonoma State, I would like to thank Kelly Colbert, whose help I have appreciated immensely, and who is not only smart, but wise beyond her years; Helen Dunn, who is the kind of mentor all scholars dream about, and who has graciously hosted many events at her beautiful house; J. J. Wilson, whose thoughtfulness in bringing to my attention books, events, and people who might help my own work has been much appreciated; and the members of my writing group: Kim Hester-Williams, Scott Miller, Lisa Nakamura, LeiLani Nishime, and Tim Wandling—astute critics all whose scholarly help is only matched by their wonderful taste in food. At Boulder, Peyton Dryden and Melissa Green were exceptional students who graced my academic life and whose intellectual and personal gifts made them a joy to work with.

A number of institutions and grants have provided support for this project since its inception. An Ahmanson/Getty postdoctoral fellowship at UCLA helped initiate this project in 1993. At Boulder, junior faculty development and impart research grants sustained it. At Sonoma State, my work has been furthered by a summer fellowship as well as by a faculty diversity development program award. My thanks also go to the publishers with whose permission some of my earlier work appears: "Who ever heard of a blue-eyed Mexican?": Satire and Sentimentality in María Amparo Ruiz de Burton's *Who Would Have Thought It?* is reprinted with permission from the publisher of *Recovering the U.S. Hispanic Literary Heritage,* Volume II edited by Erlinda Gonzales-Berry and Chuck Tatum (Houston: Arte Público Press/ University of Houston, 1996); "'I think Our Romance is Spoiled,' or Crossing Genres: California History in Helen Hunt Jackson's *Ramona* and María Amparo Ruiz de Burton's *The Squatter and the Don*" originally appeared in Valerie Matsumoto and Blake Allmendinger, *Over the Edge: Remapping the American West* (Berkely: University of California Press, 1999) and is reprinted here with permission from the University of California Press.

And at Palgrave, my thanks and appreciation go to Kristi Long—fastest and best editor in East *or* West—Ella Pearce, Rick Delaney, Amy McDermott, and Karin Bolender, for their help preparing the manuscript.

Finally, this book is for you, ideal reader, without whom, of course, there would be no reason to write at all. Thank you for reading this.

# Preface

What does American literature beyond the Mason-Dixon line look like? From the perspective of the Old North Church, there really isn't one. Like the deft self-parody of New Yorker maps that reduce life beyond Eighty-second Street to a flat horizon line, the literary West cannot be readily discerned from the vantage of the East Coast. And because the *federal* United States remains with its center conceptually fixed as the aggregate of the original 13 stars and stripes, the national map stays two-toned, a conflict of North and South in black and white.

The literary topography is correspondingly monochromatic. While writers have begun in the last decade to critique the pervasiveness of the black-white dialectic, we are generally less inclined to honor the discrete particularities of local places than we are to interpret "the local" as metonymic of some conception of the national "whole."[1] The power of what Barry Lopez calls this "homogenized national geography" ensures our continued reliance on a calcified iconography for regional division in the U.S.: the Liberty Bell for New England, the auction block for the South, the mission arch for New Mexico and Arizona, the gold nugget for California.[2]

And so, the West: since Frederick Jackson Turner's elegy for the American "frontier" a century ago, both intellectual formulations and popular conceptions frame the desert as deserted, an unremitting wasteland softened only by a crepuscular sun poised in freeze frame at the horizon. From the prairie's "forgotten plough" magnified "black against the molten red" in Willa Cather's *My Ántonia,* to the eastbound train "diminished against the evening sky" in the "unfeatured wilderness" of *The Virginian,* to the "Evening Redness in the West" that subtitles Cormac McCarthy's *Blood Meridian;* from literary critic Jane Tompkins's geologic vacancy where "technology was primitive, physical conditions harsh, the social infrastructure nonexistent," to historian J. S. Holliday's precultural desert in which life is nasty, brutish, and short,[3] the West has been reduced to an exercise in self-imaging, the philosophical equivalent of the climbing wall at a city athletic club, a place existing to be scrambled up or ridden over, to be camped upon by scouts playing imaginary Indians or skied through by athletic "pioneers" longing for unbroken fields of powder.

Consider the West in what remains its most famous novel, Wister's *The Virginian*. Like California in Henry James's *The American Scene*, or the western landscapes of Stephen Crane's "The Bride Comes to Yellow Sky" and Cather's *The Song of the Lark*, we view the region from inside the window of a railroad car. Wister's first sentence positions reader and narrator as voyeurs onto the strange scenes of a remote land: "Some notable sight was drawing the passengers, both men and women, to the window; and therefore I rose and crossed the car to see what it was" (11). He closes the introductory chapter by rewriting the wide open space of a Wyoming sky as the sea, the departing eastbound train as a Pilgrim ship, and his narrator as William Bradford without the consolation of his own errand into the wilderness:

> The East-bound departed slowly into that distance whence I had come. I stared after it as it went its way to the far shores of civilization. It grew small in the unending gulf of space, until all sign of its presence was gone save a faint skein of smoke against the evening sky. And now my lost trunk came back into my thoughts, and Medicine Bow seemed a lonely spot. A sort of ship had left me marooned in a foreign ocean; the Pullman was comfortably steaming home to port, while I—how was I to find Judge Henry's ranch? Where in this unfeatured wilderness was Sunk Creek? (15)

Essentially travel narratives, such fictions paste western scenes into the pages of literary albums conceived and produced in New York and Boston.

Such is the potency of this iconography that it gets invoked by writers native to the West as often as by eastern travelers. In "Leaves from the Mental Portfolio of an Eurasian," Sui Sin Far celebrates the courage of her Chinese American heroine while recalling and revising the exhortation to "go west, young man": "I believe that some day a great part of the world will be Eurasian. I cheer myself with the thought that I am but a pioneer. A pioneer should glory in suffering."[4] If such literary recycling provides insights into the gap between discursive formation and regional social practice, it also continues to zone the literary West as a whites-only space. As Robert Shulman argues of Wister, the novelist "substitutes a mythic West for the workaday realities of cowboy life and the practices of big corporate ranchers in conflict with small ranchers, farmers, and townspeople" thereby contributing "to the enduring image of the West as predominantly white" (xvii, xxiii). As conventionally figured, diverse U.S. regions all too often are framed as the equivalent of time zones in a chronology of empire, the eastern wildernesses chastised by the Puritans, the western spaces made penitent a little later by their pioneer descendents.[5]

Since the discursive "local" cannot help but be scripted in relation to national stories, it would be naïve, as Steven Tatum reminds me in his essay "The Problem of the 'Popular' in the New Western History," to attempt to "get 'beyond' the mythic West."[6] I am not trying in this book to escape narrative configurations of region. Rather, I wish to argue that as described by conventional literary historiography, their outlines are overly confined. The two-dimensional template often used to map regional relations is simply not plastic enough to represent the contingent and shifting relationships between these "united" states. This book understands the interconnections between sections as complexly dynamic, more like the travel routes of an urban rapid transit system or the constantly shifting ratios of energy bundling between urban areas, rural locations, states, and regional areas that compose our nation's interconnected electrical systems.

Like Anna Deavere Smith, who sees in California an "opportunity" to reconsider "the American character," I wish to foreground the (literary) West as the perspective from which to figure American literary history more generally. The essays in this volume juxtapose African American, Mexican American, and Anglo American fictions produced in the wake of the Civil War and the U.S.-Mexican War—contiguous national conflicts that remain segregated in critical practice—as a case study for rethinking American raced formations and regional inflections. They also juxtapose regions, by comparing narratives set in Boston and San Diego, New Mexico and Washington, D.C., South Carolina and San Francisco. I argue here not only "for inclusion of the United States-Mexico border experience within cultural studies," as José Saldívar suggests in *Border Matters*, but also for an understanding of the inextricability of this region's tensions with other sectional issues in the United States.[7]

Being a local does not mean that our understandings of the rest of the world are by definition insular or provincial. We need not jettison thick description of particular places, but rather substitute a more flexible metaphor in place of the lingua franca current in American Studies, a vocabulary that has itself been appropriated from the disciplines of geography and cartography: of borders and zones, of maps and sites, of locations, locations, locations. On the one hand, this self-consciousness about point of view is critically productive, admitting the possibility of different perspectives. On the other hand, despite the collective agreement to honor the liminality of border zones and the complications of multiple sitings, such cartographic metaphors recall both the colonial past we are ostensibly critiquing and the integrity of the nation-states we affirm, over and over, to be political fictions. Despite the celebratory affirmation of "no borders here," a mission statement for companies like MCI and Sprint as much as for scholars who vilify the ills of global capitalism, the result is often not a complicating of identity and loyalty but a constricting of both: "subversive" or "accommodating," "nationalistic" or "resistant" to patriotism, "central" or "marginal."

Just as the pattern of light and dark in a photographic negative resolves into intelligibility only when we look at individual shadings in relation to the entire gray scale, so the regional narratives that make up American literature cannot be appraised in isolation. Any geographical or literary site is the locus for the articulation of many different understandings of home, and these expressions are themselves informed by ideas about what is *not* home. This book understands location as relation rather than as fixed center, by investigating regional narratives at their crossings. The railroad provided many turn-of-the-century Anglo American writers with a potent metaphor for Manifest Destiny, but as Genaro Padilla reminds me, it also provided African American men in the South and the North with work as dining car chefs and Mexican American fathers laboring in western yards with the opportunity to take their children on vacation trips to see the rest of the country.[8] Notwithstanding the myth of pilgrims' progress that animates both historiographic and literary understandings of the United States ("Go west, young man!), Americans have always traveled across the continent in more than one direction.

While the essays in this volume treat literature by women and men, by sojourners, recent immigrants, and western natives whose families have lived in the region for more generations than the Daughters of the American Revolution can count on their fingers, they are collectively sustained by a focus on rhetorical patterns and metaphors of travel across (ostensibly) separate domains: public sphere and private home, feminine drawing room and masculine war theater, foreign policy and domestic law. Taken together, the narratives they consider plot marriages between races and religions, develop class affiliations across regional divides, and point to political interests that transgress normative social and geographic understandings. Ultimately, my arguments are designed to question critical sectionalism as much as regional divisions, by blurring generic distinctions, by reading across literary periods, and by juxtaposing writers who explore the same set of social issues during the same historical moment, but who are nonetheless conventionally segregated into separate literary "traditions"—sentimental literature, the African American novel, literary modernism, early Mexican American fiction.

The late nineteenth-century writings of María Amparo Ruiz de Burton, whose novels foreground the social and political problems framed by the U.S.-Mexican War and the Civil War, constitute the narrative backbone of this study. Accounting for her life and work demands a more complex model of American identity than is admitted by the schematics of conventional regional parameters. As a Californiana who championed the rights of Mexicanos but who lived for over a decade on the East Coast, Ruiz de Burton's experience shows up the limitations of the separate-but-equal theory of sectional divides. She protested as vociferously of the illegal appropriation of Mexican land in her fictions, written in English, as in her Spanish-language correspondence with longtime friend General Mariano Vallejo. As a descendent of one of the oldest and most respected families in Mexican California, she identified with what was essentially an aristocratic political tradition; nonetheless, she campaigned successfully at the White House to obtain an audience with the president himself to ask for a raise in her husband's pension. An intimate of President Lincoln's wife Mary, she simultaneously maintained a friendship with Verena Davis, the wife of ex-Confederacy President Jefferson Davis.

Her novels likewise flout the regional quarantines established by literary historiography. Where the path of American heroes in fiction and chronicle is fixedly westward, her Californiana heroine in *Who Would Have Thought It?* travels east to Boston, while her young protagonist's New-England-bred-neighbor goes south to Mexico. And where California's contributions to the national scene until the mid-twentieth century are typically restricted to natural wonders (Ansel Adams, John Muir, and Jack London compose a triumvirate of spokesmen for the state), Ruiz de Burton forgoes Half Dome and mountain passes to focus on the domed ceiling of the Opera House and the social altitudes of San Francisco high society.

Besides proving a cogent metaphor for the overlapping boundary lines of race and region the book investigates, Ruiz de Burton's fictions, with their convoluted sentimental plotting and rapier-sharp satire, their lampooning of feminine vapors and masculinist political institutions alike, their merciless parody of Brahmin pretensions and their championing of "Spanish" bluebloods, suggest that the literary "best in the West" need not always be conflated with the "wild West"—whether this be Joaquín Murrieta's or Buffalo Bill's.

In fact, literature west of the Mason-Dixon line is both far more complicated and a great deal more varied in tone, genre, gender, and argument than both the trade and academic presses make out. [9] It is also far more connected with other regional formations. The thinly populated western landscapes of Owen Wister's novels and Frederic Remington's paintings, for instance (artists who have defined the region) are developed in response to their antipathy—explicitly voiced and collectively shared—toward the immigrants crowding Ellis Island's holding rooms and New York's tenements. Such efforts at regional distancing in their turn help to shape the direction of travel endorsed by Ruiz de Burton's fictions.

But this book, as Forrest Robinson says of his own essay in *The New Western History*, is not designed to be "all-embracing."[10] The survey is a scholarly necessity, but it has its limitations. Descriptions of the literary landscape as it has been conventionally agreed upon are useful teaching tools because they train readers to navigate the field by looking for a standardized set of literary signposts. But in establishing and agreeing upon such conventions, we risk forgetting that they have been imposed upon a landscape so that we might find our way through it more quickly. Claims of representative status to the contrary, any survey to some extent assumes what it sets out to prove as normative. If we substitute another set of western texts in place of the groupings conventionally framed as "western," we see a different series of literary signposts, which in turn leads us to a different description of the field.

At this point, new scholarly landscaping seems warranted. A certain conceptual laziness continues in large part to characterize both popular and scholarly assumptions about the West and western literature.[11] The livid hues of the Grand Canyon in ads for sports utility vehicles and the "Evening Redness in the West" that is perennially the standard of fiction have colored our regional understandings for too long. While contemporary political assessments examine California as a kind of test-tube culture for predicting and diagnosing the nation's ills, such sunset accounts of western cultural practice seem congealed in a history textbook that has not made it past a first edition. This book selects a new collection of narratives about region in place of the masculine terrain synonymous with muscularity, dynamism, and the virile rhetoric of Marlboro Men from Jack London's Klondike adventurers through Jack Shaefer's Shane to Cormac McCarthy's soulless, if critical, reappraisal of westward expansion in *Blood Meridian*.[12] Finally, while essays delineate the itineraries that connect American places, they also privilege a close focus to develop what Barry Lopez in "The American Geographies" calls a knowledge of regional relationships that is "intimate rather than encyclopedic" (133).

The book's opening chapter provides a theoretical introduction for reading American literary historiography interregionally. Merely filling in that part of the map that has been inadequately colored and contoured will not radically shift its skewed center, the introduction argues. The chapters that follow develop comparative cultural readings that revise American history from locations west of the continental divide, gloss texts that represent the West from urban "centers" like Boston, and consider novels that explore the national government in Washington, D.C., as a primary site for interregional exchange. In all of these fictions, multiple vectors of travel contrast pointedly with linear myths of our national origins.

Chapter 1 juxtaposes Henry James's *The Bostonians* with María Amparo Ruiz de Burton's *Who Would Have Thought It?* to demonstrate that their literary common ground describes a national space more complex than the regional absolute values we construct when we "map" discrete regions. Just as Ruiz de Burton's Lola embodies regional relations by traveling east to occupy the paternal heart of the "blue Presbyterians," so James's Basil Ransom is a pale substitute for the "tatterdemalion darkies" who migrate north after the Civil War, the transplanted southerner who figures the nation's "black" contradictions and in so doing, defuses the immigrant threat to East Coast shores.

Succeeding chapters further this exploration of national identity as it is defined over and against regionally scripted notions of the "native." Chapter 2 looks closely at two literary assessments of the right of way in post-1848 California. Censuring the raced laws of primogeniture affirmed by contemporaries like Gertrude Atherton, Frank Norris, Josephine Clifford McCrackin, and Josiah Royce, María Amparo Ruiz de Burton's *The Squatter and the Don* invokes political scandals and contests over land with legal precision. If Helen Hunt Jackson's story of *Ramona* inflects justice differently, the novel nonetheless frames critique and apology as historical corrections necessary to settle political accounts. Both fictions represent the post-1848 literary West as a place of contending forces.

Chapter 3 considers Ruiz de Burton's *Who Would Have Thought It?* within another American literary milieu—Spanish-language newspapers published in the U.S. following the Treaty of Guadalupe-Hidalgo. By foregrounding the travels of a Yankee veteran freed from southern imprisonment who chooses to live in Mexico rather than return to New England, this novel critiques the nationalist discourse of the Civil War as a cover for the same commercial interests that catalyze the U.S.-Mexican War. When, having become disenchanted with the federal policy he learns is the root cause of his confinement in a southern jail, Isaac chooses Mexico over the Northeast, Ruiz de Burton indicts what looks like a sectional corruption—the secession of the South—as a systemic evil. This defiant itinerary complicates the ethnic dichotomies written into the history of the United States at the same time as it stands as a metaphor for its gendered polarities. The book's sentimental battleground—occasioned by what to do with Lola, the Californiana raised in the Norvals' Boston home—allows Ruiz de Burton to parody the masculine war theater and to conflate two spheres kept separate, namely, the domain of political event and action and the private, feminized world of marriage and family life.

Even in narratives that are ostensibly structured upon divisions between North and South, the West, like a close-mouthed politician, carries a cultural weight in excess of its tangential plot value. The final two chapters consider relationships between Washington, D.C., and California in order to expose conventional representations of "center" and "periphery" as cultural fictions. Chapter 4 considers two novels that plot congressional proceedings in the capitol as inextricable from the lives of westerners who appear to poach upon New England's territory. In *Senator North,* Gertrude Atherton defuses class-based anxieties about the nation by exploiting the figure of the western senator, whose political aims define themselves over and against the interests of the New England aristocrat. On the other hand, in her serialized novel *Hagar's Daughter: A Story of Southern Caste Prejudice,* Pauline Hopkins embodies the West through gendered figures that speak simultaneously for racially coded values. Conceived on a southern plantation, bred on a western ranch, educated in a northern school, Hopkins's heroine Jewel Bowen embodies Hopkins's revisionary regional dialectic, providing her with a means to interrupt the apparently calcified iconography of North and South. And as a "western girl" with her pistol in her hand,[13] Jewel plays upon the dime novel, a literary form produced out of the New England publishing establishment, which remains in the critical literature virtually synonymous with western writing.

While these novels frame the center of government as a switching station for the traffic between regions, Willa Cather's *The Song of The Lark* uses the figure of the train operator to fulfill the nationalist mandate "Westward the course of Empire takes its way."[14] The final chapter considers the racialized figures Cather exploits to establish a relationship between empire and sexual difference. At the heart of this intersection is the effeminized figure of the Jew, the domesticated but "exotic" "stranger" who cannot be adopted into the nation's "family circle."[15] Conventional history rewrites the conquest of Mexican land as a domestic "annexation;" Cather exploits the metaphor of home (recall the title of *The Professor's House*) to cement this relationship. That is, she uses a gendered metaphor of domesticity as a civilizing force to simultaneously justify *and* cover over imperial relationships. Considered more closely, Cather's sexualizing of imperial appropriation provides opportunities for examining relationships between sectional conflict, nationalism, and imperial designs.

Notwithstanding their different resolutions of sociocultural conflict, all of the writers examined in this study unequivocally politicize "home." Since the private cannot be made public without risk to middle class femininity, these authors bring the world to the confines of the drawing room, exploiting the feminine domain as a place where political ills can be articulated and resolved. In its turn, this conflation of spheres becomes a metaphor for the inextricability of domestic politics and international affairs. As American Studies scholars, we can read the pointedly gendered language such writers use to connect the political spaces of public and private in order to explore relationships between the languages of nationalism and empire, two kinds of political expression all too often framed as separate endeavors.

The epilogue considers a number of other representations of cultural theft from the turn of the century to its closing, in order to contextualize Cather's depictions of cultural appropriation and to look more generally at narrative efforts to fashion an American aesthetic native to the western region. From Zane Grey's delineation of Cliff City pottery shards through Cather's reworking of this scene on the mesa, to Barry Lopez's musings on his own interest in native pottery, writers have explored indigenous cultural practice as an index for the relationship between the western desert and conceptions of nation.

As a whole, the book's six chapters examine representations of the West as it is constituted by the people who move into and out of this region, traveling not only from East to West and North to South, but also from and to Mexico, against those directions of regional traffic mythologized as the historical norms. By invoking the West as a third geographical register, the novels considered here encourage us to consider political imperatives that are invisible when framed conventionally in two regional dimensions. In its ability to generate difference, by fracturing the national space along several regional axes that is, the West circumvents the unshaded "solutions" produced by the reductive regional "either/or" of North over South.

# Introduction ∽

# Location, Location, Location

## Complicating Transnational Readings of American Literary History

### I: Beyond Black and White Readings of American Culture

Question: "Why were the Mexicans at the battle of Buena Vista like good wine?" Answer: "Because they both run from the grape." Hardly a distinctive riddle in the wake of the 1848 Treaty of Guadalupe-Hidalgo that closes the U.S.-Mexican War. More surprising, however, is its publishing venue: this anti-Mexican puzzle, reproduced in Eric Lott's 1993 study *Love and Theft*, is printed at the bottom of a page of lyrics for the song "Why does dat Darkey follow me so?" in the *Minstrel Songbook* of 1848. If we consider that the popularity of the minstrel show, according to Lott, peaks in 1846, we can read this kind of performance not only as working out the tensions surrounding the slavery question, but as a way of handling the repercussions of the Mexican War as well.[1]

Lott does not pick up on the interregional play provided in the illustration he reproduces, but its caption and accompanying riddle are worth considering more closely. The text of the song occupies most of the page; at the bottom, separated from it by a line divider, are printed the riddle and its answer (172). The question alludes in several ways to the title of the song; the opening "Why" echoes the first word of the song and establishes itself as a parallel interrogation, while the central pun of the riddle, "run from" mirrors the title's verb phrase "follow me." The syntactical play of the question and response set the two conflicts in structural and thematic opposition. The Mexican soldiers and the black man of song and riddle are both described in relation to a white interlocutor; the former threatens to "follow," while the latter—recall that this is 1848, the year of the signing of the Treaty of Guadalupe-Hidalgo—has already "run." Represented as mirror images, the "darkey" and "the Mexicans" of top and bottom of the page implicate the two conflicts as twin sides of the same nationalist coin.

In fact, late nineteenth-century literature frequently plays out such inter-regional cultural formations. Californiana writer María Amparo Ruiz de Burton stages a meeting of frontier hero and blackface performer in her 1872 novel *Who Would Have Thought It?* The narrative conflates the captivity narrative and the minstrel show through its heroine, Lola, a Mexicana born into an Indian captivity in California who is taken into the abolitionist household of a Boston physician. In *Blackface, White Noise: Jewish Immigrants in the Hollywood Melting Pot,* Michael Rogin plots the shift from captivity narrative to minstrelsy as a telos charting two centuries of national growth; as "the first American national literature," the former gives way to minstrelsy as "the first . . . form of nineteenth-century mass culture." [2] But Ruiz de Burton's deft restaging of both, in the character of the Californiana she transplants to Boston, suggests we upset this traditional literary chronology in favor of a more flexible historiography that can account for relations *between* such cultural phenomena.

Nor is Ruiz de Burton alone in establishing links between political conflicts treated as absolute values by scholars. Lott's argument about the origins of minstrelsy on the docks and waterfronts of northern and western cities corrects a misguided notion of blackface as the product of the plantation South's aristocratic big houses. But this attention to region simultaneously links continental expressions of Manifest Destiny with national articulations of empire. Even a cultural romantic like Frank Dobie reminds us of the relationship between southern secessionists and westward expansionists when he describes the political ambitions of nineteenth-century vigilantes in *San Francisco: A Pageant* to found what they hoped, following the aspirations of southern gentlemen, would become "an independent Pacific Republic."[3]

What might American culture look like if we read it from the perspective of such interregional exchanges? This study begins with the premise that regional relationships in both the nineteenth- and twentieth-century United States are more complicated than the scheme literary historiography traditionally maps around North-South conflicts. Despite repeated calls for revision, much work in American Studies continues to envision the nation as plotted around the Mason-Dixon line, with the Civil War as its privileged metaphor. My book considers fictions published in and about California and the West post-1848 as a way of enriching the regional and raced patterns that inform our assumptions about literary America. Its chapters explore issues in American Studies through comparative readings: They consider how the "center" is regionalized in books like Henry James's *The Bostonians* and in Californiana writer María Amparo Ruiz de Burton's critique of New England in *Who Would Have Thought It?* They examine rhetorical and conceptual links between representations of Manifest Destiny in the turn-of-the-century sentimental novel and modernist reworkings of the relationship between race, region, and empire in the Southwestern novels of Willa Cather. They ask how we read the classed registers of abolitionist discourse when we speak from a western space. They survey the late-nineteenth-century historical romance to examine how mixed marriage in books by Gertrude Atherton and Helen Hunt Jackson, and in short fictions published in *The Century* and *The Overland Monthly* attempt to resolve land litigation, and they examine arguments about citizenship made by Californians appealing land grant cases before the Supreme Court in Washington, D.C.

In the process, my book critiques some contemporary models of nineteenth-century literary historiography. By situating the United States as a colonial power, the increasing internationalization of American Studies acts as a corrective to provincial studies of American culture. I locate my own work alongside such projects, which reappraise "regional" practices once framed as peripheral (narratives of border regions or of the Pacific Rim, for example), over and against the rhetoric of the national "center." By refusing to exoticize such locales as marginal, the new regional studies discourages oversimplified models of "difference" framed as distinct from "normative" conditions of American life. Notwithstanding such provocative work in border studies, however, much transnational theory runs the risk of oversimplifying the rich web of raced relations that constitutes the United States. American Studies scholars who rely too heavily upon European postcolonial models often misread or ignore the historical idiosyncrasies of the American continent. Furthermore, focusing upon the legacy of slavery as the primary form of global imperialism can lead to models of literary history that privilege the Civil War as paradigmatic of American difference, reducing the complicated patterning of race relations to a single debate between North and South. This iconography of regionalism does little to unseat New England's continued status as cultural center of the United States and originary metaphor for national identity. Instead, it sustains what José Saldívar in *Border Matters* aptly calls "the great discontinuity between the American frontier and *la frontera*."[4]

This book examines fictions that revise ideas about American history and culture from locations west of the continental divide, not to "fill in" a part of the map whose topography has remained inadequately contoured, but to rethink the regional relationships that constitute the United States as a whole.[5] Although the language of "remapping" occupies pride of place in contemporary reformulations of American Studies, perhaps cartography is the wrong metaphor, a two-dimensional image too flat to register the shifting relations between sections, a practice too steeped in imperial mapmaking to recognize intercultural reference sufficiently.[6] Rather than coloring in regions, we might instead focus upon their interrelation: the political and social pressure points that originate in one area but that prompt similar fractures in other sections; the stresses that develop in different regions simultaneously, but whose implications are not confined to a particular geography.[7] Like Jesús Velasco-Márquez, who asserts that we "cannot understand the Civil War without understanding the U.S.-Mexican War," my interest is in demonstrating the political, social, and cultural inextricability of the multiple geographic fractures that divide and connect the nation.[8] Rather than call for greater inclusiveness per se, or substitute one regional mapping for another, I want to examine the extent to which regional identities, like the Hegelian self and other, produce one another.

This book considers western literature from a variety of locations; nonetheless, I wish to emphasize its local inflections as a case study. While I hope it can engage with corollary projects on Hawaiian narrative, midwestern culture, the arts of the eastern seaboard, and southern cultural studies, this book is rooted in observations made from my own vantage point as a scholar of African American, Jewish American, and Chicana/o cultural practice and as a resident of urban Northern California. The San Francisco Bay Area is home to immigrants from Cambodia and India, longtime Italian residents, recently arrived Russian Jews, Chicanos whose families have lived and worked here for generations, first- and second-generation Californians from Vietnam and Mexico, Laos and Guatemala. Yet the nuanced relationship among and between our cultural practices does not get discussed—in any sustained way—in much of the most visible work in American cultural studies, those projects framed as centrally located within the Academy. This is not to point to any paucity of scholarship: my work on María Amparo Ruiz de Burton is indebted to other critics in Chicano Studies who think within and through the multiple junctures and intersections of American cultural practices, scholars including Jesse Alemán, José Aranda, Amy Doherty, John González, Erlinda Gonzales-Berry, Ramón Gutiérrez, María Herrera-Sobek, Douglas Monroy, Amelia de la Luz Montes, Genaro Padilla, Vincent Pérez, Tey Diana Rebolledo, and José Saldívar.[9] These scholars call attention to the fact that the literary map continues to be framed in black and white. Contemporary models in American Studies gesture toward more expansive theories of raced and regionalized values, but the fact remains that cultural studies work that does not concentrate upon the North-South conflict is often denied the wider circulation and institutional support that projects focused upon the Anglo American and African American canons enjoy.[10]

## II: "the New England homogeneous"

If the cultural script of the "Gas, Food, Lodging" sign is a constant across freeways from I-80 to I-10, critical assessments in American literary historiography maintain a similar fixity. Notwithstanding heralds of a "dramatic transformation in the self-understanding of American Studies,"[11] this book argues that "our national literature" remains centered within the culture of New England. From William Bradford to James Fenimore Cooper to Nathaniel Hawthorne to Henry James, literary America occupies only a small part of what since the end of the U.S.-Mexican War we designate as the continental United States. Contemporary work in American Studies continues to skew the topography of region so that Chicago, Denver, San Francisco, Los Angeles, and other points west and south of New England remain vanishing points on the horizon line.

Is there a way to recontour the map of American literature so that its regions interlock without buckling and without forcing one area, like some overworked tectonic plate, to direct the rest? To comment on the provincialism of the literary canon hardly constitutes a paradigm shift, but if the cultural coordinates of "region" and "nation" are as familiar for contemporary criticism in American Studies as Paul Revere's ride has been for American history, they remain in a cherished academic condition: contested, that is, without being displaced. Historians and literary scholars celebrate methodological "border crossings" as inroads to a less parochial regionalism, examining empire as the invisible third term in the region-nation equation. New Western historians such as Patricia Limerick, Richard White, Brian Dippie, and Michael Malone call for a "politics of location" to defend against critical recolonization, while literary scholars including Donald Pease, Carolyn Porter, Rob Wilson, and Philip Fisher invoke "transnationalism" as a response to provincial studies in cultural geography.[12]

But introducing the workings of "empire" as a third term in the region-nation quadratic does not necessarily nuance the equation. However promising in theory, calls for resituating the United States over and against global imperialism are in practice little more accommodating than the calcified opposition they are designed to supplant. Just as "region" stood in relation to "nation" (the former less significant because "narrower" than the latter), so "nation" in contemporary theory is slighted in favor of "empire." There are, of course, exceptions to this scholarly rule. The subtitle of Amy Kaplan's introductory essay to *Cultures of United States Imperialism* comments upon "The Absence of Empire in the Study of American Culture." "How would this Eurocentric notion of postcoloniality apply to the history of American imperialism," Kaplan asks, "which often does not fit this model?" (17). This important acknowledgement of the European perimeters of postcolonial study opens space for more historicized assessments of the imperial United States. Likewise, Paul Gilroy argues for considering "the ethnohistorical specificity of the discourse of cultural studies itself," and notes that "it is hard not to wonder how much of the recent enthusiasm for cultural studies is generated by its profound associations with England and ideas of Englishness."[13] In "Nationalism and Contemporaneity: Political Economy of a Discourse," Alok Yadav insists that "the overwhelming focus on the dangers of nationalism" are "often drawn from European experience, but applied to the non-European world."[14]

For the most part, however, writers who invoke global models of empire in American Studies borrow heavily and indiscriminately from postcolonial theory without acknowledging its geographical and intellectual roots in the histories of British and European imperialism. Just as U.S. literary scholars tend to look eastward, defining the canon in relation to its European antecedents but ignoring how it characterizes itself over and against indigenous American literatures, so European intellectual configurations all too often function as the methodological North Star for theorists in American Studies, effacing what Eric Lott calls "peculiarly American structures" (18).[15] Moreover, thanks in part to postcolonial theory's failure to historicize its intellectual origins, the European example of imperialism has become a metonym for global forms of empire. I will explore the implications of this borrowing in the sections that follow; suffice to say here, however, that the results for contemporary paradigms in American Studies are unrewarding. Insufficiently attentive to class differences between British and American models of cultural studies, such projects exploit the "diasporic" to explain patterns of immigration to the United States that do not conform to postcolonial definitions of "the exile" and "the nomad." By mistakenly conflating "nation" with (official, as opposed to insurgent forms of) European "nationalism,"[16] they do not transform this relationship but simply effect a substitution of terms, leaving the central equation intact.

As I have suggested at the opening of this essay, filling in the contours of those sections of the literary map dismissed as beyond the pale will not shift its skewed center. The regional metaphors contemporary scholars of American Studies invoke to interrogate the relation between the two terms that make up the "United States" are simply not plastic enough to describe border dialectics. Surely this "union" is itself a metaphysical conceit (unlike political constructs yoked by violence together) requiring an equally dynamic critical rubric to accommodate its tensions. We need to consider the ways in which sectional borders are traversed—not only from east to west and north to south, but against those directions of regional traffic mythologized as the historical norms—so that we can arrive at more satisfying accounts of the relationships between them. Rather than practicing a kind of critical postmortem by sticking colored pins into the national map, we might instead focus upon the *movements* between such points and spaces.[17]

Insisting upon travel does not in and of itself correct the center-periphery model, however. In *Questions of Travel: Postmodern Discourses of*

*Displacement,* Caren Kaplan examines the ideological work this metaphor provides for postmodern theory: "Topography and geography now intersect literary and cultural criticism in a growing interdisciplinary inquiry."[18] But they "do not necessarily liberate critical practices from the very conundrum of aestheticization and universalization that spurred a search for alternative metaphors and methods in the first place" (144). Like Kaplan, I would insist we historicize the critical terrain we traverse. But a substantial shift in point of view will not be accomplished simply by rewriting "place[s] on a map" as "place[s] in history" (24). Since "place" can only be glossed contextually, it is the entire field of places and their relations to one another that we need to reassess. Rather than discard the chronological grid in favor of a spatial metaphor, we might reconsider the conventional relationship literary study assumes between the two. While science has long since moved beyond Newtonian physics to embrace flexible models like chaos and string theory, scholarly work in literature remains obdurately devoted to a Cartesian model that forces all movement to conform to a single telos. Hence the centrality of a narrative like *The Pilgrim's Progress* to the British canon, where each step the protagonist takes coordinates with an ethical register to reproduce a scale of values. Or, on U.S. shores, consider a story like Nathaniel Hawthorne's "Young Goodman Brown"—again, we are in the world of Euclidean geometry and Cartesian geography, one where spatial coordinates plot moral "intentionality." Interregional and international travel in the texts this book discusses flout the kind of linear movement easily congruent with such a telos. The multidirectional quality of border crossing clarifies the constructed nature of distinctions between center and margin, suggesting we put less interpretive pressure on such definitions.

Nor will celebrating the permeability and instability of decontextualized "borders" correct this reliance on fixed coordinates. Fetishized as the sites of contested and "third" spaces, border zones all too often become generic markers—geographic ciphers for citing postmodern theory. Notwithstanding its fine examination of a transnational black cultural practice, Paul Gilroy's *The Black Atlantic: Modernity and Double Consciousness* provides a case in point. Gilroy exploits the ship as an icon for cultural affiliations that operate in defiance of national borders ("sailors . . . crossing borders in modern machines that were themselves micro-systems of linguistic and political hybridity" [12]), in order to consider the cross-Atlantic connections of writers like Richard Wright and W.E.B. DuBois. In the process, he critiques "Historians of ideas and movements" who "have generally preferred to stay within the boundaries of nationality and ethnicity and have shown little enthusiasm for connecting the life of one movement with that of another" [186]). The relations Gilroy establishes between movements suggest we reconsider racial identity as defined by nationalism. In order to span the nautical miles, however, these intellectual crossings blur the vagaries of particular coastlines. Statements like this one: "Whether their experience of exile is enforced or chosen, temporary or permanent, these [African American and Caribbean] intellectuals and activists, writers, speakers, poets, and artists repeatedly articulate a desire to escape the restrictive bonds of ethnicity, national identity, and sometimes even 'race' itself" (19) run the risk of oversimplifying the complex relationships between such forms of self-identification.

More importantly, the pan-African affiliations Gilroy uncovers are cemented through a shared critical practice as much as they are named by an "essential" cross-Atlantic cultural patterning in the primary texts themselves. What in part enables the transnational focus of this study, in other words, is the set of canonical texts that comprises its backbone. Their widespread circulation, and the shared assumptions of the intellectual community within which they are read, is a *metaphor for* rather than an *argument of* transnational cultural practice. Without figures like Wright and DuBois as international currency, these cross-Atlantic linkages look more tenuous.

In this book I wish to work toward a trans*continental* rather than a trans*national* critical practice, by juxtaposing narratives that image travel across the continent, in order to articulate the raced coordinates of sectional conflicts and their relation to imperial tensions. In its insistence that regionalist discourse serves as an acronym for a constellation of ideas about racial identity, cultural practice, class positioning, and nationalist and imperialist projects, my own project develops out of the work of many scholars in American Studies. In particular, Carolyn Porter's wide-ranging critical survey, "What We Know that We Don't Know: Remapping American Literary Studies," has helped shape my thinking. But to my mind, this and other fine readings of region—classic studies like Henry Nash Smith's *Virgin Land*[19] and contemporary reevaluations like Amy Kaplan's "Nation, Region and Empire"—exoticize regional literatures distinct from the Northeast by defining them with reference to the publishing industries of Boston and New York. If we grant the hegemony of eastern literary enterprises like Beadle's western dime novel series, we need not dismiss those narratives about the West published within it.[20]

Despite their condescension toward the regional arts they exported, writers like Frank Dobie and Mary Austin represent the cultural practices of the West and Southwest in relation to a nationalist agenda. In turn, they define this agenda with an eye toward the network of intracontinental relations that characterize it—a purview it would serve contemporary scholars to reconsider. Where much current work sets the regional in opposition to the national, Dobie's 1933 study of the history and literature of California effectively regionalizes the history of the East Coast and gestures toward the sectional affiliations that constitute the nation. "In . . . 1834," he writes, "[T]he roster of voters [in the legislative body of the territory of California] is filled with names borne by the soldiers who under Anza and Moraga had entered California in the same year that the Liberty Bell in Philadelphia was announcing the birth of a nation" (73–74). Insofar as it establishes parallel "creation stories" of the United States on either coast, we can read Dobie's comment as refusing the metonymic relation of region and nation in which the eastern seaboard comes to stand in for the country as a whole.

Nor should we forget to locate books published out of the Northeast as themselves regionally constituted. Few glosses of Frank Norris's *The Octopus* fail to insist upon the text as a California product. The most recent Penguin Classic edition, introduced by California historian Kevin Starr, appeals to the growing number of contemporary readers interested in American regional literatures.[21] But how many critics of Nathaniel Hawthorne's *The Scarlet Letter* concentrate their attention on the local history out of which its central romantic plot unfolds, namely the Indian conflicts known as King Philip's War?[22] My point is not to discredit interdisciplinary projects like the Penguin edition—far from it—but simply to highlight how critical glosses of nineteenth-century literature may reproduce the distorted regional map.

The late nineteenth-century California writer María Amparo Ruiz de Burton's own fictions, for instance, situate us within the wake of two ruptures typically framed as regional absolute values: the U.S.-Mexican War and the Civil War. Her novels constitute themselves within and against a number of discourses: Manifest Destiny, the closing of the American frontier, the romance of the Spanish Conquest, the affirmation of Gilded Age technologies as raced business practices. Ruiz de Burton's first book, *Who Would Have Thought It?*, published during the middle of her ten-year residency on the East Coast, indicts federal policy during the Civil War and connects this conflict with American imperialism in Mexico. The novel pushes us to consider how American literary history appears if we decenter the Civil War from its privileged position, substituting, in its place, multiple interruptions and breaks in the national map: the conflict over Texas resolved a mere quarter of a century before it; the U.S.-Mexican War almost simultaneous with it; the disputes over water rights that continue to shape western politics to this day.

Consider such western fictions alongside narratives like those of Henry James, and texts produced out of New England also resonate to the repercussions of these midcentury national conflicts. James's lexicon invokes what look like different languages about nation: Anglo American anxieties about increased immigration to the West and the Northeast, changing definitions of the citizen sparked by pressure from what the Boston expatriate consistently calls "the alien," racially-inflected revisions of labor and leisure in the

Gilded Age. Like Ruiz de Burton, however, he uses sectional conflicts to explore the United States as a locus for global power. For both writers, the language of region becomes a metaphor for arguments about the raced inflections of our national vocabulary.

### III: Local or Locale?
### The Cultural Work of "Regionalism" in Transnational Theory

*The boundaries of the local need to be kept open (or porous) if the local is to serve as a critical concept. The contemporary local is itself a site of invention; the present is ultimately the site for the global.*

—Arlik Dirlik, "The Global in the Local" in *Global/Local: Cultural Production and the Transnational Imaginary*[23]

*The emergent discourse of "global-localism" proposes the most challenging critique directed against the pre-constituted categories anchored in the discourse of anti-imperialism. It argues against the colonizer's power to construct the "other" out of figures within an ethnocentric unconscious. Because of its capacity to violate national boundaries, imperialism, according to this critique, should be understood instead as a phase in the process of globalization that, in disrupting the coherence of the geopolitical entities called nation-states, thereby enabled their openness to interconnection with all other nation-states.*

—Donald Pease, "New Perspectives on U.S. Culture and Imperialism" in
*Cultures of United States Imperialism* (26)

*Such rediscoveries of identity can function as forms of fundamentalism, leading to local ethnicities that are as dangerous as national ones.*

—Caren Kaplan, *Questions of Travel* (159)

"Porous" and "open," "ethnocentric" and "fundamentalist"; the only clear principle here is the amorphous range of identities provided "the local." If they have nothing else in common, the formulations cited above all refuse to consider locality in relation to any discrete place. None advocates the kind of intimacy with place we see in the Monterey novels of John Steinbeck, the poetry of Robert Frost, Jimmy Santiago Baca, or Lorna Dee Cervantes, the personal narratives of Lorene Cary, Gary Soto, or Barry Lopez.[24] Instead, "the local" acts as an objective correlative for all that is not "global." If neither term is defined, their opposition categorically places locality in the position of what is to be defended against: essentialism, nationalism, a "narrow" angle of vision "on the internal lineaments of American culture" that "leaves national borders intact instead of interrogating their formation" (Kaplan, 15). For Kaplan "the local" is a euphemism for what is, a priori, considered "dangerous";

that is, cultural nationalism, here equated with identity politics. For Pease, "localism" is an attempt to make "the global" resolve out of a critical fog. But despite itself, Dirlik's definition is most to the point: in much contemporary theory, I would argue, "the local" is indeed "a site of invention" in some relation to "the global." In other words: these representations of the local suggest that it serves a structural rather than intellectually substantive function in contemporary criticism. How else can we make sense of a phrase like this one: "The contemporary local is itself a site for invention; the present is ultimately the site for the global?"[25] unless to understand "the contemporary local" as a shorthand form for identifying a critical position?

My interest here is to move the local toward the locale: to readmit it to history, to insist that it assume a particular face, in order to correct American Studies's diffuse, too expansive focus on the intersections of "nation" and "empire." Rather than invoke transnationalist theory as a physic for scholarly provincialism, we might better assess imperialism as a framing term in the region-nation equation through a critical peripheral vision whose angle of sight is not concentrated on empire as an abstraction (a totalizing formulation that undermines efforts to specify its various forms), but instead on how a particular cluster of texts refracts historically and geographically discrete political practices. Instead of deconstructing nationalist discourse by conceptualizing a global theory that flouts institutionalized borderlines, I wish to stay within national borders in order to rethink the cultural work "region" performs.

Despite the persistent invocation of region in contemporary formulations of American identity, an emphasis that promises a renewed interest in locality and "thick descriptions" of discrete spaces, regionalism is too often a placeless construct that denies the specificity of the languages that circulate within a given area. The "regionalist" literary gaze, that is, remains perversely farsighted, focused upon the blurred horizon line of nation rather than the sharp, clear-etched details of foreground locales. When the critical lens is turned upon particular American places, it is not with the eye of Eliot Porter—whose photos detail and dignify the humble particulars of light dappling ferns or insects crossing a leaf—but with the epic address of Ansel Adams, where regional spaces are icons for national grandeur. "National reunification" is not only "the cultural project that would inform a diversity of American fiction for the following three decades" (240), as Amy Kaplan argues, but the underlying agenda prompting critical reflections on this literature.

When Carolyn Porter charges Philip Fisher's regionalism as "not finally a name, but a rhetorical device . . . charged with a good deal of 'cultural work'" (Porter, 484) she cogently calls attention to the way in which contemporary ideas about region mimic the fictions they unravel. Although her response to Fisher is exhaustive, I would like to return to his essay because it exposes the regionalist unconscious so clearly. Part of the "cultural work"

Fisher's "regionalism" performs is to act as a coded figure for American race relations. "In early twentieth century America," he argues, "a new regionalism that was not geographic but ethnic appeared as a result of massive immigration. The local 'color' was not that of climates and regions, but of hyphenated Americans" (xiii). By rendering race in spatial terms—"ethnic" Americans substitute for the geographic fringe—Fisher responds to fears about the outward spreading of inner cities (populated by "ethnics") by establishing a cartography that pushes others back to the (regional) margins.[26] Contemporary regionalism encodes the same racial resonances in *The New American Studies*. Fisher reduces the complex affiliations between race, gender, and queer theory programs by amalgamating them under the umbrella of identity politics, then concatenates them further by defining every "counter element to unitary myths within American Studies" as demonstrating "the force of regionalism" (viii). This management approach to American Studies reflects anxieties about the specter of literary balkanization following the institutionalization of programs like Ethnic and Women's Studies. Meanwhile, the "new American Studies has stood outside this regionalism by locating a set of underlying but permanently open national facts around which all identities are shaped and with which the many rhetorics of our culture are engaged" (xiv).

Fisher's celebration of "national facts" provides other scholars with cultural work of their own. Amy Kaplan uses the ending of *The Octopus* in "Nation, Region and Empire" to point to "an important but overlooked historical context for American literary nationalism: America's shift away from continental expansion to overseas empire at the turn of the century" (263). Carolyn Porter reiterates this interest in the imperial agenda of late nineteenth-century discourse and suggests that transnationalist theory may help "distinguish between the overlapping social formations in the nineteenth-century of nationalism and imperialism" (515).

Overlapping, indeed. The conquest of the Southwest, naturalized with the euphemism of "continental expansion," is itself an imperial act, as contemporary writers are quick to indicate. Henry Nash Smith cites this 1846 letter of Henry Gilpin's: "The untransacted destiny of the American people is to subdue the continent—to rush over this vast field to the Pacific Ocean . . . to regenerate superannuated nations . . . to stir up the sleep of a hundred centuries—to teach old nations a new civilization" (Nash, 37). Here as elsewhere, nationalism must transgress its own borders to make itself known. Gilpin's violent rhetoric implies that a nationalist "pedagogy" cannot be achieved through mere "annexation." Waking up "sleepy" nations like Mexico is not the natural consequence of internal political gravity, but a deliberate act of imperial destruction. A half century later, "The Making of California" advertises the gold rush as the "material conquest of California." Here, in the pages of *The Century*, "the Anglo-Saxon movement to California" is simultaneously imperial maneuver, regional exercise, and nationalist foray whose "lines of sympathy and interest . . . reached to every quarter of the country."[27]

One hundred years after this 1890 paean to the imperial grandeur of continental expansion, scholars frame American conquest with the same vocabulary of intercontinental colonialism. In "'Left Alone with America,'" Amy Kaplan reveals the global frame of reference erased in earlier critical versions of American literary historiography by charting the "imperial dimensions of [Perry Miller's] founding paradigm" (5). Arguing that *Errand into the Wilderness* develops a vision of the New World that rejects and displaces "competing cultural histories . . . onto the site of Africa" (4), she demonstrates the ways in which "a demarcation of the domestic from the foreign is central to Miller's conception" (7). Contemporary versions of this geographical translation of the American "wilderness" into an African "jungle" metaphor substantiate the canniness of this critical insight. In Ivan Doig's 1987 novel *Dancing at the Rascal Fair*, for instance, Montana missionary transforms into Congo missionary: "her larklike smallness looked like someone unexpectedly being carriaged along the banks of the Congo."[28] Because it implicitly draws upon theories that posit the British Empire as structural paradigm for global forms of imperialism, however, Kaplan's revisionary map overcorrects for Miller's mystifying paradigm. Since the model her work draws upon assumes that the pressures of empire operate intercontinentally, she must displace indigenous populations beyond the borders of the United States in her efforts to call attention to the exertions of imperialism upon them. Accordingly, she cites Toni Morrison's thesis about canonicity in *Playing in the Dark* ("'one can see that a real or fabricated Africanist presence was crucial to their sense of Americanness'") to underwrite her critique of Miller, whose own "sense of Americanness" is predicated upon his trip to the Congo and his relation to Africa. But this translation of Morrison's focus on a "real or fabricated Africanist presence" moves the field of inquiry from the United States to Africa (Morrison's focus on the relationship that Anglo American writers have to black Americans and black American literature that they can only represent as "Africanist"), a remapping that hides from view the operations of colonialism within the United States itself.

Similarly, Kaplan invokes a domestic culture in Chicano Studies, only to move this cultural field beyond the border. A U.S. literary and artistic set of practices is in this essay linked with "the borderlands" that connect

> the study of ethnicity and immigration inextricably to the study of international relations and empire. At these borders, foreign relations do not take

place outside the boundaries of America. . . . Chicano Studies has brought an
international perspective to American Studies in part by reconciling the concept of ethnicity (traditionally treated as a self-enclosed entity) through the
theory and politics of postcoloniality (16–17).

Despite the essay's scrupulous and intelligent decoding of the mystified op-
erations of American imperialism, both black Americans and Mexican
Americans are nonetheless "internationalized." However deft, Kaplan's critique of Miller's imperial "City on a Hill" exoticizes and displaces African
Americans by drawing out the "international and spatial dimensions of
Morrison's argument" (5). And in conflating all Latinos with (U.S.-born)
Chicanos, her invocation of "America," if revisionary in intent, nonetheless
situates itself within a continuing history of obfuscation about immigrant
versus native-born Mexicans.[29]

   This is the difficulty with talking about Empire. Invoke this abstraction
but once, and the richly complicated relations between distinct social systems blur in favor of Foucauldianesque generalizations that, despite themselves, compress distinct political-cultural strata under the weight of a single
granite monument to power.[30] Hence Kaplan's domestication of United
States foreign policy in the mid-nineteenth century as a southwestern version of the Homestead Act. But even in those instances where the nuances
of intercultural relations are maintained, referencing them with "imperialism" tends to reestablish the "center-periphery" model in which the institutional norm—despite being introduced as an oppositional or ironized
term—effectively resituates difference in relation to itself. Philip Fisher's celebration of regionalism as "the counter element to unitary myths" (viii)
clearly totalizes race relations, but by eliding Latin American literature and
Chicano literature, Carolyn Porter's use of José Saldívar's *The Dialectics of
Our America*[31] also threatens to flatten out the very "border"(s) she urges
critics to cross:

> Saldívar's remapping of the field fundamentally changes the way one reads
> both Chicano literature and "the border" as a cultural formation within the
> larger hemispheric picture of structural economic dependency . . . a Latin
> American vantage point might serve to fracture and destabilize the normative
> assumptions of an American Studies whose clear focus has traditionally been
> achieved at the cost of its nearsightedness (505, 509).

Using a single "border" to abbreviate the complicated relation between "internal" schisms and international disputes threatens to write out the (often)
unspoken regional differences inflecting Chicano literature and literary criticism as well as the sovereignty of individual nations: Guatemala and Chile;

Argentina and Mexico; Puerto Rico and Cuba. Calling the United States "America" certainly bespeaks ethnocentrism, as Porter indicates, but amalgamating the rest of the continent under the designation "Latin America" will hardly resolve the problem.

The "problem" with global models is that they aren't, properly speaking, global at all.[32] Rather, they tend to originate out of the most institutionally entrenched departments (English, not Ethnic Studies) and the most powerful nations (those who wield imperial authority, or, in other words, those who get to exercise their "transnationalism" upon others). When deracinated from its historical and political ground, transnationalism can become a form of intellectual tourism that blithely refuses to acknowledge how the traffic signals at border crossings make freeways look like one-way streets.[33] The premature celebration of "[T]he dissolution and disinvention of *e pluribus unum* narratives," in Rob Wilson and Wimal Dissanayake's introduction to *Global/Local* provides a particularly ebullient example. Their paean to "transcultural hybridity" pans the globe as swiftly as do the continent-hopping television advertisements of multinational corporations like MCI: "The nation-state . . . is being undone by this fast imploding heteroglossic interface of the global with the local: what we would here diversely theorize as the *global/local* nexus" [2–3]).[34]

Paul Bové's conclusion to this collection illustrates even more strikingly the work the "global/local nexus" affords transnational theory. He eulogizes Masao Miyoshi's essay "A Borderless World? From Colonialism to Transnationalism and the Decline of the Nation-State" in language that reads like a scholarly version of *The Terminator;* that is, a masculinist fantasy of the critic as cyborg: "Miyoshi's essay strikes one over and over again for its ascetic effect. Oddly, here is an essayist who has stripped away the apparatus of theory, the knowledge of literary history, of aesthetic form to take on something like a hard body: tough, clean, glaring examination of the unjust processes and transformations that occur in global economy, passing almost unnoticed by 'literary critics'"(376). Yet as much as literary critics yearn for the "hard body" of economic "fact," they seem less than willing to put in the necessary hours at the gymnasium to acquire the appropriate intellectual "toughness." Connecting literary study with global economics requires more than the scholarly equivalent of a half-day beachcombing economic theory.

Notwithstanding the fruitful and provocative work that has been done in "border studies," then, indiscriminately affirming and conflating such crossings without acknowledging their sometimes crippling effects reproduces the euphemistic tonalities of overly optimistic theories of the "global economy."[35] Instead of practicing this international "boosterism," let us risk looking provincial and concentrate on tending our own gardens. Like American Studies scholars more generally, I am interested in exploring how writers have used region as a metaphor for difference ("difference" itself an overdetermined term), but I prefer a close angle of vision rather than a panoramic overview as best suited for remapping the historically distorted survey that has characterized American literary cartography.

## IV: New Directions?
## The Persistence of the "Center/Periphery" Model
## in American Literary Historiography

*My dearest girl, you do not hear California mentioned in New York once a month. It might be on Mars. The East remembers California's existence about as often as Europe remembers America's. They don't know what they miss.*

—Gertrude Atherton, *The Californians*

*The clinching argument for the colonial model is this self-consciousness about their status within the historical profession. . . . Told that their traditional concerns belong to the "cactus and sagebrush" school of history (literally the bush leagues), Western historians are apologetic. . . . A little assertiveness might be more in order. Historians who spend a life-time studying the varieties and vagaries of seventeenth-century Puritanism or putting a New England town under the microscope feel no compunction in dismissing Western historians as parochial, their concerns as glorified antiquarianism.*

—Brian W. Dippie, "American Wests: Historiographical Perspectives," in
*Trails: Towards a New Western History*[36]

As Europe is to America, so New England is to the United States: anyone who has spent time in Boston can confirm the equation Gertrude Atherton establishes between the immutability of East Coast provincialism and the sustained undervaluation of American cultures. One hundred years separate her critique from Dippie's exhortation, but New England's status as originary metaphor for national identity remains largely untroubled. Nor is this definition of nationalism limited to literary study. Historian Patricia Limerick astutely scrutinizes Frederick Jackson Turner's thesis as an effort to authorize the United States as an imperial power by distinguishing "native" from European antecedents. Turner's frontier mythography exists in Oedipal relation to the Puritan creation story it seeks to supplant; reassessment of Turner as the father of American regionalism accordingly focuses upon the ways in which his historiography, like the Puritan narrative founded at Plymouth Rock, serves a nationalist agenda. As Brian Dippie explains this, "when western history developed into a separate field of study under Turner's tutelage, it involved isolating not a portion of America from the rest but all America from Europe" (117).

New Western historians have provided trenchant criticisms of Turner's thesis, but their revisions have kept the regional parameters of the national map intact. (To use a global metaphor, we might say that Turner, for historians of the West, is the equivalent of Greenwich mean time: we may not all be in his time zone, but we all set our watches to calibrate with it.) For instance, Patricia Limerick's critical reassessment relies on a vocabulary that assumes one direction of colonization (an initial remove from Europe to America, a second westward movement from Boston through the heartland to Eureka), and in so doing naturalizes the assumptions she wishes to call into question. Her argument rethinks but also resurrects the same stories by and about "pioneers" and "settlers" that Turner legitimized as axiomatic for his own representation of the West as a synecdoche for the nation. Likewise, Donald Worster hopes that contemporary work will "restore to memory all those unsmiling aspects that Turner wanted to leave out" (117).

By censuring rather than celebrating the westering impulse his thesis eulogized, such correctives supply Turner with a conscience. But, like Turner, the New Western historians put the West on the national map to redress a patronizing definition of "regional history." What is important about the New West is precisely what Turner argued was significant about the old one: its ability to model America. Worster, Limerick, and other scholars who redefine this region as a distinctive section point to its special relationship to the federal polity; the West is unique in its dependence on national government. "Government had a greater impact upon the West than the West had upon government," Gerald Nash argues, and so "the myth of the individualistic, isolated self-sufficient Westerner is largely that—a myth" (77). Richard White's own conclusion, excerpted below, speaks to the nationalist agenda that underlies these collective efforts at sectional individuation: "The American West, more than any other section of the United States, is a creation not so much of individual or local efforts, but of federal efforts. While the federal government shaped the West, however, the West itself served as the kindergarten of the American state."[37]

Kevin Starr's *California Dreams* illustrates this Mount Rushmore model of regionalism by citing turn-of-the-century descriptions of "'The face of Los Angeles'" as "'the truest conceivable representation of the whole American face, urban, rural, big town, little town, all together'" and as a synecdoche for the nation, carrying "'to the final degree of caricature the various traits of American society.'"[38] Other recent appraisals circulate the currency of regionalist discourse only to call attention to the resiliency of the national metaphor. Hence the perennial critical attention to Turner, who, as Patricia Limerick reminds us, enabled "the West [to enjoy] its few moments of celebrity in mainstream American history as the necessary stage setting for the last big sweep of national expansionism" (19). Ultimately, if the New

Western historians take up Gertrude Atherton's claim in order to clarify how the "national" encodes an eastern regional agenda, they stop short of questioning the relation between region and nation itself. Limerick underwrites Gerald Pomeroy's national demographic even as she corrects his vision of the West. Just as Owen Wister's introduction to *The Virginian* styles the influx of Anglo Americans into Wyoming as "a colonial romance" (6), so Limerick responds to Pomeroy's claim ("citizens resented the territorial status . . . not only because they were Westerners, but also because recently they had been Easterners"[80]) by assuming the same New England point of departure: "[b]ut Western Americans did what most travelers do: they took their problems with them" (90). If her own formulation is critical, it repopulates the West with the same tourists granted citizenship by historians both before *and* after Turner.

The pull of this traditional iconography is strong. Statements like this one: "the fact remained: the West never went to war for its independence" (23), write out the conflict in Texas and dismiss the U.S.-Mexican War even as Limerick's *Legacy of Conquest* as a whole works hard to keep the notion of conquest in view. Likewise, Richard White's history, a provocative reassessment of traditional western historiography, moves against traffic but stays on the same well-traveled critical highway. His study censures visions of a citizenry "unified" under "nationalist doctrine" like Manifest Destiny: "But the United States was, in fact, a country whose citizens were not fully united but were instead divided into two distinct and antagonistic sections: the North and the South" (74).

The reappearance here of North and South in a book that treats neither section is a stunning testimony to the resilience of traditional figures for the nation. The West is reduced to an object of the regional gaze, spoils to be trafficked: "When the North and South struggled for dominance in the Union, they clashed over the distribution of land in the West" (140). That the North-South conflict continues to speak as the paradigm for sectional tensions in this reappraisal of a section so far removed from the Mason-Dixon line suggests that as long as New England remains fixed as the center of the United States, other "regions"—in their shared conceptual equidistance from the heart of the "nation"—remain generic markers of difference from it.[39]

Literary scholars in American Studies draw from a different vocabulary in their own discussions of the relation between region and nation, but substitute "margin" for "region" and "center" for "nation" and their revisions mirror those taking place in history. Just as local history remains a "subfield" of American history, so, despite efforts to "decenter the field," as Carolyn Porter notes, the "'center/periphery' model by which 'traditional' versus 'marginalized' texts are arrayed in the curriculum" remains "ever resilient" (500) in American literary study. Notwithstanding their re-visionary claims—Donald Pease's critical anthology is part of Duke University Press's "New Americanists" series—contemporary formulations of literary historiography continue to invoke the Civil War as paradigmatic of American difference.[40] Like a compass, the regional focal point inevitably drifts back to the northern question. Porter commends Michael Rogin for shifting direction in *Subversive Genealogy: The Politics and Art of Herman Melville* when he invokes "the American 1848." Yet his own 1848 is obstinately bent on serving a European comparison: "Just as Henry Adams saw 1848 'in America as the culmination and defeat of . . . 1776,' Rogin sees a similar 'relation between 1789 and 1848 in Europe' . . . the Mexican War and ensuing struggle over slavery it served to refuel" (as cited in Porter, 518–19). Slavery—defined in relation to the Mason-Dixon line—remains politically emblematic of all imperial tensions, including those played out on different directional axes.

Scholarship frequently reiterates this exercise in geographical translation. Henry Nash Smith glosses the "westward movement" (132) in relation to slavery and interprets the "American seizure of California" as "an act of defiance to England rather than to Mexico" (24). Amy Kaplan's wide-ranging essay on "Nation, Region and Empire" factors California literature into the region-nation equation and provides a more nuanced representation of literary geography. Yet, like *Virgin Land,* it reinstates the center/periphery model by focusing on writers "published by a highly centralized industry located in Boston and New York" (251). Because Kaplan reads texts that thematize distinct regions without attention to the locality of the places they represent, her own definition of regionalism remains in service to a discourse of nationalism that uses the Civil War as its universalizing foundational metaphor. At the same time, she focuses on the eastern publishing establishment in order to develop a provocative argument about regional literature, namely that it allows an "urban middle-class readership" to locate itself as national "by consuming images of rural 'others' as both a nostalgic point of origin and a measure of cosmopolitan development" (251).

But if we shift our focus away from Boston-based writers and New York publishing houses toward writers in Denver, Santa Fe, and San Francisco, and California publishers like Hubert Howe Bancroft, this conflation of regionalism with what is "rural" looks less natural. Priscilla Wald echoes Garry Wills in arguing that "the most potent official story of the United States . . . is the legacy of Abraham Lincoln and a product of the Civil War."[41] Likewise, Philip Fisher invokes "the spatial structure of slavery" as the template for the "New American Studies." In his revisioning, as in previous periods of American revivalism, the Civil War carries a great deal of weight:

Periods of civil war are periods without ideology because two or more
rhetorics of self-representation, national purpose, and historical genealogy are
in wide enough circulation to elicit complete support. . . . The condition of
civil war can be taken as the fundamental alternative to the condition of
monarchical power, self-display, uniform discourse, ideology, and controlled
representation (xv).

The academic equivalent of Civil War encyclopedias and PBS's series of the
previous decade, this rosy political assessment is itself mythic in its celebration of a period "without ideology." Nor is using the Civil War as the "chief
'example of a damaged social space'" (as cited in Porter, 493) innovative. On
the contrary, "the mythic figure of Lincoln [and] . . . the railroads and tele-
graph that reconquered a geography" (xii) continue to circulate in ever-pop-
ular survey courses like "American Literature After 1865," a fact that
underscores how the Civil War has for some time functioned as a structur-
ing metaphor for literary historiography.

This does not mean that we should dismiss it as a literary value; rather, if
we decenter and rehistoricize its iconography we will produce more nuanced
readings of texts ostensibly designed single-mindedly around this rupture.
How else explain the antebellum politics of Pauline Hopkins's *Hagar's
Daughter: A Novel of Southern Caste Prejudice,* unless we keep in view the
East-West polarity invoked to describe its southern daughter, a black woman
raised in California as a "western girl," with a frontier paternity to match?
How else understand the travails of the young Mexican Californiana who
goes east in María Amparo Ruiz de Burton's indictment of federal corruption during the Civil War in *Who Would Have Thought It?* except as a deliberate rewriting of the gender and geography of imperial exhortation? By
correcting the critical gaze, which continues to view the United States out of
New England eyes, we produce richer critical descriptions of region, nation,
and the relation between them.

# Chapter One ∼

# Beasts in the Jungle
## Regional "aliens" and Boston Natives

### I: Two Portraits of Parochial Boston

*The types and faces bore them out; the people before me were gross aliens to a man and they were in serene and triumphant possession. Nothing, as I say, could have been more effective for figuring the hitherward bars of a grating through which I might make out, far-off in space, "my" small homogenous Boston of the more interesting time.*

—Henry James, *The American Scene* (172)[1]

*The doctor's most unnatural liking for foreigners . . . was the cause of [his] sending his only son Julian to be educated in Europe,—as if the best schools on earth were not in New England. . . . That liking was also the cause of the doctor's sending Isaac to be a good-for-nothing clerk in sinful Washington, among foreigners, when he could have remained in virtuous New England. . . . And finally, impelled by that liking, the doctor betook himself to California, which is yet full of "natives."*

—María Amparo Ruiz de Burton, *Who Would Have Thought It?* (8)[2]

I was halfway between Cheyenne and Laramie driving east on I-80 when I saw the sign for "Little America." I remember Wyoming from the summer my family spent on a dude ranch near Jackson Hole when I was nine. Together with my brothers and sister, I rode slow ponies around a corral and wore out a pair of heavy-heeled, tan-colored cowboy boots I kept in my closet for years afterwards. Now, 30 years later, I thought I might buy another pair at this truck stop. But the view opening up around the curve of the exit smothered my nostalgia: faux colonial red brick buildings cluttered the wide horizon, disparaging its booted and hatted visitors as ill suited for the occasion—Paul Revere's ride? The battle of Lexington and Concord?—

the architecture revisited. Twenty-five hundred miles away and four thousand feet higher than the crooked Concord streets, surrounded by tumbleweeds rather than the unfurling fronds of Boston ferns, the iconography for "America" remained faithful to what Henry James calls in *The Bostonians* "the heroic age of New England life . . . the reading of Emerson and the frequentation of Tremont Temple."[3]

If popular wisdom frames regionalism and urbanity as a contradiction in terms (consider the visual logic of Little America, which grafts a New England frieze onto a Wyoming truck stop to reassure shoppers that what they purchase here measures up to the "national" standard), the critical imagination likewise characterizes region as rural retreat. But what happens if we regionalize an urban center like Boston? James's "homogenous Boston of the more interesting time" is clearly an invented geography, the sort Amy Kaplan calls "the projection of a desire for a space outside of history, untouched by change."[4] For the expatriate writer, Walden Pond is a reservoir for memory and nostalgia; at the same time, the "deep Concord rusticity" is a "medium for our national drama" (*The American Scene,* 195). In "Nation, Region, and Empire," Kaplan distinguishes rural color from urban capital;[5] the center produces locality, then pushes it to a geographic remove. In *The American Scene,* by contrast, the center is *itself* "painted with 'local color.'"[6] Here as in *The Bostonians,* James eulogizes the "native" American as an endangered species in his own birthplace: " . . . what the old New England spirit may still . . . give; of what may yet remain, for productive scraping, of the formula of the native Puritanism educated" (178–79). Set in opposition to James's Italian, Irish, black, and Jewish "flagrant foreigner[s]" (196), the Puritan remains the "ghost" of "old social orders," of "a closed circle that would find itself happy enough if only it could remain closed enough" (*The American Scene,* 21). Notwithstanding its narrow political parameters,[7] James's lament locates the placeless "distended industrial nation" (Amy Kaplan, 251) of contemporary critical imagining, assigning it distinct geographical coordinates. His unapologetic insistence on keeping the circle "closed enough" corrects scholarly representations of nationalist discourse that forget its local origins and mythify it as a master narrative.

In this chapter I juxtapose James's and Ruiz's parochial portraits of Boston in order to outline a critical methodology that refuses to reduce the productive tension between American regions and the federal polity to a question of center and margin. Coupling *The Bostonians* with *Who Would Have Thought It?* encourages us to reappraise the stratified oppositions (texts "central" to the canon over and against "local colorists" taught as electives in English departments) through which we conventionally interpret narrative. I wish to defamiliarize *The Bostonians* and to make more readers familiar with *Who Would Have Thought It?,* not because the latter needs dignifying—

anyone who reads Ruiz de Burton's 1872 novel will recognize the wealth of references to Greek and Roman history that provide the writer with one of her richest sources of parody—but rather to indicate how glossing them together produces more complex readings of both.

Reading *The Bostonians* alongside María Amparo Ruiz de Burton's novel *does* require that the former be wrenched from the critical history that has accreted around it; if the American canon is the literary equivalent of Mount Rushmore, this study temporarily pries *The Bostonians* loose from its face. But in bracketing the critical apparatus I do not mean to be dismissive of this long-standing scholarly history. Nor do I wish to suggest that the literary coupling of James and Ruiz de Burton positions a "major writer" over and against a "subaltern voice." On the contrary, Ruiz de Burton's republished fictions are reshaping the Chicano literary canon; her 1885 novel *The Squatter and the Don* is the inaugural volume of the Recovering the U.S. Hispanic Literary Heritage project, a project that will have as far-reaching effects on its own discipline as the Schomburg Series has had for the study of nineteenth-century African American literature.[8]

Read side by side, correspondences between James and Ruiz de Burton clarify themselves. However distinct their arguments, both writers satirize "the Puritan code" (*The Bostonians,* 36), drawing on a raced iconography to establish the city's parameters. James's "gross aliens" (figured in *The American Scene* as the "remorseless Italian," the "Jew in a dusky back-shop," and the "tatterdemalion darkies" [197, 195, 276]) have made Boston and New York uncomfortable places for Emersonian natives precisely because such "immigrants" are at home there. Like James's interlopers, the "Indians, Mexicans, or Californians" (9) of Ruiz de Burton's *Who Would Have Thought It?* are indigenous foreigners; American citizens who, from the point of view of the "blue Presbyterians" satirized here, can never be Americans. Both the New Englander and the Californian play upon the regional character of literary abbreviations for national identity, describing Boston as a parochial location from which to examine the contested term "American." The focus on movement into Boston by immigrants racialized in *The American Scene, The Bostonians,* and *Who Would Have Thought It?* and excursions out of the city by Yankees who question the equation of its parameters with national borders clarifies the constructed nature of these dividing lines. In the introduction to this book I have suggested that travel in American literature is often read as the index of a controlling intellectual design, but the multiple travel vectors in these novels confound any notion of "forward" and "backward," contrasting pointedly with linear myths of our national origins.

I wish to take a closer look at the paths James and Ruiz de Burton traverse in and out of New England and the United States in *The Bostonians* (1885) and *Who Would Have Thought It?* (1872) to explore the implications of thinking "regionally" about national conflicts like the Civil War and the U.S.-Mexican War.[9] James and his readers have defined *The Bostonians* as an "American tale" because it explores "the situation of women, the decline of sentiment of sex, the agitation in their behalf." My reading contextualizes the book's gendered arguments by considering this "most salient and peculiar point in our social life" as indivisible from the peculiar regional institutions James will explore more directly in *The American Scene.*[10] Likewise, my discussion of *Who Would Have Thought It?* registers the contingent nature of Ruiz de Burton's feminist critique, where a spinster Yankee heroine goes to Washington to demand of Congress "a right" (146). Through this critique, Ruiz de Burton indicts a federal government distinguished by its hypocrisy, a sin she regionalizes as a Puritan fatal flaw. In both books, national identity develops from regional formations: Basil Ransom is a pale substitute for the "tatterdemalion darkies" who migrate north after the Civil War, the transplanted southerner who James uses to embody the nation's "black" contradictions and in so doing, to defuse the immigrant threat. Lola Medina is also an embodiment of regional conflicts, a young Californiana who in going east occupies the paternal heart of the "blue Presbyterians" (55) of Boston and through whom Ruiz de Burton yokes together conflicts over race and land. Like James's peregrinations, Ruiz's interregional plots suggest we look more critically at the way English departments package American literary history by assigning political movements distinct regional coordinates.

## II: A Foreign Beast in the (Urban) Jungle:
### *The Bostonians*

While James invokes a gendered metaphor to characterize *The Bostonians* as an "American tale," his equation of femininity and nationalism is disingenuous, since Ransom's forays into his cousin's Boston drawing room are not only masculine predations but also regional agitations of "closed circles." James reminds us again and again of Ransom's "Southern complexion" (162) and of his consequent inability to cultivate "the artistic sense" so evident in the "interior" of Olive Chancellor's house, a feminine space whose "organized privacy," books, and "culture" make it "Bostonian" (15). Along with scholars like Sara Blair and Jonathan Friedman, I wish to look more closely at the racial inflections that structure such faces in James's work.[11] Like *Who Would Have Thought It?*, which uses the battle of the sexes to parody military exercises so as to make visible the raced contours of American life, *The Bostonians* is a novel of manners that exploits gender as an in-house metaphor for more "public" arguments between "species" (157). James's satire on the misguided adventures of the suffragettes, I wish to argue, also allows him to obliquely ward off the encroachments of black "foreigners" (26).

If the soul of New York finds concrete expression in the upraised hand of the Statue of Liberty, the mind of Boston is incorporated in spinster suffragettes like the "frumpy little missionary" Miss Birdseye (157) and "the little medical lady" Doctor Prance, who is a "perfect example of the "'Yankee female:'" "[s]pare, dry, hard, without a curve, an inflection or a grace" (36). This New England answer to England's Florence Nightingale is refracted through the "unregenerate imagination" (36) of Basil Ransom. But James endorses this plainness as well; to speak of the "Yankee female" in this book is to be redundant, for we don't see a single male in its environs. Doctor Prance and Miss Birdseye make up the "last link[s] in a tradition" (157), that originally masculine golden age of New England in which Emerson figures so prominently. Since New England men have migrated from the drawing room into the boardroom, Boston's interiors have become peopled only by "the sex."

This is how Miss Birdseye's frail form comes to embody Culture, and why James taxonomies her death so elaborately. When this American vestal virgin has passed, the "unquenched flame of her transcendentalism" (157) will have nothing to feed upon. Transcendentalism characterizes the "air and 'tone'" (*The American Scene,* 178) of Boston, but Margaret Fuller is not included in the pantheon; her absence in *The Bostonians* as a reference for the "modern maidens" who cluster around Miss Birdseye speaks more loudly than does Verena Tarrant in her New York stage appearances. Like James's humiliating exposure of Olive Chancellor (meant to chastise the feminine desire for authority), the writer's erasure of the most celebrated feminist name in Transcendentalism is partial compensation for commercialism's evacuation of men from the New England drawing room.[12]

By writing out Fuller, James prostrates suffragism at the feet of abolition, privileging the racial foundations of the "closed circle" over the gendered oversoul. Owen Wister lampoons the suffragist progressive in *The Virginian* as a "manly-lookin" hen in a drawling anecdote that recalls Hawthorne's extended play on the ancestry of the Pyncheon family in *The House of the Seven Gables:* "There's an old maid at home who's charitable, and belongs to the Cruelty to Animals, and she never knows whether she had better cross in front of a street car or wait," the narrator asserts, "I named the hen after her. . . . I think she came near being a rooster" (55). By contrast, James provides his own "modern maiden" with a degree of dignity. Despite his derision for Miss Birdseye's myopia—her name ironically announces this—he affirms her unwavering devotion to the "heroic age of New England life." "[T]he only thing that was still actual for her" (157), he muses, "was the elevation of the species by the reading of Emerson" (157). Like Ransom, who clumsily but successfully makes her his ally, Miss Birdseye is demoored, temporally adrift from the main currents of contemporary American life.[13] Region speaks as much for racial conflict as for the battle of the sexes, for Miss

Birdseye's reforming impulse is dedicated not to suffrage, but to "the other slaves," "the negroes" for whom she carried the Bible (186):

> Her best hours had been spent in fancying that she was helping some Southern slave to escape. . . . It would have been a nice question whether, in her heart of hearts . . . she did not sometimes wish the blacks back in bondage. . . . For when causes were embodied in foreigners (what else were the Africans?), they were certainly more appealing (26).

Here we arrive at the novel's real cultural work, which, in spite of James's satire of Miss Birdseye, is to look longingly backward toward the closed Emersonian circle, a circle that would be happy enough if only it could stay closed enough, a circle that has been irreparably rent, in the final decades of the nineteenth century and the opening years of the twentieth, by "The Ubiquity of the Alien," with whom "there is no claim to brotherhood" (*The American Scene,* 91–92).[14] Miss Birdseye's lapse of insight is not, at any rate, shared by James, who repeatedly laments the "'ethnic' apparition" who sits "like a skeleton at the feast" (*The American Scene,* 101). Just as "the Hebrew conquest of New York" threatens to dilute the city's "American" value, so the "tatterdemalion darkies . . . could absolutely not fail to be, intensely 'on the nerves' of the South." Like the burgeoning population of the Jewish ghetto, the "darkies" refuse to stay within the confines of the South: waiting in a Washington railway station, the sentimental tourist visiting stateside is equally "discomposed" by this "beast that had sprung from the jungle" (*The American Scene,* 277, 276).

In *The Bostonians,* the beast is more tactfully and tactically hidden, but it is there, nonetheless, in the person of Basil Ransom. Like Vanderbilt's Biltmore, contaminated by the southern "niggery wilderness" its foundation rests upon,[15] Ransom's "sultry" complexion is proxy for blackness. From the outset, with his "dark, deep and glowing" eyes and "his thick black hair" (6), he is a polite expression of anxiety for the "foreigners" who are invading *The American Scene* (98). Ransom is the novel's Euphemism— a ragged and rudimentary but distinctly more appealing substitute for the "African type[s]" (*The American Scene,* 276) James finds in the capital city.[16] This nervousness is pitched at a higher note in the travelogue than in the novel: because the writer trains his irony upon himself more than the objects of his (discomfited) eye, their alienating properties stand out in bold relief. *The Bostonians,* on the other hand, is not so highly colored. As if in obeisance to the distaste the city's finest have for garish portraiture, James tempers his expostulations, cloaking northern feminist and southern conservative in a satiric mist that blurs their silhouettes. Still, "the reader . . . is entreated not to forget" that Ransom

prolonged his consonants and swallowed his vowels, that he was guilty of elisions and interpolations which were equally unexpected, and that his discourse was pervaded by something sultry and vast, something almost African
in its rich basking tone, something that suggested the teeming expanse of the
cotton-field (6).

Read this passage on Ransom's speech alongside the sustained attention
James gives to "foreign" accents ten years later in *The Tragic Muse,* and it becomes more difficult to dismiss the earlier "entreaty" as forgettable nostalgia
for the Old South. As Sara Blair notes, Miriam's Jewishness is scored in the
"marked alterity of [her] speech, which . . . departs from the 'conventional'
in 'the foreign patches,' the 'little queernesses and impurities' that identify
her as one who has 'lived abroad too much.'"[17] (138). Blair's insight suggests
we listen carefully to the ways in which "impurities" like Ransom's register
James's arguments about the nation.

As in *The Tragic Muse,* the coded references to racial difference in *The
Bostonians* also speak for desire; Ransom's "sultry" blackness is a figure for his
aggressive sexuality, a sexuality as foreign in Olive's drawing room as it is familiar to her sister, who James upbraids by keeping undressed. "Mrs. Luna
was drawing on her gloves," Ransom observes, then notes he "had never seen
any that were so long; they reminded him of stockings, and he wondered
how she managed without garters above the elbow" (7). Mrs. Luna is an appropriate subject for this speculative seduction. A moon (her name, in Spanish) to Ransom's sun (recall his "rich basking tone"), she also registers a
"foreign" difference. Tonally, both characters are too "vast" and "basking" for
the cold watercolor light of Boston's Back Bay; too seductive to be illumined
by the hesitant clarifications of the northern sun in Beacon Hill interiors.

James references blackness as a conventionally racist metaphor for uncontrolled sexuality; Ransom is "guilty" of "unexpected" "interpolations"
and of suggesting the "teeming expanse of the cotton-field" (6). But the
"African" (6) otherness of his speech also speaks for sexual difference. His
presence in the Boston drawing room jars, not so much because of its pal-
pable eroticism—Mrs. Luna, I have suggested, radiates this as well—as for
its obliviousness to the hedging the suffragettes wish to impose upon feminine sexuality. This refusal to accommodate resonates with Olive Chancellor's own unwillingness to mask her passionate, uncontrolled interest in
Verena. While James sanctions the former, however, he does not underwrite
the latter; if Ransom's observation of Mrs. Luna is a seduction, James stages
Olive's intervention in Verena's life as a rape:

Verena had learned . . . what a force of will [Olive] had, what a concentration
of purpose. Olive had taken her up, in the literal sense of the phrase, like a

bird of the air, had spread an extraordinary pair of wings, and carried her through the dizzying void of space. . . . From this first interview she felt that she was seized, and she gave herself up, only shutting her eyes a little, as we do whenever a person in whom we have perfect confidence proposes, our assent, to subject us to some sensation (69).

Like Leda, Verena surrenders, but what is most remarkable here is the unchecked "force of will" James registers in Olive. If Ransom's figure, is, like the minstrel, oversexed, Olive's metaphorical posture recalls another bird "species" (recall Miss Birdseye!) in such a way as to frame sexual difference as inappropriately and perversely gendered.[18] This mirroring suggests we read the intimate, potent hatred that Olive holds for Ransom in their contest over Verena as an oblique kind of self punishment, his own (racialized) difference a way of articulating her (sexual) otherness.[19]

Ransom's "elisions and interpolations" provide us with a troubled figure for lesbian desire, but they also speak in less ambivalent terms of James's anxiety over the "teeming" foreign interlopers who occupy the New York streets as aggressively as Ransom does Olive's Boston drawing room. Olive names Ransom an "enemy of her country" and "the wretched coloured race" (140). Ransom is inextricably "bound up" with the "horrid heritage" of "the afflicted South" James will dwell upon in *The American Scene* (277). If the southern black man in Washington looks "ragged and rudimentary," (*The American Scene,* 276) so too does Ransom in Boston, who wonders if "there were not a prejudice against his Southern complexion . . . whether he were stupid and unskilled" (162). In fact, his northern stay only makes his own "Africanness" more visible, for "Basil Ransom's interior" is a "low-ceiled basement, under the conduct of a couple of shuffling negresses, who mingled in the conversation and indulged in low, mysterious chuckles when it took a facetious turn" (161). The racial merging in this passage is all the more striking for the break in tone it reveals; in place of the sustained irony that characterizes the novel as a whole, readers are treated to a discomfited sentimental prose whose shaky control reflects the misgivings of the expatriate who will comment nervously upon the black and Jewish presence in *The American Scene*. Like the parody of sentimentality in minstrel theater, a spectacle that Eric Lott argues "glossed not white encounters with life on the plantation . . . but racial contacts and tensions endemic to the North and the frontier" (38), Ransom's (punned upon) "interior" and travel from the South to the North exploits this character as a stand-in for James's "darkies," and for the Great Migration to cities like Boston. Moreover, the "shuffle" James appropriates from the minstrel stage uses racial difference to indicate class distinctions.[20] The relationship between white tenant and black proprietors is grotesque not only because it unites the races under one roof, but also because of the low plane of the conversation itself. Ransom's quarters are unpardonable, so much so that James's own prose stumbles by too sumptuously insisting on the gradient of decline: he repeats the word "low," then unnecessarily underscores the cultural impoverishment of Ransom's room by locating it in the basement.

No wonder that by contrast, the unimpeachably rarified and fully enclosed spaces of Olive Chancellor's Charles Street house look so "American," her "agitation" on behalf of women "a very American tale" (back cover, 1978 Penguin Modern Classics edition). It is this "mingling" that James will pity but not pardon, this poverty of culture that threatens and for which Ransom is made to serve, this provincialism that illustrates the raced coordinates of James's regional mapping, for Ransom's own distance from "the air of the greater world—which was the world that the North . . . had comparatively been" is a polite reminder of the distance "the negro" has traveled from the South, the Italian from Sicily, and the Jew from the Pale.

### III: A "fondness for foreigners:"
### María Amparo Ruiz de Burton's
### *Who Would Have Thought It?*

*Now, George Mechlin was making his second visit to his family. He had found New York so very dull and stupid on his return from California.*

—María Amparo Ruiz de Burton, *The Squatter and the Don*[21]

The California skyline Ruiz de Burton delineates in *The Squatter and the Don* shares little with the topography James dismisses in *The American Scene* and *The Bostonians*. His Yosemite is a vulgar efflorescence that interrupts the sweep of western expanse, not the tempered expression of a decorous landscape. For James, the West is all Death Valley: a space rather than a place, and one characterized by absence. Verena Tarrant's attraction for Mrs. Farrinder has less to do with the veteran speaker's intrinsic majesty than for her own starved state. Like Owen Wister, who in *The Virginians* dismisses the region as a cultural wasteland (Vermont native Mrs. Woods sends her westering daughter the books she has requested, exclaiming "'How her mind must be starving in that dreadful place!'"), so Verena "was excited by the company in which she found herself," the narrator tells us, "a fact to be explained by a reference to that recent period of exile in the West . . . in consequence of which the present occasion may have seemed to her a return to intellectual life" (40).[22]

Ruiz de Burton's 1885 historical romance rebuts such representations of California life as a contradiction in terms; Mechlin's dismissal of New York, for instance, looks more studied when read against James's impoverished view of the western American scene. Like James, who sees California as a brainless beauty ("that wondrous realm," he calls it ingratiatingly in *The American Scene,* "kept suggesting to me a sort of prepared but unconscious and inexperienced Italy, the primitive plate, in perfect condition, but with the impression of History all yet to be made" [340]), the majority of commentators continue to describe the golden state as a vacant wonder.[23] By contrast, Ruiz peoples California, providing the state with a mature genealogy. The southern Californians who travel east in *The Squatter and the Don* through restaurants and through opera houses (not minstrel shows) enjoy countless social triumphs, leaving a gratifying admiration in their wake. Even the railroad magnates who ruin the state's financial health are sophisticated, witty, and cultivated. With its excellent wines, its polished social life, its cosmopolitan manners, Ruiz de Burton's California—unlike the exoticized "Spanish" feudalism celebrated in Helen Hunt Jackson's *Ramona* or the dilapidated foreign glamour described by Gertrude Atherton in her California romances—is both a distinct American region and distinctly American. As if in response to estranging ethnographies like Jackson's and Atherton's, the travels of the "party from San Diego" demonstrate the class-based links that shape relations between the best of East and West.[24] The Californianas of *Who Would Have Thought It?* and *The Squatter and the Don* insist on the cultural superiority of their home, it is true, by sweeping victoriously through the ranks of New England's social élites, but the paths they trace back and forth across the continent establish connections between regions framed to this day as foreign to one another.

By legitimating California culture in *The Squatter and the Don,* Ruiz de Burton accords the Californios cultural "title" over the Spanish land grants stolen from them after the Treaty of Guadalupe-Hidalgo in 1848. But defending their claims also means defending the country as a whole against those eastern inhabitants who patronize the West as second-rate. When Clarence and Hubert praise the "flavor of the real genuine grape which our California wines have," they are really critiquing the provincial sensibilities of Bostonians like the Norval ladies, who insist that Europe provides the standard for judgment:

> "I think sooner or later our wines will be better liked, better appreciated," Clarence said. "I think so too, but for the present it is the fashion to cry down our native wines and extol the imported. When foreigners come to California to tell us that we can make good wines, that we have soils in which to grow the best grapes, then we will believe it, not before" (171).

Given the depredations of the railroad, whose shining ties trespass the country from land's end to land's end, the point is not to keep the circle "closed enough" but to understand how distinct "old social orders" can make class-based alliances across race and region. Both *The Squatter and the Don* and *Who Would Have Thought It?* cement interethnic affiliations through mixed marriages. Like Ruiz, who married an Anglo military officer during the American occupation of California, the Californianas of her fictions effect what José Aranda calls a "symbolic . . . resolution of all social and political contests by forcing opposing parties to become related, a family, if you will."[25] In defiance of the norms of the romance genre, where marriage is idealized as a union uncontaminated by the demands of practical life, Mercedes and Elvira Alamar fall in love with Anglo American men, who, if not born to wealth and culture, at least know how to create it through wise investments. The orphaned Lola Medina, their literary precursor in *Who Would Have Thought It?,* goes even farther by marrying one of three well mannered Bostonians (the other two are her fiancé's father and her mother-in-law's brother Isaac, who escapes to Mexico after release from prison during the Civil War).

This high-born young lady's stay in Boston affords as sardonic a perspective on the drawing rooms of the "blue Presbyterians" (55) as does Basil Ransom's clumsier entrance into the "organized privacy" of Olive Chancellor's Charles Street house.[26] When Dr. Norval brings his new ward to his middle-class household, her dark skin provides his wife with an excuse to relegate her to the servant's quarters. In *Who Would Have Thought It?* as in *The Bostonians,* abolitionism is a social index that registers class pretensions and speaks to racial differences in excess of the black and white distinctions the Mason-Dixon line plots between free and slave states. Verena Tarrant's low birth is equally marked by her mother's social affectations and her father's "ignoble" position as "the detested carpet-bagger" (51). "Mrs. Tarrant," we are told, "had passed her youth in the first Abolitionist circles, and she was aware how much such a prospect was clouded by her union with a young man who had begun life as an itinerant vendor of lead pencils" (62). For James, this class status marks Verena's stay in Boston as a "foreign" agitation of the closed circle—and it is by sacrificing her at the novel's close that he can shore up the fragments of its precincts.

In *Who Would Have Thought It?* the language of abolitionism resonates with similar class values. The proof of Mrs. Norval's precarious social positioning, a woman nouveau riche at Lola's expense and whose fortune she diligently siphons off, is her failure to circulate this gilded tongue with any facility. "Mrs. Norval is a good abolitionist in talk," one of her neighbors sneers,

> but she ain't so in practice. . . . The night the doctor arrived with Lola, Mrs. Norval insisted that the child should sleep with Hannah, or with the cook,

but as she, the cook, despises niggers, she plainly told Mrs. Norval that she "wouldn't have sich a catteypillar" in her bed (47).

A complex language for Ruiz de Burton as for James, abolitionism defines social groups and regional affiliations as much as it signifies political identifications. The writer lampoons abolitionism as the rhetorical equivalent of a ladies committee for the Boston Museum of Fine Arts, but she does not evacuate it of raced values. On the contrary, we are first introduced to "Wendell Phillips's teachings" (19) at the same time we are introduced to the child Lola; that is, through the diseased imagination of Mrs. Norval and her daughters, who mistake the "Spanish" child for a "nigger girl" (15). Ransom is figuratively associated with the South's "tatterdemalion darkies," but Lola, born into an Indian captivity, is literally blackened by her mother to ensure her safety. Four decades later, Zane Grey will whiten the genre by instating Mormon despots in place of Indian abductors in *Riders of the Purple Sage* and Mississippi pioneers in place of Californio natives. Milly Earn's daughter Elizabeth is, like Lola, born a captive, but instead of passing as an Indian, she plays a boy, discovered only when the "whiteness of skin" below the brown tan line shows "the graceful, beautiful swell of a woman's breast."[27] In the 1872 novel, however, Lola's "black skin" (31) moves the Norval daughters to revile her using standard racist tropes; she is a "specimen" of the "animal" kingdom" (16) whose dark skin entitles her to share the kitchen and the "blackened pillow" (38) of the Irish servants, but not the front rooms the family occupy.

In the hands of some writers, translating "blackness" to the Irish workers would destabilize it as a racial signifier, but Ruiz's exploitation of blackness, like James's play on "African" speech in *The Bostonians,* does not liberate it from racist hierarchies. Instead, the physical begriming of the servants in *Who Would Have Thought It?* mirrors their comportment. The brogue of the "sensitive Irish ladies" (31) is audible in the novel, as is their distaste for the girl they think is black. Their lack of hospitality toward Lola resonates with their lowly social station, which Ruiz naturalizes through metaphors that play upon color. Divested of her feminizing hoop skirts, the "repulsive" (38) cook stands in the center of her fallen clothing "like a stubby column in the middle of a blackened ruin" (37). Her stockings, similarly soiled "black . . . had the privilege of ascending to her ankles, where they modestly coiled themselves in two black rings" (37).

This "blackening" of the Irish is of course not idiosyncratic to Ruiz. Even before the massive waves of immigration from Ireland at midcentury, Eric Lott notes, "Irish and black tended to share the same class niche. . . . 'smoked Irishman' was nineteenth-century rural slang for 'Negro'" (95). Clearly, the raced metaphors of *Who Would Have Thought It?* play off of such discursive conventions. But Ruiz de Burton's besmirching of the Irish also indicates her desire to foreclose upon potential affiliations between two populations whose Catholic practices have afforded others an opening for vilifying them both as "foreign." In 1909, Sui Sin Far will gesture toward connections between marginalized groups in California in "Leaves From the Mental Portfolio of an Eurasian" when she describes a woman who prefers to pass as a Mexicana rather than suffer the censure of the "yellow peril" by turn-of-the-century anti-immigrant groups: "It is not difficult, in a land like California, for a half-Chinese, half-white girl to pass as one of Spanish or Mexican origin. This the poor child does, though she lives in nervous dread of being 'discovered.'"[28] But despite their shared position as a religious minority in the land of the "blue Presbyterians"—Ruiz calls our attention to this when she satirizes the cook's hostility toward Lola (" . . . being a good Catholic and a lady of spirit, [cook] crossed herself earnestly but hurriedly, shook her fist threateningly at Lola, and bolted into bed" [31])—the gap between Irish servant and Californiana ward is unbridgeable in the 1872 novel. Ruiz's anxiety about the possibility of a religious cross-racial alliance is serious enough that she distinguishes Lola from the kitchen workers she is forced to sleep near with a metaphor that threatens to locate the aristocrat in the position of the black slave—another elision she is at pains to deny throughout the novel. Forced by Mrs. Norval to sleep with the Irish servants, Lola chooses instead to throw herself down in the hall on a mat positioned directly outside the bedroom door of the matron herself.[29]

But Lola's blackness is only skin deep, and Ruiz de Burton, writing from a racially defensive position herself, is impatient for it to wear off. If, according to Eric Lott, "those who 'blacked up' and those who witnessed minstrel shows were often working-class Irish men" (35), the feminine "minstrel" of *Who Would Have Thought It?* figures the conventional massing together of different Catholic populations in New England in order to distance herself from just this "servant" class. So we are reminded by Dr. Norval, who has rescued Lola from captivity, that her "blood . . . is as good as, or better than" his own; that she is "neither an Indian nor a negro child," but that her blood "is pure Spanish" (29, 33). Ruiz de Burton insists upon the ignominious social position of "Indian[s]" and "negro[s]" to celebrate the "highly born" (33) Lola. Like the dismissive stance taken by California's 1856 Colored Convention movement, whose newly inaugurated black newspaper the *Mirror of the Times* desired to "tell [white] Californians that Negroes appreciated and understood [the principles of republican government] more than many of the state's foreigners and [Irish] illiterates,"[30] Ruiz de Burton's own unattractive representation is designed to undermine the assumptions white Americans hold about Mexicans. Nevertheless, it distinguishes one California population only to demean others en masse.[31]

Yet Lola's whiteness, as Amelia de la Luz Montes indicates, points also to the vexed relation between Native Americans and Mexicanos. "Like [Lydia Maria] Child," whose novel *Hobomok* "does not quite describe a world where the Indian and Puritan can coexist equally . . . Ruiz de Burton subsumes her own indigenous heritage when she insists upon the 'whiteness' of Mercedes's skin in *The Squatter and the Don* as well as Lola's whitened skin in *Who Would Have Thought It?*"[32] Lola's transformation from "little black child" (46) through the "spotted" condition that makes the Reverend Hackwell think she "must belong to a tribe of Mexican Indians called 'Pinto'" (78) to the woman whose skin is so "white and smooth" it made the doctor's "kind heart beat with pleasure" (79) is remarkable even within the forgiving conventions of the sentimental genre. Taken as a metaphor for the complex network of intimacies and disaffiliations that characterize American race relations, however, Ruiz de Burton's use of blackface complicates Eric Lott's argument that "minstrelsy . . . reinstit[utes] with ridicule the gap between black and white working class even as it reveled in their (sometimes liberatory) identity" (71). In so doing, it calls our attention to the insufficiency of bipolar models of race relations.

When the Norval ladies cast (and cast off) Lola as black, they not only allow the writer to exploit the value of abolitionism as a social currency, but also to undermine its regional coordinates in a manner unavailable to the satire of provincialism afforded by a text like *The Bostonians*. By comparing the political repercussions of the U.S.-Mexican War with the unjust civil conflict that follows it, Ruiz de Burton suggests that defining the United States and its citizens using the rubric of North over South is itself a misapprehension of grand proportions—a misreading of all the people, at least, of all of the "Roman Catholic" (8) people, who live and work in the West. It is the Civil War booster Beau Cackle (of whom the narrator comments that "a long war was good for the Cackle family") who defines the western region as preyed upon by federal policies designed to favor the Puritans residing on the other edge of the continent. "[A]s soon as we take their lands from them they will never be heard of any more," this worthy predicts, "and then the Americans, with God's help, will have all the land that was so righteously acquired through a just war" (9).

What is politically radical about this book happens here, when Ruiz de Burton unhesitatingly juxtaposes two American wars—critically segregated to this day—to undermine both as national values. The ironic cadence strips the U.S.-Mexican War of glamorous rhetoric. It is not, after all, a peaceful annexation (under the terms of Manifest Destiny) or a "just" and glorious conquest (the elegy at the Alamo). Instead, the war is a prosaic matter of gaining real estate for the personal betterment of the New England incompetents who control the federal machine. While Ruiz de Burton is not the first to censure

U.S. imperialism during the war against Mexico—recall that in New England this conflict was, if not roundly condemned, at least partially contested—her insistence that readers acknowledge the relationship *between* this conflict and the Civil War opens a space for comparing, and so reevaluating, a wide range of nationalist discourses. Lazy military men like Beau Cackle, who use the sectional turmoil that follows in the wake of the Treaty of Guadalupe-Hidalgo to line their pockets and to further their political careers, do a lot of cultural work in this novel, because they allow Ruiz de Burton to move beyond the indictment of discrete actions to expose systemic flaws in the federal government. The capsule description Ruiz de Burton provides of the first "just war" of 1846–48 anticipates the extended ironic treatment she will give the second. It is the interpretive key through which readers gloss the military exploits and domestic squabbles that will occupy the rest of the novel, and a briefer version of the argument embodied in the person of Lola Medina, whose journey east and north reverses the geographic and gendered descriptions of Anglo American travel and whose presence undermines the ostensible centrality of "virtuous New England" (8).

The domestic triumphs Lola enjoys over the provincial prejudices of the Bostonians remind readers of the regionalized and raced frame through which the Civil War is filtered in this sardonic parody of northern virtues. We leave the shores of California behind us when Dr. Norval rescues Lola from her Indian captivity, but her graceful drawing-room victories inevitably resonate with the fumbling military exploits of the Yankees in the Civil War. Their own veniality during this apparently sectional crisis is in Ruiz de Burton's satire of nationalist rhetoric indistinguishable from the imperial fantasies that motivate the appropriation of Mexican land; the logical extension, that is, of systemic federal corruption. We can see her exploitation of military metaphors for the social battles fought over the daughter of California as a reminder of the contiguities between these two conflicts, traditionally distinguished as foreign and domestic policy. The "separate spheres" Ruiz conflates when she likens the wars between the Presbyterian Norval ladies and the Catholic daughter of Mexico to the military conquests the descendants of the "Pilgrim fathers" enjoy over their southern neighbors crosses ideological boundaries as well.[33]

Just as James uses Ransom's regional forays to figure the violation of national borders, so Ruiz de Burton's "blue Presbyterians" are chastised by western eyes to foreground relationships between imperial designs and sectional tensions.[34] In *The American Scene* and *The Bostonians*, ethnic Americans are "foreign" precisely because they exist beyond the pale of the Emersonian circle, and it is this geographical confusion Ruiz de Burton plays upon in *Who Would Have Thought It?* Provincialism in her book does not characterize national identity so much as corrode it. Mrs. Norval dismisses California residents as beyond the pale, presciently laments her son Julian's "fondness for foreigners" (18) and identifies her brother Isaac's penchant for "gallantry . . . Havana cigars . . . and those miserable sour wines to a good drink of whiskey" as "tastes . . . which the well-regulated mind of a New Englander repudiates" (72–3). It is this kind of regionally defined prejudice that makes honorable soldiers like Julian and Isaac expatriates in twin removals that leave the American political field open to the misappropriations of Bostonian philistines like the Cackles.

Granted, Ruiz de Burton's satire of New England manners celebrates the superior culture not only of Mexicanos native to California, but also of Mexico itself. Isaac's international pilgrimage following his release from prison destabilizes the authority of the Mason-Dixon line as regional index; rather than return to his Boston home, he opts for further travel in the South. This move deconstructs New England authority from within the nation, of course, but it also recontextualizes the imperial agenda of the United States. Through the vision of a reformed Yankee, Ruiz de Burton develops a political critique that is itself articulated using culture as metaphor. Compared with their Mexican social equivalents, the best citizens of New England have few social resources. Like Henry James, who exploits house and garden as metaphor for the quality of consciousness its inhabitants enjoy, Ruiz de Burton's novel of manners describes interiors in order to sit in judgement upon the ethical conduct of American homeowners.

James may call Washington, D.C., the "City of Conversation," as Susan Luria indicates in "The Architecture of Manners," because of its "'social indifference to the vulgar vociferous Market'" (303–4), but for Ruiz de Burton, Lincoln's federal seat is merely tacky, as is the Boston home of the Norvals. *Their* overstuffed mansion looks tawdry when glimpsed from the well-appointed haciendas of Mexico's upper classes. While the President of the United States chews on tobacco and thumps his foot "like a ballistic pendulum" in time with the "base drum" of the band music he admires, California's relations del otro lado "sit in the library" reading "papers, books, reviews" and "pamphlets" in four languages and dining on "the best wine" their guest Isaac "had ever tasted in his life" (279, 286).[35] If the Mexican elite were less well-mannered, one suspects they would enjoy a guffaw at the expense of their plebeian neighbors to the north.

Ruiz de Burton's comparative reading of culture accords a select few of Mexico's citizens a prestige hitherto unregistered in the American literary landscape, but it would be a mistake to assume that the Californiana writer's critical location is synonymous with that of Lola's relatives. The domestic tableaux in *Who Would Have Thought It?* register the social altitude of the Mexican elite, yes, but they do so from the vantage point of a Californian who, after living for a decade on the East Coast as the wife of a military officer, was intimately connected with the highest authorities of United States federal government. It was she, after all, who obtained a promotion for her husband by appealing personally to President Lincoln. Counting on the support of Mary Lincoln, she urged Mariano Vallejo to come to the capital in 1860 to further his interests:

> No deje de venir, y yo quiero tener el placer de presentarlo a Mr. y Mrs. Lincoln. Ella y yo somos muy buenas amigas y yo sé muy bien que si yo lo presento será muy recibido—Venga pronto [Don't hesitate to come, and I want to have the pleasure of presenting you to Mr. and Mrs. Lincoln. She and I are very good friends and I know very well that if I present you, you will be very well received. Come quickly].[36]

Originally published in Philadelphia in 1872, *Who Would Have Thought It?* is produced out of this social milieu; the portraits provided readers of systemic incompetence and corruption are accordingly indigenous representations, not the musings of an armchair traveler.[37] Put another way, the glimpses we get into the drawing rooms of the two nations are interior ones not only because they use a domestic metaphor to describe political conflict, but because, along with the California-based historical romance Ruiz de Burton will publish out of San Francisco in 1885, they are internal critiques designed to make readers reconsider the legislative and cultural monopoly northern cities like Boston and Washington enjoy over United States citizens as a whole. When "the people of California take the law in their own hands" in order to "seize the property of . . . [t]hese monopolists" (*The Squatter and the Don,* 366)—legislators whose corrupt policies remake national policy into a provincial image—then the nation will be home not only to the descendants of emigrants like the Pilgrim Fathers, but to its regionally defined "natives" as well.

Chapter Two ~

# "I think our romance is spoiled"

## Mixed Marriage and Land Loss in Nineteenth-Century Historical Romances of California

### I: Representing the Right of Way:
### Literary Eulogies and Litigious Novels

W hile the Treaty of Guadalupe-Hidalgo appeared to settle who could cultivate, capitalize, and control the land, literary representations of the right of way continue long after 1848 to adjudicate cultural title to the state. Regardless of their political positioning, fictions produced in the wake of the U.S.-Mexican War struggle to reestablish primogeniture within a troubled space. The editors and writers assembled in San Francisco in 1868 to discuss the inaugural cover illustration of the new western magazine, the *Overland Monthly*, settle upon "a growling young California grizzly bear, the mascot of the state."[1] The bear is "'objectless,'" Mark Twain recalls, until Bret Harte draws the lines of a railroad track under its feet. "'[B]ehold he was a magnificent success! . . . the ancient symbol of California savagery snarling at the approaching type of high and progressive Civilization, the first Overland locomotive!'"(9). Twain's salubrious recoloring of this icon contrasts strikingly with Mariano Vallejo's pointed recollections, where the conquering bear, lampooned as an index of American barbarism, looks more like a hog.[2] For both writers, however, defining who is "native" means appealing to history.

This chapter surveys California's turn-of-the-century historical romances to appraise how different writers legitimize their retellings of land loss and social upheaval. It also considers closely two exceptions to the willful amnesia that characterizes much late nineteenth-century fiction: Helen Hunt

Jackson's *Ramona* (1884) and María Amparo Ruiz de Burton's *The Squatter and the Don* (1885), narratives that foreground the "land grab" despoiling the state's natives of territory rightfully their own.[3] By writing history as a phenomenon of the literary present, Jackson and Ruiz de Burton expose the larger narrative project working to produce social stability and cultural authority in a space characterized more by ruptured lineages than by gentle breezes and burgeoning fruit trees. Their own insistence on the unfinished and contentious nature of western social life reveals how literary work at the turn of the century, even as it appears to obliterate history, is constantly rewriting it.[4]

## II: Monumentalizing the Past

I would sooner pray under the red-tiled roof of a Southern Pacific railroad station as see the bell tower rising above the cement adobes of Taco Bell as a link to the history of Mexican California. Yet this commercial symbol, ubiquitous along the sprawl of fast-food restaurants and gas stations that run the length of the old El Camino Real, is but the latest in a series of icons that have for a century provided Anglo boosters with a mythic cultural legacy for the state. Less than 30 years after the Treaty of Guadalupe-Hidalgo consigned Alta California to the United States in 1848, writers for magazines like *The Century Magazine,* the *Atlantic Monthly,* and the *Overland Monthly* represent the buildings of Mexican California in the style of Shelley's "Ozymandias": old as the pyramids, fragile as the crumbling turrets of a crusader's stronghold, the missions are the "monuments of an epoch already past" "crumbling into ruin," passing away grandly yet definitively "in the long procession of the centuries."[5]

More striking even than the undifferentiated uniformity of this kind of representation is its tendency to hurry the passing of the elderly. Or rather, the middle-aged: for when one considers that 40-some years mark our own distance from the civil rights struggles of the sixties, the three decades between the end of the United States-Mexican War and the flourishing of literature celebrating its repercussions hardly seem long enough to justify relegating the culture of the Californios to a dusty museum shelf. Repeatedly, however, as Cecil Robinson asserts in *With the Ears of Strangers: The Mexican in American Literature,* Mexican California is figured as an anachronism, its archaic "Spanish" past revered, its Mexican present "scorn[ed]" or "simply ignore[d]" (67–8). In the South, as Sandra Gunning demonstrates in *Race, Rape, and Lynching,*[6] plantation and local color fiction lullabied white readers jittery over the (temporary) black political gains of Reconstruction. These fictions literally reconstructed the antebellum South's big houses, celebrating their rigid social hierarchies while vilifying the black men and women whose labor built the foundations for their graceful columns and broad verandas.

Narratives by and about California during this period jettison the material past with equal aplomb. In the hands of Owen Wister, whose 1906 novel *Lady Baltimore* champions the slave South, *The Virginians*—perhaps the single most important shaping influence on cowboy fiction—creates a racially circumscribed old West as a "great playground" of young Anglo American men looking for "American adventure" (51). Just as this popular romance helps to define the cowboy novel as the West's answer to the plantation fictions of Thomas Dixon, so the California of aristocratic dons and humble peones Robinson describes as characteristic of its pastoral tradition vies in feudal luster with visions of the old South (135).[7] Yet they naturalize political conflict—the ongoing contest over land deeded the Californios by the Spanish Crown—by rewriting Californio history less as antebellum than as antediluvian. The crumbling monuments represented in these fictions mask political work-in-progress by providing the American West with an antique cultural finish. Such literary retouching reduces complex cultural negotiations to a one-dimensional story of advance and decline. Imposing this kind of chronological template allows writers to defuse ongoing struggles by figuring contests over land, resources, and capital as a fait accompli, already over.

Elizabeth Haas astutely argues that "the monumentalization of the California missions that took place in the early 1900s . . . is only one side of the story. For the Californio and Indian town residents, the mission's new prominence fostered the articulation of versions of their history and identity that expressed deeply held interpretations of the past."[8] From the point of view of its Anglo American visitors, however, the pervasive charm of the Californio mission is never more appealing than when it begins to deteriorate. Consider Josephine Clifford McCrackin's 1877 story "La Graciosa":

> The warm light of the spring-day shed a soft glimmer over the crumbling remnants of the monuments that the patient labor of the mission fathers have left behind them—monuments of rock and stone, shaped by the hands of the docile aborigines into aqueducts and fountains, reservoirs and mill-house; monuments, too, of living, thriving trees, swaying gently in the March wind, many of them laden with promises of a harvest of luscious apricot or honey-flavored pear. The hands that planted them have long fallen to dust; the humble adobe that gave shelter to the patient toiler is empty and in ruins, but the trees he planted flourish, and bear fruit, year after year; and from the shrine where he once knelt to worship his new-found Saviour, there echoes still the Ave and the Vesper-bell, though a different race now offers its devotions.[9]

The literary work that creates this picture of idleness is considerable: quarrying looks less like breaking up boulders and more like a laying on of hands.

"[D]ocile" natives "shape" the material of nature into the monuments of civilization, but their bone-wearying labor, twice referred to as "patient," shades into contemplation of the "mission fathers" who direct rather than perform it. What survives are not the people who have created this earthly paradise (their hands have "long fallen to dust"), but the garden itself: "living, thriving trees" with the promise of a harvest to be enjoyed vicariously by the reader. This wilderness-in-reverse metaphor efficiently kills off the "aboriginal" and "Spanish" inhabitants of California's fertile soil, leaving "a different race" to sample the edible and visual delights of their land lease.

In his 1906 *Casa Grande: A California Pastoral,* Charles Stuart frames Californio life as equally anachronistic:

> Through the drowsy night-gloom, lime-washed adobe walls showed clean and distant, their massiveness draped by vaqueros' trappings, with here and there quaint relics of former soldier occupants. Casa Grande, sturdy and red-tiled, had been a fort when Rancho Aguas Frías in Sonoma County, was the northernmost Mexican outpost of California. Now, some ten years later, it was the dwelling of John Miller, who had converted the abandoned outpost into a prosperous cattle range.[10]

While only ten years have elapsed since the "fort['s]" conversion into a "dwelling" (note this masculine version of the feminine nomenclature that makes a "house" into a "home"), Stuart stages the simultaneity of Mexican and Anglo life at Casa Grande as a disjunctive shift from the rustic past to modern times. The fading picture of adobe walls at twilight carries a temporal as well as visual logic, as does the word "distant," which instructs readers to view the house's outlines from a chronological and a spatial remove. The image of "quaint relics" speeds up Stuart's literary equivalent of time-lapse photography as it transforms articles of use (the clothing and gear of the vaqueros) into souvenirs. Most importantly, compelling readers to see homes unwillingly and only recently quitted as long-abandoned outposts denies responsibility for the imposition of new borders and dismisses the possibility of future intercultural contact.

Even as they struggle to efface history, such representations refashion it. Owen Wister's Virginian captures and hangs his old friend Steve and another cattle rustler in executions that, as Robert Shulman points out in his introduction to the novel, condone and "echo the 1889 vigilante lynching of 'Cattle Kate' and her partner. Accused of prostitution and of being a fence for stolen cattle, 'Kate' (Ella Watson) seems to have been an intelligent, independent woman whose mistake was to own land one of the big ranchers was determined to get hold of" (xix). While Josephine Clifford McCrackin's contributions to the *Overland Monthly* invoke a variety of subjects: feminine bravery, border violence, and romantic liaisons, the struggle for land title remains a constant. In "Juanita," she calls Mexicans who cross the border transgressors and claims Alta California as the property of "Uncle Sam."[11] "La Graciosa" describes the "Spanish population of California" as maintaining a "distrust" and "wholesome horror of the law" (122) as well as of the "sharp-witted land-shark[s]" skilled in finding its "loophole[s]" (144). Like her contemporary Gertrude Atherton, whose romances call attention to their historicity (she subtitles her 1890 novel *Los Cerritos* "A Romance of the Modern Time,"[12] to emphasize its timeliness), McCrackin insists that historical veracity is paramount in her fiction.

Historian Josiah Royce's novel *The Feud of Oakfield Creek: A Novel of California Life* is likewise indebted to history: it plots a battle between squatters and landholders predicated upon an actual conflict. Oakfield Creek, as the introduction reminds readers, can "easily be identified as Walnut Creek in Contra Costa county," scene in the 1870s of "some of the bloodiest fights in California history." Even Frances Fuller Victor's story of border life, "El Tesoro," invokes Mexican California, if only to focus on its material and linguistic erasure:

All search for, or belief in, gold mines, had been abandoned, even before the land [Tesoro Rancho] came into the possession of American owners, and now was only spoken of in the light of a Spanish legend; but the name was retained, partly as a geographical distinction of a large tract of country, though it was sometimes called the Edwards Ranch, after its present proprietor, and after the American fashion of pronunciation."[13]

### III: Making (Her) House (Your) Home, or, Domesticating Empire: Conquest as Seduction in the Mixed Marriages of Gertrude Atherton

*"My dear madam, you must not deprive the United States of the pleasure of protecting California. Pray grant my humble request to walk behind you and keep off the dogs."*

—Gertrude Atherton, "The Ears of Twenty Americans"[14]

Like the fictions of contemporaries Frances Fuller Victor, Helen Hunt Jackson, and Josephine Clifford McCrackin, the sun in Gertrude Atherton's narratives perpetually threatens to dip below the horizon. Her crumbling missions and rotting bell towers pit Yankee "enterprise" against the "Splendid Idle Forties," but they also clarify the relationship between imperial complacency and nostalgia. In Atherton's work, as in the late-nineteenth-century sentimental novel in the United States more generally, the Anglo

American presence is justified by a sustained and purposeful blurring of the boundaries between the federal exercise of power and social design.[15] Atherton effects this transgression through a series of gendered figures that metaphorically link imperial design and nation building.

Californios recalled the aftermath of the war as a bitter time of loss. In *The History of Alta California: A Memoir of Mexican California,* Antonio María Osio remembers the lowering of the Mexican flag in Monterey as "a painful ceremony" that the "Californios, people who loved their country and were proud of their nationality, were forced to witness."[16] By contrast, the stories Atherton republished in *The Splendid Idle Forties* and *Before the Gringo Came*[17] describe the American seizure of Mexican land as a kind of dowry, the logical conclusion of an international courtship.[18] For Atherton as for Ruiz de Burton and Jackson, the story of California is a marriage plot. In her short story collections as well as in novels like *The Californians* and *Los Cerritos,*[19] Atherton develops the same prototype to represent the conflict between Anglo and Californio. In it, a strong-minded Californiana, wooed by caballero and gringo, eventually overcomes her hostility to the "enterprising United Statesian" (*The Californians,* 10); her rejection of the Californio and her altered disposition toward the Yankee are a romantic allegory sanctifying the U.S. invasion. "The Ears of Twenty Americans" plays this amorous contest out most energetically, but many other pieces in *The Splendid Idle Forties* echo the paradigm: the best of the Californios—who can only be feminine, in Atherton's scheme, must marry the best of men—always Anglo.

While Antonio María Osio rejects the possibility of even fraternal affection between Mexican and Anglo ("the inhabitants of Monterey experienced the sorrow of seeing the stars and stripes wave for the second time from the flagpoles that had been erected for the tricolor flag of the three guarantee . . . For experience has always shown that conquerors never have been able to maintain a brotherhood with those they have conquered" [232]), Atherton rewrites the rape of Mexican land as a seduction. Never one to make too fine a point of it, she ensures we understand the lesson by calling attention to the politics of anthropromorphization.[20] Nor does she hesitate to invoke the names of the real historical actors of this drama. Pío Pico, Mariano Vallejo, the de la Guerras—all the most well known names of Mexican California are trotted out—not to lend credibility to her narratives, but to personalize the political, making history the vehicle for romance. Like many of her contemporaries, Atherton frames international conflict as a domestic problem in order to naturalize it; or, as Cecil Robinson, notes, to "soften . . . the embarrassing fact of military conquest" (137).[21] In this way history is evacuated of its content, and violence is aestheticized as sentiment. The agenda could not be more conservative here; or, to speak precisely, more invested in justifying the workings of empire.

Atherton's blessings on mixed marriages do not defy the discursive conventions of the period. As in *The Squatter and the Don* and *Ramona*, liaisons between Yankee and Californiana are condoned only under specific social circumstances. Robinson explains these provisions:

> The California myth maintains that the fine, old California families are of purely Spanish descent and not to be confused with the later, mongrelized immigrants that came up from Mexico. This myth allows "Anglos" in California to associate on equal terms with a few wealthy descendants of the old stock on the grounds that they are "Spanish," while maintaining segregationist policies toward the great majority of Mexican-Americans (152).

Like Mercedes Alamar of *The Squatter and the Don,* or Don Manuel of Josephine McCrackin's "La Graciosa," whose "clear blue eyes" reflect "[a]ll the sunshine of his native Spain" (132), the Californios of Atherton's work are of "pure Castilian blood" (131); from families, in "the northern provinces of Spain, where the fair type is preserved."[22]

Providing that she "re-create[s] the Andalusian type of loveliness,"[23] Atherton urges the Californiana to marry an "American." While the choice speaks well of her discernment (in "The Doomswoman," for instance, Atherton celebrates "the women of California" as "admirable in every way— chaste, strong of character, industrious, devoted wives and mothers, born with sufficient capacity for small pleasures" [*Before the Gringo Came,* 216]), its primary function is to indict the Californio as incapable of self government. In *California, An Intimate History* (the title itself calls attention to her privatization of political life), Atherton praises Californianas for their "sensibility" in recognizing the "quick terse common-sense . . . of the American" (*The Californians,* 11):

> California women seem to have married foreign men,—Americans in particular, whenever the opportunity was offered them; frugal, sensible, and virtuous, they no doubt recognized the inferiority of their own men as soon as they had a new standard of comparison (*California, An Intimate History,* 72).

Yet we hear less about the virtues of Anglo American males than we do about the vices of "the caballero." Even the rasp of the ugliest Yankee accent is pleasanter than the euphonious melody of a Mexican serenade. "Doña Eustaquia and Benicia Ortega are not the only ones to wed Americans," Atherton tells us in "The Wash-Tub Mail": "Listen! La Tulita is mad for this man, who is no more handsome than the palm of my hand when it has all day been in the water" (*The Splendid Idle Forties,* 143). In another story, "The Conquest of Doña Jacoba," the Doña counsels her daughter to marry one of the "men who belong to that island of the North" because "our young men—are a set of drinking gambling vagabonds" (*The Splendid Idle Forties,* 163).[24]

But the romantic "conquest" in the title of Doña Jacoba's story encodes an argument about gender as well as culture. Feminine counsel here, as in the work of the nineteenth-century American women writers this book considers as a whole, signals an opening for authority—provided the speaker is invested with the mantle of maternity. Husbands are repeatedly pushed to the narrative margins when they fall sick (consider Alessandro in Helen Hunt Jackson's *Ramona,* and Don Alamar and son Gabriel in María Amparo Ruiz de Burton's *The Squatter and the Don*); get bamboozled (Senator Bowen and Cuthbert Sumner in Pauline Hopkins's *Hagar's Daughter*);[25] or, simply, die (*Ramona's* Señor Moreno and Harold Madison of Atherton's *Senator North* are both dispatched before the curtains open). The father's prerogative is unenthusiastically reinstated in all of these books by story's end, but it is the mothers who truly command. In Atherton's work these women speak to further nationalist and imperial aims, but within this rubric, the writer allows them impressive latitude. It is Doña Jacoba, not her husband, who punishes son Santiago with a whipping in a thinly-disguised scene about the seizure of male authority and Doña Pomposa who directs her daughter to further the Anglo conquest of California in "A Ramble with Eulogia" when she insists "let it be an American you marry." (*The Splendid Idle Forties,* 227).[26]

Working for money: this gilded age equivalent of husbanding the soil properly extends the standard "use" argument circulated in the service of Manifest Destiny: "natives" do not use land productively, so Anglo Americans must make something of it in their stead. In The *Californians,* Atherton makes the land-grab argument explicit. Here as elsewhere, stealing land is the logical termination of the fantasied Californio good life:

> A caballero! . . . who will serenade you at two o'clock in the morning when you are dying with sleep, and lie in a hammock smoking cigarritos all day; who will roll out rhetoric by the yard, and look like an idiot when you talk common-sense to him; who is too lazy to walk across the plaza, and too proud to work, and too silly to keep the Americans from grabbling all he's got" (8).

Surely this is the apex of efforts to whitewash conquest, when the Treaty of Guadalupe-Hidalgo is described as the by-product of "silliness."

American aggression is glorious in "The Doomswoman" (*Before the Gringo Came*) where Atherton has Diego Estenega killed off at the end of the novella to prevent his marriage with one of the "admirable" Californianas: "But in American occupation lies the hope of California," he asserts. "What have we done with it in our seventy years of possession? Built a few missions, which are rotting, terrorized or cajoled a few thousand worthless Indians into civilized imbecility, and raised a respectable number of horses and cattle" (222). That these "rotting" missions have provided cultural capital for Anglo American writers since the first stone was dislodged from their foundations is, not, of course, recognized here. Nevertheless, the speed with which what is charmingly crumbling becomes merely decrepit speaks volumes about the political drift of nostalgia.

If the spite with which Atherton invokes California Indians here distinguishes her work from Ruiz de Burton's own slighting references to "savages," both politicize "home." This yoking of ostensibly "public" and "private" spheres speaks as well to the affiliations between this domestic politics and international affairs.[27] As Amy Kaplan frames this relation,

> [t]he binary opposition of the foreign and the domestic is itself imbued with the rhetoric of gender hierarchies that implicitly elevate the international to a male, public realm, and relegate the national to a female, private sphere. Foregrounding imperialism in the study of American cultures shows how putatively domestic conflicts are not simply contained at home but how they both emerge in response to international struggles and spill over national boundaries to be reenacted, challenged, or transformed.[28]

Despite her own best efforts to the contrary, Atherton is useful here because she so explicitly directs our attention to the relationship between gendered divisions and political geography. In "The Ears of Twenty Americans," she rewrites the Bear Flag Rebellion as a two-step between Anglo officers and their Californiana dance partners: "The officers . . . looked with much interest at the faces, soft, piquant, tropical. . . . The girls returned their glances with approval. . . . Ten minutes later California and the United States were flirting outrageously" (62). Like Ruiz de Burton, Atherton consistently introduces military terms into the drawing room, but to different effect. Ruiz de Burton, as I will argue at more length in chapter 3, gives serious thought to the enforced incapacity of "ladies" while using their social victories to critique political hypocrisy. Transporting the vocabulary of war into a feminine space does not so much dignify the private domain in her work as demean masculine enterprise as mock-heroic. Contemporary readers may be tempted to credit Atherton's use of military image as a similarly satiric strategy, but her arsenal does not include irony.

Lines like this one from *The Californians:* "The two men left the ball-room,—where the handsome and resentful señoritas were preparing to avenge California with a battery of glance, a melody of tongue, and a witchery of grace that was to wreak havoc among those gallant officers,"—(11) may be hard for contemporary readers to dignify any other way, but the conflation of spheres here is merely coy, an attempt to "grace" the political with a rhetorical figure.

When Atherton imports the vocabulary of war into "The Ears of Twenty Americans," she does little to endanger national celebration over the results of the U.S.-Mexican War. No feminist parody, this story is merely a kinder, gentler feminization of the machine. Atherton incorporates actual historical events to ensure we take both vehicle and tenor seriously: "The Californian beauty was like no other woman he had known, and the victory would be as signal as the capture of Monterey. "More blood, perhaps," he thought, "but such a history is a poor affair unless painted in red" (77). However insipid, Atherton's differently gendered West contrasts strikingly with standard representations of the region as exotic outback. With its "swift, tumultuous life, its truth, its nobility and savagery, its heroism and obscenity,"[29] the "Song of the West" Frank Norris's Presley writes in *The Octopus* remains conventional for critical approaches to the region. If the West is imagined as (masculine) epic here and elsewhere, it is as often dismissed as cultureless, the geographical equivalent of a bachelor's flat far removed from the artful drawing rooms of New England.

## IV: Requiem for Native California:
## Helen Hunt Jackson's *Ramona* as Elegy

Helen Hunt Jackson's perennially best-selling *Ramona* (1884) and María Amparo Ruiz de Burton's self-published *The Squatter and the Don* (1885) issue political judgements at odds with their era, which celebrates the new regime's right of primogeniture more often than it decries the seizure of formerly Mexican territory. In accordance with the conventions of romance, both books chart the uphill progress of suitors forced to contend with familial prejudice and social obstacles. But in keeping with the state's complicated history of colonialism, these versions of the California pastoral racialize the marriage plot. In *Ramona* and *The Squatter and the Don,* as in Gertrude Atherton's *The Californians* (1898) and *The Splendid Idle Forties* (1902), lovers struggle against conventions that prohibit mestizaje at the same time as, historically speaking, they bear witness to it. Ramona, the daughter of an Indian mother and an Anglo father, is raised as the ward of an old Californio family. After she falls in love with Alessandro, a full-blood Indian, she is forced to leave "the privileged life of the Moreno ranch" and is "plunged into the tragedies and poverty of life among the Indians."[30] The suitors of Ruiz de Burton's narrative—Clarence Darrell, newly rich son of a squatter, and Mercedes Alamar, daughter to the once wealthy Don Mariano—must overcome Mrs. Alamar's disapproval and resist the manipulations of squatters who harass and humiliate the Alamar family.

The difficulties these couples face are not stylized versions of romance, but instead representations of an overtly historical struggle to redefine borders. Jackson (author of *A Century of Dishonor,* a treatise on federal Indian policy), stages this conflict as a tragedy for both "the fading Spanish order" and native peoples, but the declining "Indian tribal communities" remain at the heart of her story. Jackson's novel describes the social effects of its heroine's personal involvement as an essentially ethnographic component of what in race-blind romances would look like psychic conflict. Love demands anthropological observation in this book rather than internal struggle. Like Jackson herself, Ramona is swept off her feet by Native American cultures, not the charm of one man's idiosyncrasies. In *The Squatter and the Don,* the contest centers upon the efforts of the Californios to maintain their land and livelihood in the face of increasing pressure from encroaching Anglo settlers.[31]

Gertrude Atherton's 1890 historical romance *Los Cerritos* justifies the American conquest of Mexican land by naturalizing it as an affair of the heart. The marriage of wealthy landowner Alexander Tremain and California beauty Carmelita Murieta (a mestiza who is herself an icon for the Spanish conquest of California), celebrates American domination of the state. But Tremain's romantic triumph is also a victory for class interests. By winning Carmelita over the protestations of Castro, the Mexican "squatter" who has fallen in love with her, he replays his legal triumph over the squatter community to which both Castro and Carmelita belong. Representing racial difference within the intimate locus of the private, Atherton uses mixed marriage to defuse the sociopolitical conflicts of post-1848 California.

By contrast, Elvira Alamar's marriage to George Mechlin in *The Squatter and the Don,* like Ruiz's own marriage to Civil War captain Henry Burton, uses the personal to politicize relations between cultures, regions, and nations. George works in New York as a bank cashier, but decides to return to California, not to scale the face of Yosemite's Half Dome, but to reinstate himself in society: "Now, George Mechlin was making his second visit to his family. He had found New York so very dull and stupid on his return from California" (69). Like Clarence, whose voyages to the East make him long for the "flavor of the real genuine grape which our California wines have" (171), George's affirmation sees mestizaje not as a union of equals, but the means by which an elite that has been *politically* dispossessed reconfirms its *cultural* superiority.[32] Since the Californios for Ruiz de Burton *are* the "real genuine" California, mixed marriage in *The Squatter and the Don* redefines provincialism with a gloss that remains revisionist to this day. Amy Kaplan argues that Charles Chesnutt's *The Conjure Woman* "exposes the broader national allegory of reconciliation through marriage that is founded on the expulsion of blacks from the national family in the Jim Crow laws of the new South."[33] Ruiz de Burton's 1885 novel complicates the figure of romantic union by presenting us with interracial alliances that produce assimilation in reverse: it is the Clarences and Georges—not the Alamares—who get converted.

In the previous chapter I argued that the historical reference point for plot disturbances is veiled in many turn-of-the-century California fictions. By contrast, Jackson and Ruiz de Burton make visible the historical parameters that drive their narratives. Both books focus unflinchingly upon struggles for land: *Ramona* bewails the suits brought by "thieves and liars" (177), while *The Squatter and the Don* defines federal land policy as "a settled purpose with our law-givers to drive the natives to poverty, and crowd them out of existence" (146). For all its passionate politics, however, Jackson's history anticipates the demise of the mission and the rancho and forecloses upon recommendations for change. Ruiz de Burton's romance develops a similar literary pathology when it invokes the "plight" of native Californians by mourning their downward slide, but the story closes with an appeal that is forward-thinking rather than elegiac.

While many Anglo American writings in the pastoral genre delineate the border between Mexico and California as distinctly as a Rand-McNally map, Jackson is less willing to grant territory to Uncle Sam and less avid to whitewash land theft as a form of natural selection. Nor does she defuse the charge political struggle carries by naturalizing violence. Her contemporary Josephine McCrackin frames border conflict as a quotidian event, a ritual that merits judgement as little as the setting of the sun. In the following passage from "Juanita," the "history of Arizona" is "pictured fittingly in pools of blood and garbs of fire"; not the crimson firelight of war, but the "rose hue" of the evening sky, which turns the clouds "a dark, sullen red, with tongues of burning gold shooting through it" (59). Or, in "Poker Jim":

> It is generally accepted that life in California, particularly in earlier days, was full of excitement and change, every day bringing with it some horrible occurrence or startling event. Perhaps, at the date of my story—about 1860—this excitement had somewhat cooled down; or perhaps it was the life of our young friend only that had flowed along so evenly while at this place. The "horrible occurrence" of her day was the ever-recurring period of her brother-in-law's intoxication—The "startling event" was the coming in of the hacks and coaches from the railroad terminus (143).

A stunning lesson in how to dispatch history, this passage invokes political terror only to reduce it to familial squabbling. The Civil War is completely submerged, while the U.S.-Mexican War is diminished as an unspecified "excitement," its aftermath described in the tone of cool amusement that slights the anguish of conflict as the product of an overheated imagination.[34] These dismissive gestures are followed by an explicit exercise in translation that instructs readers how to rewrite the past by substituting personal skirmishes for military maneuvers and traffic problems for more "startling event[s]."

Jackson's refusal to ignore the repercussions of conquest documents the seizure of land that has let Anglo American readers from Eureka to San Diego call California their own. Instead of exoneration, the "Americans" are scorned by Señora Moreno as "hounds . . . running up and down everywhere seeking money, like dogs with their noses to the ground" (8, 10). Jackson counsels readers to empathize with people humiliated on their own ground, an attention to U.S. injustice witnessed frequently in the Spanish language press[35] but only rarely in Anglo American writings, where, even today, the Bear Flag Rebellion is described as welcomed by the Californio elite, and the war euphemized as an "annexation:"

> The people of the United States have never in the least realized that the taking possession of California was not only a conquering of Mexico, but a conquering of California as well; that the real bitterness of the surrender was not so much to the empire which gave up the country, as to the country itself which was given up. Provinces passed back and forth in that way . . . have all the ignominy and humiliation of defeat, with none of the dignities or compensations of the transaction (12–13).

Oblique references to dispossession ("The Father knew the place in the olden time. He knows it's no child's play to look after the estate even now, much smaller as it is!" [5]) open to full-throated denunciations of injustice. Alessandro recounts a particularly telling incident for Ramona: "One man in San Bernardino last year, when an Indian would not take a bottle of sour wine for pay for day's work, shot him in the cheek with a pistol, and told him to mind how he was insolent any more!" (279).

Yet for all its willingness to extend sympathy to the bereaved, Ramona's representation of historical grievance as inevitable tends to negate the potential for redress. The despoiling of native Californians may be a tragedy, but it is one authorized by federal law, racial law, and natural law nonetheless.[36] Lamentation rather than exhortation characterizes this sunset picture, while the recognition of loss favored by the text's moral system is not the angry call for revenge voiced by the demonized Señora Moreno (whose hyperbolic language and cruel treatment of Ramona discourage readerly sympathy), but the wistful resignation of Alessandro and Father Salvierderra, the novel's figures of heroism and grace. Alessandro's response to the fact that the Americans "are going to steal all the land in this country" is, simply, to despair: "we might all just as well throw ourselves into the sea and let them have it" (177). This image, which echoes in minor key the triumphant westerly march from sea to shining sea, is confirmed when Alessandro loses his reason and is murdered as a horse thief. Father Salvierderra, too, bows to the results if not the tone of Manifest Destiny, when he counsels "We are all alike helpless in their hands, Alessandro. They possess the country, and can make what laws they please. We can only say, 'God's will be done,' and he crossed himself devoutly, repeating the words twice" (67). The padre's litany furthers the imperial program he decries, as he mourns the cruelty of Anglo despotism only to sanctify Manifest Destiny as God's law.[37]

Framed in the language of faith, this kind of victimization furthers distinctly secular work as well. It assuages guilt over American imperialism at the turn of the century, soothes the jangled nerves of readers harried by the frenetic pace of the Gilded Age, and reconstructs, if only imaginatively, an urbane culture lost to urban sprawl, where "old mission garden" and "proud avenue" are cut up into "building lots" ("La Graciosa," 30) and steel trespasses on land "tilled for two centuries" by people of the same blood.[38] "The pulse of to-day beats at a fever heat," Elizabeth Hughes complains in her own elegy for Mexican California, turning for a moment from "the calm quiet of the California of the Padres to our more stormy period" (28). Writing of Mexico itself, an anonymous observer for *The Century Magazine* draws on the same language of disdain for the indignities of commercialism, decrying gringos with the accent of one: "One shudders to think of street-cars in the *Calle Real*, of sharp American voices among the sunset shadows of the *paseo*, of American boot-heels on the sandal-worn pavement, of American Spanish!"[39]

According to Señora Moreno's son Felipe, the "fast incoming Americans" count success to the vulgar clink of metal on metal. Clearly, the frenzied "passion for money and reckless spending of it, the great fortunes made in one hour, thrown away in another" (359) are as unpalatable to the writer as to her character. Hence the appeal of Father Salvierderra as the remnant of gentility, whom Jackson characterizes using ethnography's standard of the dying savage: "He was fast becoming that most tragic yet often sublime sight, a man who had survived, not only his own time, but the ideas and ideals of it" (35–36). A Mexican Ishi, the priest's devotion is attractive by virtue of his nearness to extinction.

This aestheticization of violence endangers what should be by rights a historicizing project. In his introduction to the 1987 edition of the book,

Michael Dorris notes Jackson's urgent desire to right political wrongs, citing a letter to a friend in which the author distinguishes between the strategies of *A Century of Dishonor* and *Ramona*. In the former she "had tried to attack the people's conscience directly," while in *Ramona* she had "sugared my pill, and it remains to be seen if it will go down" (xviii). Bittersweet, finally, may be the palliative that Jackson's descriptions of Mexican California provide, but passages like the following are also therapeutic for harassed visitors from the "modern" states:

> It was a picturesque life, with more of sentiment and gayety in it, more also that was truly dramatic, more romance, than will ever be seen again on those sunny shores. The aroma of it all lingers there still; industries and inventions have not yet slain it . . . it can never be quite lost, so long as there is left standing one such house as the Señora Moreno's (12).

Jackson's image of decaying architectural grandeur recalls late-nineteenth-century European landscape paintings in which well-dressed figures stroll through the magnificent but ruined buildings of capital cities—a visual parable of the rise and fall of civilizations. Just so are we, her readers, situated with respect to "Old California": moralizing with the aid of hindsight upon the crumbling structures of an apparently ancient history. Dispossessed of its urgency, history is deprived of its political antidote as well.

## V: The Limits of Genre

*I hope . . . that the time will come when some faithful historian will chronicle all the deeds of daring and service these people have performed during this struggle, and give them due credit therefor.*

—Frances Harper, *Iola Leroy* (1892)[40]

*" . . . I dun know nothin' 'bout buyin' lan', an' I'se 'fraid arter I'se done buyed it an' put all de marrer ob dese bones in it, dat somebody's far-off cousin will come an' say de title ain't good, an' I'll lose it all" (173).*

—Frances Harper, *Iola Leroy*

Anger rather than wistfulness characterizes María Amparo Ruiz de Burton's own chronicle of Mexican California. What Lorna Dee Cervantes will characterize a century later in her "Poema para los Californios Muertos" as "the pure scent of rage"[41] is articulated in *The Squatter and the Don* in the controlled tones befitting the turn-of-the-century historical romance. Nonetheless, outrage and not mournful complacency drives the narrative. If *Ramona* is a romance that takes place in history, then Ruiz de Burton's narrative is a history spoken in several languages: of romance, yes, but also of the law and the political tract, as well as of a specifically feminine judgement that eludes the conventions of the romantic. Such languages permit a more sustained critical evaluation than is generally possible within the constraints of a genre whose political indictments typically do not extend beyond accounts of individual rapaciousness to accommodate testimony about systemic failure. The exoticized picture of "sunny shores" Jackson paints in *Ramona,* a geographically indistinct coastline that could as easily be Hawaii or Cuba as California, mythologizes regional boundaries and mystifies their relation to nationalist projects and imperial goals. The topography and topicality of *The Squatter and the Don,* on the other hand, indicate how local politics are underwritten by corporate interests and furthered by the federal government. By insisting upon the federal relationship to California, Ruiz de Burton refuses to participate in language that represents the state as a dilapidated paradise whose pre-industrial charms distinguish it from the busy activity of the twentieth-century East (itself a synecdoche for "nation"). In place of the booster's tourist brochure that figures the region as a lotus land immune to the ravages of time, Ruiz de Burton's novel locates the state squarely within a national chronology.

Even the chapter titles signal the book's historiographic project. The opening chapter, "Squatter Darrell Reviews the Past," announces the book's interpretive paradigm shift. Darrell is not glamorized as a sturdy "settler" making good land that lies fallow, but instead is revealed as morally compromised, a man willing to overlook the ethical problems posed by locating "claims on land belonging to any one else" (57). Succeeding chapters acknowledge romance, but alternating with laments of "Shall It Be Forever?" and celebrations like "Reunited at Last," are headings like "Pre-Empting Under the Law," "Why the Appeal was Not Dismissed," and "The Fashion of Justice in San Diego." These titles provide clear-eyed assessments of political scandal and depict contests over land with legal precision.

The Darrell-Alamar courtship evolves within a context of political corruption so thoroughly detailed that it competes with the narrative's romantic trials for center stage. Historical romance most often frames its political lessons as digressions from the movement of the suitors toward union. Biographical sketches of Frederick Douglass and explanations of the three-fifths suffrage rule disrupt the story of familial reunion that unfolds in Frances Harper's *Iola Leroy* (1892), for instance, but they never succeed in usurping the reader's loyalty for the main text. In *The Squatter and the Don,* laments over Mercedes's tears and Clarence's travels alternate with the Don's chronicle of dispossession. In chapter after chapter, Ruiz de Burton writes a history at cross purposes with the ethnocentric, blindly optimistic boosterism of state growth charts like Charles Nordhoff's "forward-thinking" *California:*

*For Health, Wealth, and Residence, a Book for Travellers and Settlers* (1872) and backward-glancing nostalgia for the conquistadores' California. Her own book graphs the ruses of an unjust "justice" system, plots federal complicity with state-sponsored violence, and charts corporate manipulations of natural and industrial resources. Ostensibly the prime mover of this textual universe, this interrupted romance becomes simply an illustration of large-scale social turbulence.[42] Ruiz's railroad of conservatively-suited entrepreneurs is a dry spectacle compared with "the galloping monster" (51) that some fifteen years later will coil its metal "tentacles" (12) around Frank Norris's *The Octopus*. In *The Squatter and the Don,* the "iron-hearted Power" (Norris, 51) is an economic fact—an office occupied by an ironical Leland Stanford who sits behind a desk taking the nineteenth-century equivalent of a conference call. Rather than destructive grandeur, what we get here is simply the Big Four "taking care of business" (318).

Where many of her contemporaries defuse political violence, moving it into a domestic space defined in opposition to the social domain, Ruiz de Burton politicizes the family circle. Home is the origin for describing national conflict. The talk of Clarence and Mercedes is as often pragmatic as lyrical, their own happiness inseparable from the aspirations of the social body. "This young couple went on discussing San Diego's chances of life or death, and their own hopes in the future," Ruiz de Burton tells us, conflating rather than distinguishing between the personal and the political. When she continues, the intimacies of romance give way to historical grievance: "They were not the only couple who in those days pondered over the problem of the '*to be or not to be*' of the Texas Pacific, which *never came!* . . . The monopoly triumphed, bringing poverty and distress where peace might have been!" (298). The documentation of political corruption plunders the vocabulary of the romance, while moral fervor and impassioned plea become part of the public domain, with a corresponding redirection and expansion of readerly sympathy.

Ultimately the sorrows of the Californios are described as frequently as the singular difficulties of Mercedes and Clarence. The author indicts political wrongs using the same vocabulary of aggravated assault she exploits to detail her suitors' sufferings:

> [The legislators] have not only caused me to suffer many outrages, but, with those same laws, they are . . . teaching the people to lose all respect for the rights of others—to lose all respect for their national honor. Because we, *the natives* of California . . . were, at the close of the war with Mexico, left in the lap of the American nation, or, rather, huddled at her feet like motherless, helpless children, Congress thought we might as well be kicked and cuffed as treated kindly (174).

Explicit denunciations of American injustice like this one recall the outspo-
ken columns of the Spanish language press, but Ruiz de Burton's frank
avowals of legal inequities target the "settlers" in their own tongue.[43] The
cleverly engineered passage I have cited above speaks to the concerns of several audiences. Ruiz appeals to the hurt feelings of westerners disparaged by
the rest of the nation as provincial by insisting that California's problems are
the product of federal disregard rather than the machinations of Joaquín
Murrieta or the San Francisco Vigilante Committee. In this way, the griev-
ances of one Californiana illustrate a systemic ill destructive to "national
honor" and "the people" as a whole. The segue from "my" complaint to "we,
the natives" resonates with "we, the people" and reminds Californios that the
author's sufferings speak for their own. At the same time, the word "outrages" speaks volumes to readers of the Spanish language press, where it encodes a pattern of abuses against Mexicano citizens of the U.S. Even eastern
readers are brought into the fold, not only by the generalized appeal of the
orphan parable, but by the way self-respect and respect for others open up
to the inclusive problem of "public morality."

Despite the fact that she is publishing in English and for an interracial
audience, Ruiz de Burton is as sharply critical of federal expedience as are editorials like the following, a eulogy for Governor Juan Bautista Alvarado
published in *La República*. Here, the Treaty of Guadalupe-Hidalgo is framed
as "cuestionable" (questionable), while the Mexicans of California are described as the "compatriotas" (compatriots) of the late governor, a community of integrity "descansaban, en vano, en las garantías ofrecidas por dicho
tratado para respetan las concesiones de terrenos" [who had trusted in vain
in the guarantees offered by the mentioned treaty to respect the conceded
terrain].[44] Don Mariano's diagnosis of political ills outlines the failure of the
U.S. government to honor the terms of the Treaty of Guadalupe-Hidalgo as
clearly as any polemical essay:

> With very unbecoming haste, Congress hurried to pass laws to legalize their
> despoliation of the conquered Californians. . . . As our legislators thought
> that we, the Spano-American natives, had the best lands, and but few votes,
> there was nothing to be done but to despoil us, to take our lands and give
> them to the coming population (175).

Rejecting the consolations of euphemism the heroes of *Ramona* are loath
to give up, Ruiz de Burton's Don Mariano discourses upon the virtues of ex-
pediency with the urbanity of his biographical namesake, Don Mariano
Guadalupe Vallejo. Through the dryly witty Don, Ruiz clarifies the racial inflections of a regional policy that is actually a product of federal venality.[45]
Counterpointing the controlled rancor with which Don Mariano exposes

unjust laws are the laws themselves. Ruiz de Burton does not merely borrow from the vocabulary of the justice system; she reproduces, wholesale, relevant legal documents. Reiterating her own 20-year suit for title to land deeded her grandfather Don José Manuel Ruiz in 1804, the author recites in *The Squatter and the Don* portions of congressional proceedings and their outcome, invoking the state's language to expose its built-in loopholes with the practiced eye of a lawyer.[46] *Ramona* demonstrates the facility with which the law becomes an abstraction; in Jackson's critique of Gilded Age mercantilism, it simultaneously decries and justifies the inexorable advance of civilization. The fact that the Californios did not, "in those happy days . . . reckon land by inches" proves their undoing in *Ramona:*

> It might be asked, perhaps, just how General Moreno owned all this land, and the question might not be easy to answer. It was not and could not be answered to the satisfaction of the United States Land Commission, which, after the surrender of California undertook to sift and adjust Mexican land titles; and that was the way it had come about that the Señora Moreno now called herself a poor woman (12).

But Ruiz de Burton refuses to rewrite the law in accordance with generic convention. Her protracted discussions of legal euphemism and evasion may tire readers expecting the pleasures of the deus ex machina rather than the pains of habeas corpus, but if this mimetic fidelity makes the narrative clumsy, it allows her to question the conventions of the romance itself.[47] Additionally, her refusal to grant the law a metaphorical register means that this language maintains an authority independent of the literary boundaries within which it is invoked. If the author gives up the aesthetic pleasures of metaphor, she underscores its political register, revealing the legal euphemisms by which the state sanctions its power.

Ruiz uses irony along with this quasi-professional exploitation of legal discourse to undermine the euphonious abstractions of local color writing. "Settlers" in particular feel the sting of the writer's scorn. The droll mirthlessness of the following repetition, for instance, dispatches them in two swift sentences: "Yet, this was the best that could be done, as his time was limited. But he was amiable, the ladies were amiable, and the gentlemen were amiable" (122). This phrase also critiques the rhetorical amiability of the genre as a whole, whose mellifluous cadences mask sordid realities. The judgement Ruiz de Burton metes out below is all the more biting for its crisp austerity:

> The stakes having been placed, Darrell felt satisfied. Next day he would have the claim properly filed, and in due time a surveyor would measure them. All would

be done "according to law" and in this easy way more land was taken from its legitimate owner. This certainly was a more simple way of appropriating the property of "the conquered" than in the days of Alaric or Hannibal (76).

A very complex kind of historicizing is operating here. Clearly, the author's indictment of the squatters depends upon historical revision; rather than romanticizing conflict as the by-product of Manifest Destiny, she focuses on the legal machinations that enable dispossession. But when she invokes "the days of Alaric or Hannibal" she is also using the discipline of history itself as metaphor. Locating contemporary events within the context of classical military conquests suggests that readers register the appropriation of Californio grants as imperial seizure rather than domestic transfer. That is, Ruiz de Burton invokes empire to correct conventional definitions of imperialism as always occurring elsewhere. Her allusion to the Eurocentric standard for American historiography also authorizes her own regional history as "central" rather than provincial. By equating her revisionary history of California with canonical classical history, she sanctifies the former as (an equally uncontestable) historical "truth."

In fact, such mannered irony aligns *The Squatter and the Don* with the sardonic deconstructions of nationalism characteristic of late-nineteenth-century Mexican American writers more generally. Antonio María Osio's parody of Anglo American military heroism in *The History of Alta California: A Memoir of Mexican California* reads with as much relish today as when it was first penned. "Apparently the meal hour had arrived," Osio remarks caustically of a cessation in battle, "and they had to fulfill that obligation first so that they might return to firing later with more vehemence." [48] When read against Anglo representations of "Pancha" as provincial village girl (in "Pancha: A Story of Monterey," the heroine "who never had been but a league away from [Monterey] in the whole seventeen years of her life-time, did not know that the city in which she lived was picturesque at all," and in "Niñita," our lady of the same name "had lived her whole life long—that is to say, a trifle less than seventeen years—in the little town of Santa Cruz" where "[t]here was . . . a perfect placidity very well calculated to produce a quiet, loving faith such as dwelt serenely in Niñita's little breast"),[49] the satire of the Californios reveals itself as a classed language whose clipped inflections show up the cloying simpletons of *The Century Magazine* as fantasies of the new ruling class.

While scholars in general have read only accommodation in this genteel, mannered language, I would argue that it is a rhetorical system that turns on the gap between a *formal,* public utterance and the more full-throated anger voiced only between intimates.[50] Such public language is unfailingly courteous despite and *to spite* insult. It masks a deep anguish expressed openly in private, however. Where Don Mariano must claim no grudge against the Americans (in order to maintain his social standing as gente de razón), Ruiz de Burton writes with bitter calmness about the American "wolves" to longtime friend Mariano Vallejo in a letter dated August 26, 1867:

Los Americanos son y serán siempre los enemigos morales de mi raza, de mi Méjico. No digo esto con odio; ellos no hacen mas que seguir la ley de su ser. Las naciones, los individuos, los animales, todos hacen lo mismo. Sin odio, los tiburnes se comen las sardinas; sin rancor los lobos se comen los borre-gos . . . Pero ni los tiburnes, no los lobos . . . deben ser amados de sus vícti-mas [The Americans are and will always be the mortal enemies of my people, of my Mexico. I don't say this with hatred; they do not do more than follow the law of their nature. Nations, individuals, animals, all do the same. With-out hatred, the sharks eat the sardines; without rancor the wolves eat the lambs. . . . But neither the sharks, nor the wolves . . . can expect to be loved by their victims].[51]

If the corrosiveness expressed in this letter is rarely voiced in *The Squat-ter and the Don*, the sardonic deftness of its conclusion is not uniformly maintained in the novel either. Like Jackson's exploitation of Alessandro and Father Salvierderra as allegorical figures, character often works in *The Squatter and the Don* as shorthand for a cultural script that forecloses upon a more complicated rendering of the relation between collective practice and individual biography. Indeed, with its quality of timeless lament, the story's prolonged account of despoliation threatens to undermine its own historicizing work. In the following passage, for instance, the trenchant ac-count of land foreclosure and corporate manipulation of public policy gives way to the consolations of abstract elegy: "It seemed to Clarence as if the little fountain was in sympathy with the dispossessed owners, but did not dare to raise its timid voice in behalf of the vanquished, who no longer had rights in their patrimony, and must henceforth wander off disinherited, de-spoiled, forgotten" (85). On the one hand, the very completeness of this list of misfortunes revises official versions of the American conquest that give short shrift to the losses suffered by the Californios. On the other hand, the acknowledgement of loss carries with it a paralyzing sense of closure and surfeit.[52] Ruiz occasionally figures cultural conflict using a generalizing lan-guage of deterioration. As he contemplates the weddings of his son and daughter to Anglo Americans, "Don Mariano was kind and affable to all, but many days passed before he became reconciled to the fact that the mar-riage of his two children was not celebrated as his own had been, in the good old times of yore" (123).

But this narrative listlessness is the exception rather than the rule. The language of mourning does not monopolize the text; pathos may be the preferred convention of the historical romance, but Ruiz de Burton never sustains this voice for long, shifting instead to modes more polemical than pastoral. The passage I have quoted above is followed on the next page by sardonic commentary that stifles lugubrious lament: "Voices calling them to dinner were now heard, and they returned to the picnic grounds. No banquet of the Iliad warriors surpassed this, showing that the settlers of Alamar had found the Don's land and the laws of Congress very good" (86). More than anything else, it is her deft manipulation of irony that allows the writer to exploit mixed marriage, as José Saldívar suggests, to "set the limits of the national imagined community and simultaneously deromanticize the traditional plot of the western U.S. romance."[53] The nostalgia voiced in Don Mariano's reminiscence of "the good old times of yore" not only "occlude[s] harsh social transformation" but also "opens toward a rhetoric of nonappeasement" (215), as Genaro Padilla persuasively argues of nineteenth-century Mexican American literature more generally. But the parody of romance encoded in the mock marriage Mercedes's mother Doña Josefa witnesses at the close of the novel, where "one of the railroad kings, who had killed the Texas Pacific . . . was giving a 'silver wedding' party to the elite of San Francisco" (361) provides another critical opening. As Jesse Alemán astutely points out, "despite the closure Clarence and Mercedes's marriage affords her, Doña Josefa's position outside the 'silver wedding' party ironically highlights the limitations of her daughter's marriage as a symbolic resolution to the narrative's historical conflict" (13).

Even where the narrative is most despairing, Ruiz de Burton builds in textual "loopholes." Don Alamar explains to Clarence:

> I don't see any remedy *in my life-time*. I am afraid there is no help for us native Californians. We must sadly fade and pass away. The weak and the helpless are always trampled in the throng. We must sink, go under, never to rise. If the Americans had been friendly to us, and helped us with good, protective laws, our fate would have been different. But to legislate us into poverty is to legislate us into our graves. Their very contact is deadly to us (177, emphasis added).

In this remarkably searching critique, Ruiz de Burton refuses to indict individual instances of corruption in order to call into question the ostensibly impartial abstraction of the Law itself. The eulogy supplies readers with enough contradictory indices to permit multiple glosses. The verb series ("fade," "pass away," "sink," "go under") transforms the Don's pronouncement into a funeral dirge: there is no hope for rallying, only the wearying certainty of imminent demise. But these synonyms for cultural extinction are undermined by the modifying phrase that closes the first sentence. The very contingency of "in my life-time" unravels the passage's fixed cultural teleology. Additionally, the equation posited by the penultimate line ("But to legislate us into poverty is to legislate us into our graves") underlines the fact that the Don's image of death is precisely that—a metaphor. The yawning grave is not unequivocal reality, but merely the means by which Ruiz figures the creation of a permanent—but still living and breathing—underclass.

This temporal window gestures toward a different future. Given the interpretive work required to uncover it, however, the opening is narrow. Loopholes may not require professional training—Ruiz de Burton's legal acumen demonstrates this—but they do demand close scrutiny and a skeptical disposition. How much more likely, then, for readers to be guided by eulogy than by those interpretive gestures at variance with generic expectation. Toward the close of the book Don Mariano attests "we are Clarence's vaqueros now" (247), a pronouncement that, if ironic, certifies the more fatalistic reading by echoing how the mighty have fallen. This acknowledgment makes explicit the political inequities other writers gloss over,[54] but within the resolutely ahistorical lexicon of the pastoral, the image of the conquerors conquered rehearses the rise and fall of civilizations in a manner more archetypal than topical.

### VI: "I think our romance is spoiled," or, Crossing Genres: The Status of History in *The Squatter and the Don*

I have indicated some of the rhetorical maneuvers by which Ruiz de Burton redirects the backwards glance of the historical romance: a sustained historicism that keeps current events current, an irony that cuts across the grain of the pastoral's tendency toward euphemism, a wholesale appropriation of legal and polemical languages in order to question the primacy of the lexicon of the romance. All of these strategies are successful to a degree, but they are nevertheless embedded within a narrative whose generic conventions encourage postmortem rather than prevention. Yet *The Squatter and the Don* is critically successful in a way that *Ramona* is not, because it calls our attention to the very generic borders its characters have difficulty transgressing. Clarence and Mercedes speak the language of romance, but Ruiz de Burton parodies their suspirations and swoons to remind readers that *their* literary aspirations do not speak *her* mind. If pastoral conventions generally take the history out of the historical romance, they are also gendered and raced in a manner that trivializes the work of women writers and condescends to Californio literature as the writings of a people disparaged as "good-natured," as Josephine Clifford McCrackin writes in "A Lady in Camp," but "not very deep" (222).[55] Time and time again Anglo American writers use "the shimmer of romance and poetry" (McCrackin, "Arizona Deserts," 307) as a foil for the drudgeries of the Gilded Age, a means of enjoying the rustic pleasures of Californio life—represented, of course, at the safe remove of the past. McCrackin's "La Graciosa," whose title conjures up images of the good life, makes this point particularly emphatically. No sooner does Nora move to the San Francisco Bay Area from the East Coast than she becomes the object of Don Pedro's attentions. Mocking Nora's penchant for the romantic, while simultaneously underwriting her rose-colored vision, McCrackin invokes the same language of rapture that D. H. Lawrence, Mary Austin, and Willa Cather will exploit to celebrate their own representations of the Southwest half a century later. Whether she is admiring the beauty of the landscape or the graciousness of Mexicano custom, Nora sighs for "the romance of it all" (34). Even the young woman's mercenary encouragement of the Don is at once chided and justified by this appeal: "Well, was it not romantic, after all, to marry the dark-eyed Don, with the haughty bearing and the enormous wealth?" (41).

When we bear in mind that McCrackin's relentless aestheticization of a "declining" culture is conventional for late-nineteenth-century Anglo treatments of "the Mexican," we can appreciate how Ruiz de Burton furthers her clear-eyed recitation of land fraud stylistically. She supplies historiographic corrective, that is, by denying the pleasures of nostalgia. Instead of maintaining with Jackson that the "picturesque life . . . can never be quite lost" (12), she insists that government corruption and illegal business practices like those that enriched Leland Stanford will bring "ruin and squalor and death . . . to people who never harmed you!" (319).[56] "[S]qualor" replaces the crimson glory of the setting sun; "ruin" and "death" stand in for loss tempered by nostalgia. [57] Refusing to render the decline of the Californios sublime, she plays instead on the romantic genre itself. Like the often biting prose of Vallejo, the honored friend with whom she kept up a correspondence for many years, or the satiric deflations of Antonio María Osio, Ruiz de Burton is at her finest when she lampoons the pretensions of the epic, a genre closely aligned with both romantic and nationalist rhetoric. Sometimes this parody is broad; whenever Mercedes's brother Victoriano describes his sweetheart Alice (Clarence's sister), his family teases him in dialogue that resembles the verbal slapstick of Laurel and Hardy or the punning confusion of a "Who's on First" routine. At other instances, Ruiz de Burton's satire recalls the finely sustained irony of her first novel, *Who Would Have Thought It?* This critique of femininity, for instance, cogently makes use of and mocks sentimental convention: "Mercedes took her hat and gloves and cloak off, and sat at the window *to enjoy* her misery in a thoroughly womanly fashion" (167). By emphasizing "enjoy," Ruiz insists on the virtues of parody. Compare this play on sentimentality with Charles Stuart's unsmiling heroine of *Casa Grande*, who sheds tears of genteel joy without a trace of satire: "Once again the little room with white curtains and white bed became silent witnesses of the girl's happy tears" (109).

Nor does such attention to the limits of genre remain implicit. Mercedes's gratification upon learning that her intended is not a squatter after all, but has purchased his land from her father, allows Ruiz de Burton to give readers explicit lessons in literary interpretation. "It isn't half so *romantic* to love a plain gentleman as to love a brigand, or, at least, a squatter," Mercedes's sister Elvira teases her. "Are you regretting that, after all, you cannot sacrifice to love your patrician pride by marrying a land-shark, thus proving you are a *heroine?* . . . Really, I think our *romance* is spoiled. It would have been so fine—like a *dime novel*"—(141; emphasis added). Romance, heroine, dime novel: the vocabulary here is insistently metatextual, directing readers to gloss this sisterly joke in the most literary of terms. *The Squatter and the Don*, it turns out, is more than a romance—or rather, as Elvira's negation indicates, is not one at all. In place of the love story, now comically deflated, we are to substitute an expressly political history: of class conflict, of racial injustice, of land theft. Playing the two terms of her generic equation against one another, Ruiz de Burton appropriates the historical romance only to use it against itself. Her characters do not entertain an audience nostalgic for a feudal paradise (ricos sampling the fruits of the California vine while peones contentedly harvest it), but instead struggle to maintain their land and livelihood in an all too squalid present.[58]

Yet her acerbic rereading of the romance has its limits. Bahktin has argued that the ideological work of the novel is to "do the police in different voices," and we can position Ruiz de Burton's multipronged rhetorical strategizing within this context. Her wholesale recirculation of the law, her reproduction of historical texts like the Huntington letters, the various satirical registers with which she voices her characters' romantic tribulations— these are unsettling, yes, but in the end they are not enough. After all is said and done in *The Squatter and the Don*, Ruiz de Burton provides us with an interpretive "key" to her story that does and says everything again—a nonfictional conclusion spoken in the register of populism that exhorts readers to political action. The forward-carrying motion of this second narrative finish is clear; from its unapologetic title "Out with the Invader" to its explicit recommendations for change, the eight-page coda makes us question the efficiency of the 309-page fiction that precedes it. Freed from the constraints of a genre enforcing plaint rather than platform, Ruiz de Burton here urges *"the people of California"* to *"take the law in their own hands,* and seize the property of those men, [the] arrogant corporation" and to "confiscate it, to

reimburse the money due *the people*" (366). By invoking actual historical figures, she reinstates the Californios as the heirs of the state and provides Mexicano readers with a model of political behavior as far removed from Father
Salvierderra's gracious resignation as from the rapaciousness of the Big Four:

> The Spanish population of the State are proud of their countryman, Regi-
> naldo del Valle, who was one of the first to take a bold stand against the mo-
> nopoly. This young orator with great ability and indomitable energy, has
> never flagged in his eloquent denunciations of the power which has so tram-
> pled the laws of California and the rights of her children (369).

Ruiz de Burton's reliance on a conclusion framed hors de texte asks us
to reconsider both the limits of genre and the ease with which we, as critics and readers, celebrate "dialogism" as a political end in itself. Under her
direction, the historical romance is elastic enough to support a plurality of
voices. But the manipulation of different registers is not sufficient, for this
polyphony is contained within a medium colored by writers who romanticize the Mexican American as a contradiction in terms and who dismiss
sentimental writing as too slight to bear the burden of political reckoning.
Ultimately, "doing the police in different voices" doesn't change the nature
of law enforcement itself.

# Chapter Three ∼

# "Who ever heard of a blue-eyed Mexican?"

## Satire and Sentimentality in María Amparo Ruiz de Burton's *Who Would Have Thought It?*

### I: "Yankee Popocatapetls": The American Scene

The opening of María Amparo Ruiz de Burton's 1872 novel *Who Would Have Thought It?* disorients readers expecting the California landscape of *The Squatter and the Don*.[1] No ranchos or railroads give breadth to its horizon line, no vaqueros or patrones people it, no cattle graze upon it, no miners speculate over it, no squatters apportion its choicest views for themselves, and, most importantly, no land grants await (unjust) settlement between its borders. The story of a middle-class New England family whose fortunes and fates are altered by the orphaned Mexican girl who comes to live with them on the eve of the Civil War, *Who Would Have Thought It?* is preoccupied with social problems that look as thematically estranged from Ruiz de Burton's later historical romance as they are geographically distant from its West Coast setting. Lola is introduced into Dr. Norval's household only to be rejected by the physician's provincial wife and jealous daughters as a "native" *and* a "foreigner"—a condition made possible by simultaneous descriptions of the West as an unpeopled vastness and an area wrested from vanquished natives. Yet she maintains her dignity through a series of complicated adventures. While her champion Dr. Norval is presumed dead in Africa, she is tormented by his kinfolk, affianced to his son Julian, accosted by Mrs. Norval's lover (the ex-divine Major Hackwell, who tries repeatedly to seduce her), and reunited, finally, with her father, a leading citizen of post-revolutionary Mexico, by her neighbor Isaac Cackle, who travels to Mexico after his disenchantment with American Civil War politics.

Despite its confinement to the overdecorated drawing rooms of the Puritan nouveau riche, however, Ruiz de Burton develops the convoluted story of *Who Would Have Thought It?* to remind us that the social corruption it exposes and the political tableaux it depicts (military campaigns generated by greed and incompetence, politically motivated scapegoating, progressive rhetoric emptied of political urgency and circulated in the service of social climbing) are not idiosyncratic to either the Boston coastline or the Washington scene, but instead are iconographic of nationalist projects and their relation to imperial designs. Lola's regional transplantation calls into question the North-South axis that conventional narratives use to plot the Civil War and the East-West dichotomy that pushes Mexicanos and Native Americans to the geographical margins of a country depicted with its center skewed at the eastern limits of its territory. When Ruiz de Burton links the genealogy of Lola (rescued out of an Indian captivity during one of Dr. Norval's travels to California) with the history of abolitionist New England, she reconfigures the terms of literary and historical debate about the post–Civil War period. *Who Would Have Thought It?* explores the triangulated relation of region, nation, and empire through the metaphor of familial conflict. Her satire collapses distinctions between two languages of war, demystifying both the swashbuckling imperial romance of Manifest Destiny at the Alamo, and the epic sweep with which the United States's domestic breach is traditionally depicted. By yoking the U.S.-Mexican War of 1846–1848 and the Civil War of 1861–1865 together in this way, she advertises to readers the fact that these conflicts are conventionally quarantined, despite their historical contiguity. What sharpens this military coupling is the edged treatment she provides the internecine squabbles of the Norval family, whose divided loyalties on the subject of abolitionism figure the conflict between North and South, and the anticipated "mixed marriage" of Lola and Julian, whose romance speaks to the conquest of Mexico following the Treaty of Guadalupe-Hidalgo.

In fact, Lola's presence on Puritan shores affirms the social authority of the Californios, those who "are mostly of Spanish descent"—if at the cost of the Indian populations of America, the "cannibals" of Mrs. Norval's inflamed imagination. In so doing, the novel anticipates the more exhaustive treatment of federally condoned land seizure in California which the author will develop in *The Squatter and the Don*. The topographical overlay in the 1872 novel not only complicates the ethnic dichotomies written into the history of the United States, however, but figures its gendered polarities. The book's sentimental battleground—the family schism occasioned by disagreement over what to do about Lola—is Ruiz de Burton's camouflage, a feminized narrative space from within which she can deliver scathing and sustained critiques of American political opportunism. Through Lola and the Norval ladies, she will parody the masculine war theater and conflate two spheres typically distinguished in Anglo American middle-class life, the domain of political event and action and the private, feminized world of marriage and family life. Ultimately, her insertion of a Mexican heroine into the social space of New England carries a political charge far in excess of readers' expectations about the work of the sentimental novel.[2]

### II: A "most unnatural liking for foreigners": The Perverse Piety of Puritan New England

*La clase ignorante americana tiene mayores vicios que los mexicanos de la misma escala social. Que el color moreno no es un indicio ni de ignorancia ni de desmoralización; que el cutis cobrizo americano cubre tan viles cuerpos como pueda cubrirlo un cutis azabachado [The uneducated class of Americans has greater vices than do Mexicans of the same social class. That the color brown is neither an indication of ignorance nor of corruption; that the copper-colored American skin covers bodies as vile as a black skin may cover].*

—"Gringos y Greasers," *La Gaceta*[3]

*Si yo pudiera creer en el "Manifest Destiny" dejaría de creer en la justicia ó la sabiduría divina. No amigo mío, el Manifest Destiny no es otra cosa q(ue) "Manifest Yankee trick" como sus "wooden hams and wooden nutmegs" del Connecticut [If I could believe in Manifest Destiny I would cease believing in justice or divine wisdom. No my friend, Manifest Destiny is nothing but a Manifest Yankee trick like their wooden hams and wooden nutmegs of Connecticut].*

—María Amparo Ruiz de Burton, letter to Mariano Guadalupe Vallejo[4]

From Francisco Ramírez's famous editorials in Los Angeles's *El Clamor Público* in the late 1850s, through poems honoring the heroes of Cinco de Mayo and essays celebrating the social and political activities of Mexicanos in *La República* circulating in San Francisco three decades later, the project of Spanish language newspapers was not only to provide Spanish speakers with information about what became in 1848 el otro lado, but also to counter the systematically racist representation of Mexicans and Mexican Americans produced in English throughout this period. In affirming the moral superiority of the Mexican working class in the face of its Anglo American social equivalents, the anonymous author excerpted above also underscores the frequency with which Mexicans of all classes are scapegoated (now as then) as the source of a variety of regional and national problems. If a Spanish language newspaper like Santa Barbara's *La Gaceta* could publish

articles that, under cover of humor, critique the "*green go*" as a "Judas" figure,[5] those writing in English were far more likely to risk censure by Eng-
lish-only readers for remarks construed as critical of anti-Mexican sentiment.

All the more remarkable, then, is Ruiz de Burton's acerbic rereading of
Yankee prejudice. From the outset of her comedy of manners, the writer
circulates all of the stereotypical traits of the Yankee, using parody to turn
the Anglo American racial aesthetic on its head. The virtues of true New
Englanders, who are "sober-minded," "economical" and "thrifty," are glee-
fully unmasked as vices when we read of worldly Puritans like Mrs. Norval's brother Isaac, whose sympathy for foreigners leads him to sojourn in
Mexico, to be "free with his money" (that is, generous) and to have "a most
lamentable penchant for gallantry"(72). As epitomized by Mrs. Norval,
whose principles dissolve precipitously when she falls in love with the
smooth-talking Reverend Hackwell, the Yankee is a hypocrite. The dissem-
bling Reverend views preaching as an opportunity for seduction. To his colleague Reverend Hammerhard's question ("Why didn't you become a
Methodist or an Episcopalian,—anything more human than a blue Presbyterian?" [55]), he responds cavalierly: "If I had left the practice of law to become an Episcopalian preacher, I would not have stopped there,—I would
have ended by being a Catholic priest. Then I could not have married; and
imagine what a loss that would have been to the ladies!" (56). The Reverend's amorous adventures—his seduction of the hapless doctor's wife and
his thwarted passion for Lola—implicitly distinguish his Anglo American
brand of "business Christianity" from the spiritual faith of the Catholic
"natives."[6] Like Cotton Mather with a sense of humor, Ruiz de Burton delights in exposing the concealed moral decrepitude of the "cutis cobrizo
americano."

The author develops one of her most scathing indictments of Puritan
hypocrisy through Mrs. Norval's spinster sister Lavinia, whose indefatigable
nursing and intrepid efforts at the Capitol building to gain Isaac's release
from a rebel prison earn the respect of narrator and reader alike. If the author grants "Lavvy" "good-heartedness," (a quality she retains a monopoly
on amidst the reptilian Puritans), she nonetheless satirizes the nurse's efforts
as engineered by self-interest masquerading as duty:

> [A]s Lavinia had been properly brought up, she loved her patients. . . . The
> more groans and sighs and lamentations she heard, the more cheerful she
> became in the sublime sense of *duty.* And when the amputating-knife had
> to be used unsparingly, then Lavvy was . . . "*jolly*" in the midst of sur-
> rounding misery. I do not mean that the good-hearted Lavvy could rejoice
> in the sufferings of others, but she rejoiced in the thought that she could al-
> leviate them (143).

With exuberant Dickensian satire, Ruiz de Burton undermines conceptual equations that link "America" with the Puritans who controlled its northeasternmost territories in order to expose the regional agenda that underlies this nationalist rhetoric.[7] Connecting the pretentious Misses Norval and their mother with the sententious oratory of Capitol Hill, she exposes the nation's verbal currency as a self-promotional, morally impoverished language that only fools suffer gladly:

> It was the arrival of some great day in New England when the Misses Norval were to make their farewell appearance in church before leaving for Europe,— some great day in which the Pilgrim fathers had done some one of their wonderful deeds. They had either embarked, or landed, or burnt a witch, or whipped a woman at the pillory, on just such a day (83).

In implicit contrast to the faith in prayer that makes Lavinia a Catholic in sentiment[8] and Lola one in fact, the eyes of those occupying the pews of the Presbyterian church are not cast heavenward, but are directed terrestrially toward the upper reaches of society. Ruiz strips the embarkation and landing of the Pilgrim fathers of its spiritual investiture. She defrocks these political entrepreneurs as the logical forerunners of the Norval sisters, whose own scrambles up the social ladder she parallels with the lauded entrance of their predecessors onto the American continent. One of the most rhetorically deft critiques in the novel is embedded in the sentence I have just cited, which deglamorizes the activities of the first of America's politicians through a list structure whose unhierarchized syntax mirrors its leveling theme. Here the grandiose landing on Plymouth Rock is the prelude not to the foundation of good government, but the scapegoating of its (distinctly feminine) citizens who are maimed and murdered through a series of violent punishments that rival the author's own ethnocentric description of West Coast "savages."

Like Pauline Hopkins, who in her 1900 story "Talma Gordon" desanctifies the "old New England Puritans who had come over in the Mayflower" by invoking the "East India trade" that has established their prominence ("All [Captain Gordon's] ancestors had been such; but when the bottom fell out of that business he established the Gordonville Mills with his first wife's money, and settled down as a money-making manufacturer of cotton cloth"), Ruiz de Burton denaturalizes the spiritual authority of the national "fathers" and reminds readers that their rise to power has been underwritten by violence.[9] Just as Hopkins's Captain Gordon profits by the death of his first wife in childbirth, Ruiz de Burton's Puritans cultivate their cultural capital through the women they pillory and burn. Parodying representation that is stuck like a broken record on the first Thanksgiving, she critiques the way in which the Pilgrims have remained icons for national identity by comparing the venality of the current crop of congressmen and churchmen with the founding politicians of the United States. Mrs. Norval's heart first thrills to the words of Reverend Hackwell when she listens approvingly to a sermon whose theme "was the hackneyed one of the sublime love of religious freedom, which made the Pilgrim fathers abandon home, civilization, friends, to come to a comfortless wilderness" just at the moment when, in defiance of Doña Theresa's dying wish to have Lola "baptized and brought up a Roman Catholic" (46) she is working hard to ensure that her stepdaughter remain a member of the "blue" school of churches. When Lavinia arrives at the seat of government to ask for Isaac's release from prison, she encounters a similar vision of hypocritical self-interest in the person of Mr. Cackle, whose dull sons have profited sufficiently from the war business to insert themselves into the Washington political élite. Appropriately enough, she finds her old neighbor "before the painting representing 'the embarking of the Pilgrims,' discoursing upon the merits of it to a large number of admirers, who listened to his words in silent respect"(149).

### III: "Who would have supposed such a Vesuvius covered over with New England snows?"

*He would contrive to induce Lola to go on board of a steamer, and take her to Cuba and there force her to marry him. And, wild and absurd as this idea was, to the heated brain of the major it seemed quite practicable (360).*

This picture of a wild-eyed Presbyterian divine entertains readers as it counters Anglo American depictions of the passionate Mexican ready "to put the dagger to the throat" (257) to end a love quarrel. In Ruiz de Burton's revision of the captivity narrative, it is the preacher who goes native, threatening the good name of an aristocratic "Spanish" Mexican rather than a Puritan blueblood like Mary Rowlandson. Ruiz de Burton's treatment plays off of Californio and New England versions of the genre, but it spotlights neither the savagery of an othered people nor the miracle of divine wisdom. Instead, the writer reappraises the maligned chastity of Mexicanas in particular and the beleaguered sexuality of women in general. While Rowlandson's *Narrative* stages the Christian captive's fraught relationship among a "godless" tribe as the locus for divine instruction, Ruiz de Burton is less interested in exploring the relationship between Lola's civil mother and her savage captors than in exploiting this abduction as a parallel for Major Hackwell's barbarous behavior toward Lola. Readers cannot help but see the resonances between Lola's mother's misfortune and the one her daughter narrowly escapes; Hackwell's licentiousness, however, far exceeds the rapaciousness of Doña Theresa's Indian captors. The ex-minister's unraveling at the hands of Lola also recalls the besotted state of Mrs. Norval, who has turned a blind eye to reports of her lost husband's existence in order to "marry" her lover. Significantly, it is Hackwell's "savagery" in exploiting Mrs. Norval, rather than her own fevered state, which the writer passes judgement upon.

Mrs. Norval provides Ruiz de Burton with a feminine analogue to the parody of Anglo American masculinity she mercilessly lampoons through Hackwell. In a volte-face that underscores the writer's indictment of Puritan hypocrisy, it is the prim and parsimonious madam who turns out, in the mocking words of Reverend Hammerhard, to be "a Vesuvius covered over with New England snows." Not to be outdone by his colleague, Hackwell embellishes the Reverend Hammerhard's description of this "Yankee Popocatapetl":

> She is a Clytemnestra, a Medea, a Sappho! She is so earnest, and her love for me so fervid, that she almost makes me forget that she is thirteen years my senior, and *compels* me to love her; yes, just kind of sucks me into her furious love maelstrom! Whew! . . . If those superb eyes of Lola were not here maddening me . . . if I did not think of that girl night and day, I believe the old woman would succeed in kindling me with her conflagration (251–2). [10]

Not the less remarkable for its exuberant critique of the sentimental prose that was the order of the day in both Anglo American serials and the Spanish language press, this overblown rhetoric undermines conventional representations of sexuality that maintained the purity of white womanhood by slandering everyone else. Mid-and late-nineteenth-century western texts authored by Anglo Americans often affirm feminine "spotlessness" not by denying the existence of feminine sexuality, but by racially quarantining such expression; white gentility is represented as sexless because it is juxtaposed against the licentiousness of women of color. Ruiz de Burton turns this raced representation on its head: Lola's triumph is that she can inspire passion without being moved by it. Mrs. Norval, on the other hand, is ignited by a few flowery compliments cast in her general direction. Nor is the author's critique limited to this matron, for even the good hearted "Lavvy," whose hysterical attachment to her canary birds substitutes for the proffered and then reclaimed attentions of Reverend Hackwell, chastises her own immodesty in language that slights New England purity and masculine integrity simultaneously: "How very wrong girls are in permitting any liberties to men to whom they are engaged! How foolish! How silly! Who can tell what miserable liars they may not turn out to be?" (48–9).

Ruiz de Burton's volcanic metaphors simultaneously revenge literary and political wrongs and broach the possibility of feminine desire. The matron's shift from beguilement into madness (she lapses into brain fever upon her husband's return) suggests that this representation—even for Anglo American women—is ultimately shut down. But however transient, however ironized, Ruiz de Burton's explicitly sexualized representation of feminine passion defies the contemporary literary standard that rules against its display. While her defensive representation of Mexican womanhood allows for no blemishes upon Lola's chastity and punishes Doña Theresa's involuntary humiliation at the hands of her Indian captors with death, she remains through the latter half of *Who Would Have Thought It?* surprisingly sympathetic with Mrs. Norval's fall from grace. The single embrace Lola gives to Mrs. Norval's son Julian when she sees her gravely wounded fiancé lying in bed is countered by the author with this lengthy apology:

> If those arms had been strong, she would certainly have kept away from them, no matter how lovingly they had been extended to her. . . . In justice to Lola, it must be stated that she had passed the greater part of the night tracing for herself a "prospectus" of her future conduct towards Julian, which was so strict and circumspect that Mrs. Norval herself could not have found a single fault with it (206).

While Lola's spotlessness must be defended with this gentle reproof, the author's remonstrance of Mrs. Norval concludes on a forgiving note. The hapless matron "had so far degenerated that she regarded her youth as misspent, her life a blank, until she loved Hackwell, until she was past forty. Poor woman! to have been a chrysalis all her days! Who would not excuse this avalanche of the snows of forty years?" (247). A curious mixture of revenge and compassion, this passage ridicules Mrs. Norval's less than decorous passion and then, having accomplished redress, forgives it.

Such ambivalent satire remains the rule rather than the exception throughout the novel. The following passage, for example, closes with an appeal to the understanding hearts of her readers:

> When that one passion—her love for Hackwell—was beyond her mastery, all her imps ran riot in bacchanalian freedom, and she was jealous of her sister and hated her, and she forgot her dying son, and she did not mourn for her lost husband. . . . All she now thought of and longed for, was to see Hackwell, to be near him. That was the all-absorbing, uncontrollable impulse. . . . Cast not a stone—no, not a little pebble—at the madam, for, after all, she was very womanly when she was so absurdly silly. And who is not silly when truly in love? (188–90).

However tongue-in-cheek, the Reverend's description of Mrs. Norval as "compelling" his love provides her with a source of authority that celebrates mature femininity and affirms its sexual nature.

I would argue that it is her own authorial remove from the Presbyterian matron that allows Ruiz de Burton to raise this erotic possibility for Anglo American women. While qualified by the narrator and racially contained by the writer, such representation is pointed when we read it against both English and Spanish-speaking contemporaries who position the 40-year old woman as a contradiction in terms. "La Mujer" [Woman], a vignette from Santa Barbara's *La Gaceta,* describes the teenage girl as beguiling (from 15 to 20 she is an "ave del paraíso" [bird of paradise]), but by 30, she is already a "cotorra" [parrot][11] and at 40, a "lechuza" [owl]. (Some things never change: her masculine counterpart, on the other hand, is a "gallo" [rooster] at the height of his power). "Una Madre" [A Mother], an essay in *El Clamor Público,* sanctifies maternity as the condition closest to the celestial, because as mother, woman sacrifices for her child both "su tranquilidad y sus placeres" [her peace of mind and her pleasures]. This celebration of motherhood as the only earthly disinterested love ("Una madre en fin es el único ser en la tierra que ama desinteresadamente" [A mother, in short, is the only earthly being who loves impartially]) is a stunning contrast to the description of maternity we are treated to in Ruiz de Burton's 1872 novel.[12]

In an era distinguished by lachrymose complaining, where femininity is "invariable" [constant], "fiel" [faithful], "cariñosa" [loving], and "generosa" [generous] but ultimately, "[s]umisa," [obedient],[13] Ruiz de Burton's satire, sustained almost without break over 443 pages, and her portraits of strong-willed, stubborn women disclose themselves as highly oppositional strategies, devices that critique gender and genre as these are imbricated in sentimental literature. Ultimately, the compelling if ridiculous figure of Mrs. Norval allows the writer to open a space for feminine authority where no such space is permitted. Just as her daughter Ruth "liked to *manage* her mother, because she was the *power* of the family" (66), so the repressed sexuality of Lavinia is a figure for the spinster's independent will: "Lavvy wanted nothing better than plenty of employment for her exuberant moral energies and redundant force of will. The prospect of a tussle with a cabinet member or two, and plenty of skirmishes with delegations, did not terrify the strong soul of Lavvy" (142). Lola's own tussles with the Norval family and its satellites may look histrionic to contemporary readers, but situated within a discursive context that consigns woman to characterlessness, her defiance of Mrs. Norval's injunctions to stay away from the wounded Julian, and her frank denunciation of Major Hackwell's attentions toward her demonstrate her exceptional presence.

## IV: "I come to demand a right":
## Lavinia's Siege of Washington and
## the Dissolution of Separate Spheres

*I think the sooner we give over to women the management of public business, the better it will be. If we did not have such brute arrogance and unblushing conceit, we would long ago have seen the justice and propriety of hiding our diminished heads. But no. Because we have the physical force to beat women at the polls with our fists, we maintain that they have no right there as thinking beings. . . . Glorious! Behold the result! How well the world is governed! (395)*

*Ah! Si yo fuera hombre! . . . Qué miserable cosa es una mujer! Decididamente la providencia debe recompensarme de alguna manera por haberme hecho muger! [sic]. . . . Como si ser mujer no fuera suficiente calamidad sin añadir otras. No, es necesario q[ue] yo no me entusiasme por el progreso del Continente. Para qué? Ni mi raza ni mi sexo mejorá [Ah! If I were a man! What a miserable thing is a woman! Decidedly providence must compensate me in some way for having been made a woman! As if being a woman was not a sufficient calamity without adding others. No, it is necessary that I do not wax enthusiastic over the progress of the Continent. For what? Neither my race nor my sex will do better].*

—letter of Ruiz de Burton's, dated February 15, 1869[14]

Major Hackwell's vilification of his sex is less philosophic than self-pitying following upon the heels of his ignominious defeat (the botched abduction of Lola, the exposure of his schemes to defraud the government of money meant for the war effort, the temporary insanity of his "wife" who succumbs to brain fever), but the critique of masculine tyranny it exposes resonates all the more strongly. What better mouthpiece for systemic despotism than this petty tyrant? Just as Ruiz de Burton publicly articulates her most radical ideas about feminine sexuality through a woman distanced from herself, her most striking indictment of masculine self-centeredness proceeds from the mouth of the male figure least likely to be associated with the narrative's values. Yet this sardonic rhapsody is only the latest and most explicitly gendered censure of the U.S. political system the writer provides us with in the novel. Hackwell's allusion to masculine battery strikes a chord with Ruiz de Burton's earlier invocation of the New England punishments meted out to dissenting women. But through Lavinia's siege of Washington and her wondering appraisal of its malign political workings, the author develops one of her most scathing critiques of governmental corruption, a critique that simultaneously burlesques Anglo American despotism and satirizes gender tyranny.

Ruiz de Burton justifies Lavinia's transgression into the masculine domain of party politics by suggesting that her fearful encroachment of the public sphere is an effort to right the private sector. That is, her efforts to locate Isaac are not political but sisterly, stemming from her wish to reestablish familial harmony rather than any impulse to find fault with government. In championing her brother's rights, however, she exposes the petty self-interest of bureaucrats masquerading as federal policy. Washington, as Lavinia soon finds, is in truth "a city very congenial to all unbottled little imps" (208), and it is none other than Mrs. Cackle, social competitor of Mrs. Norval and proud mother of two "distinguished Congressmen" and "two renowned generals" (225) who personifies this statement when she affirms "[a] long war was good for the Cackle family" (234). Through this smug matron and her mock-heroic sons, Ruiz shows up American politics as a theater of the ridiculous. By contrast to the hasty retreats beat by these generals at the scene of battle, Lavvy's hesitant advancements on Capitol Hill appear Napoleonic.

Of course all of this reorganization is tongue-in-cheek, its object to parody conventional representations of sectional politics, satirizing both male and female actors in the process. But the writer's consistently ironical voice has a double purpose, sustaining this novel of manners and undermining the authority of sentimental convention at the same time. Such comic deflation of both the sententious rhetoric of political life and the high moral tone affected by the sentimental novel is never more successfully achieved than when Ruiz de Burton transports the language of war across generic lines in order to blur gendered distinctions between the public and private spheres. Her personal correspondence plunders military vocabulary to give her struggles the dignity and valor typically reserved for masculine endeavors. This December 1875 letter to George Davidson, for instance, chronicles her conflicts with the legal system as a "contest with hard fortune" and transforms the widow herself into a soldier under siege: "Even now surrounded by difficulties and discouragements of all sorts, I persevere and fight the fearful odds against me."[15] In her fiction, however, such lexical borrowings are comic rather than epic. Images of war circulate in the following description of feminine service, a paragraph all the more resonant because it follows a battle scene:

> Lavinia's heart pranced like a war-horse at the sound of martial music, making the chest of the maiden resound with its galloping. Her patriotic fire spread to the Misses Cackle, until nothing but making sacrifices for their country's cause would satisfy them. . . . They made underclothes, and large, very large night-shirts; for these patriotic ladies seemed to take measure by their enthusiasm, and very possibly imagined that the heroes for whom the shirts were made must all be as large in size as in deeds (105).

In a few phrases Ruiz de Burton shells the willful naiveté of women kept so far removed from public life they transform boorish neighbors into "heroes," the tedium of a middle-class existence spent pickling vegetables and tailoring shirts, the facility with which the brutality of war is obscured by the smoke and haze of nationalist rhetoric, and finally, the small minds—not to mention small body parts—of the cavaliers themselves, arrested through the prose of *Who Would Have Thought It?* in midflight as they canter toward their own trenches.

Ruiz de Burton exploits this lexical transplantation repeatedly, in one instance to lampoon the social pretensions of the Norval sisters (" . . . several Saratoga trunks . . . stood there, all packed full of the dry-goods which composed the elegant costly outfits of the Misses Norval for their summer campaign. Julian, though weak yet and very pale, had left the day before, just in time to arrive at Gettysburg before the firing commenced" [217]) at another to ridicule the Civil War and its domestic parallel, the family battle over the courtship of Julian and Lola that constitutes the sentimental plot of the novel itself ("Julian saw [Lola] politely received in her house before he returned to camp. Mattie was an ally of theirs, Ruth a neutral power, acting occasionally as spy, and the madam, flanked by Hack and Em, was at present in *status quo*," 259).

More direct assaults accompany such oblique but merciless exposure of Anglo American policy makers and their feminine satellites. Major Hackwell's denunciation ventriloquizes Ruiz de Burton's own assessment of antifeminist federal policy and preempts rhetoric like Father Gasparri's 1877 editorial in *La revista católica,* which anticipates a social meltdown with the advent of female suffrage: "'the family will be destroyed, it will lead to juvenile delinquency, and increased abortions and eventually the destruction of the human race.'"[16] Ruiz de Burton satirizes predictions like these through an ensemble of Cackles and Blowers, the former an ineffectual sycophant who disparages a like ability in the female sex ("Women are so foolish! They never know how to make a good use of their capital, either in money or influence. Bah! and they want to vote!" 152), the latter a pretentious sophist who in condescending to instruct Lavinia in the fine art of diplomacy exposes the moral vacuum at the heart of government. Prisoners are not exchanged, he explains, because by remaining in the South they hasten the anticipated starvation of their rebel captors along with themselves. When Lavinia stares "in silent amazement" (157) at this policy, the diplomat can only retrench, citing the incapacity of ladies who "can't well grasp great ideas, or understand the reasons that impel men in power to act at times in a manner apparently contrary to humanity, to mercy, to justice" (157). Ruiz de Burton's irony deflates the puffed-up rhetoric of the Washington policy maker to disclose him performing puppet theater behind a curtain, gendering his disguise in the process. Lamenting "how little woman was appreciated, how unjustly underrated" (179), Lavvy reflects that "no matter how much a woman, in her unostentatious sphere, may do ... after all she is but an insignificant creature" (145–6). Through Lavinia's reproach Ruiz de Burton not only provides a lesson in the gender of geography but opens the possibility of its remapping as well. Thus Lavvy mourns female powerlessness in order to correct it, transforming plea into command: "for the first time I come to ask a favor,—a favor, do I say? No. I come to demand a right,—" (146).

But what of Lola? The writer's experiments with transgressive feminine authority are sustained at the cost of her Mexican heroine, whose behavior she restrains, lest it risk the censure to which even reformable Yankee women are subjected. Where Lavvy can work in a hospital with relative impunity, Lola's own nursing service remains restricted at home. Ruiz de Burton displaces anxieties about raced representation of women working in the public domain through a social distinction; Lavinia insists that it is "*ladies* with hearts and brains" who "were absolutely necessary to her country's cause. Not merely *paid menials* should attend the sick and wounded, but thoughtful women, who could judiciously order as well as obey" (179).[17] In fact, such classed cautions retrace the shifting status of nurses in the nineteenth century. Darlene Clark Hine indicates in *Black Women in White* that prior to the Civil War, nursing was a "'low-paid, low-status job for laboring-class women.'"[18] Just as, according to Anne McClintock, British women "who were ambiguously placed on the imperial divide [nurses, nannies, governesses, prostitutes, and servants] served as boundary markers and mediators" and were "fetishized as dangerously ambiguous and contaminating" (48), so American nurses prior to professionalization were typed as degenerate. But beginning with the advent of the first nursing schools in 1873,

> self-conscious élite white nurse leaders heralded nursing as ideal work for middle-class women. They argued that formal nurse training and practice provided an attractive outlet to white, native-born, middle-class, private sphere-restricted women, especially those respectable ladies who needed something to do before marriage or who were widowed (Hine, xviii).

Like Gertrude Atherton's blue-blooded Miss Carter, who expresses her support for American imperialism in *Senator North* by announcing her intention to go to Cuba to nurse American soldiers, Lavinia can exercise her patriotic duty through nursing.[19] By contrast, Lola's own ministrations are limited to the care of her fiancé. The writer's refusal to afford Lola the same access to public space that Lavinia enjoys is hardly surprising given the extent to which Anglo texts single-mindedly define all Mexicanas as maids. Still, within the confined space of the drawing room, Lola's superiority is unquestionable. If Lavinia *becomes* genteel through her goodness, Lola is *born* aristocratic, "her mother being of pure Spanish descent," as Dr. Norval notes, "and her father the same, though an Austrian by birth, he having been born in Vienna" (33). However unpalatable to late-twentieth-century readers, such class-bound representation defends against the discriminatory language of Anglo America, that, as the Spanish language press often notes, types all Mexicanos as crude and licentious. In "Gringos y Greasers," Santa Barbara's *La Gaceta* asks rhetorically: "Cuantas veces oímos hablar a un americano, de que tal o cual sujeto no era mexicano sino que era white man (hombre blanco) como si el color blanco fuese desconocido entre la raza latina." [How many times do we hear talk by an American, that this or that person was not a Mexican but a white man, as if the color white were unknown among the Latin race.] This complaint counters racist representations like the following excerpt from Susan Shelby Magoffin's 1846 Santa Fe Trail diary: "The women slap about with their arms and necks bare, perhaps their bosom exposed (and they are none of the prettiest or whitest)."[20] While the press responds to such discriminatory statements in Spanish, Ruiz de Burton uses her characters to exact literary recompense in Magoffin's own tongue. "Talk of Spanish women being dark!" Mattie Norval exclaims in *Who Would Have Thought It?* "Can anything be whiter than Lola's neck and shoulders?" (333). Even Mattie's sister Ruth makes grudging concession to Mexican refinement after Lola's money frees her from the monotony of the Yankee middle classes. Her "new elegance" allows her to see "that the reason why Spanish ladies have small feet and delicate ankles is because they walk so very little" (70).

By flying in the face of Anglo American discourse that situates high culture between Boston's Old North Church and Washington's Capitol steps, this apparently inconsequential observation contributes to the novel's most important cultural work, which is to describe American political geography using a less provincial longitude. A conventional grid of class markers becomes the "stable" reference point for Ruiz de Burton's reorganization of the skewed racial axes through which Yankees have surveyed the United States and maintained their political title. By sending Civil War veteran Isaac to Mexico, she simultaneously dismantles the North-South meridian that generally defines this war and yokes it with the conquest of Mexican land that precedes this domestic schism. When, having become disenchanted with the federal policy he learns is the root cause of his imprisonment, Isaac chooses Mexico over New England, we understand that what looks like a sectional corruption—the secession of the South—is in fact a systemic moral failing.

## V: Into Mexico

*¡Pedir reclamaciones al gobierno Mexicano! No faltaba otra cosa. Este país ha sido
el teatro donde han sufrido los ciudadanos mexicanos toda suerte de ultrajes, atro-
pellamientos e injusticias. Nuestras columnas serían muy limitadas si nos
pusiéramos a dar una lista de las injurias sufridas por los mexicanos, desde '49, en
California. ¿Cuántas víctimas inocentes de entre ellos, no han sido sacrificadas ya
por el furor brutal del populacho? . . . puede ser que en la opinión del diarios
citado la sangre mexicana no vale. . . . El gobierno Americano ve la paja en el ojo
de su vecino pero no mira la viga que tiene en el suyo. [To request reclamations
from the Mexican government! That's the last straw. This country has been the theater where Mexican citizens have suffered all kinds of outrages, abuses and injus-
tices. Our columns would be very restricted if we were to give a list of the injuries
suffered by Mexicans, since '49, in California. How many innocent victims from
among us, have not already been sacrificed to the brutal fury of the crowd? . . . it
could be that in the opinion of the newspapers cited Mexican blood has no
value. . . . The American government sees the mote in the eye of its neighbor but
it doesn't see the beam that it has in its own.]*

> —*El Clamor Público*, 12 April 1856, responding to an essay
> from the *Alta California* asking for financial compensation
> from the Mexican government for grievances against
> Americans in Mexico following the U.S.-Mexican War.

*He was disenchanted. He . . . felt that it would take a long time before he should
again believe that in America there is not as much despotism as in Europe,—
"despotism of a worse kind, because we pretend so loudly the contrary. If we didn't
say so much about the freedom, the thing wouldn't be so bad. We are hypocrites
and imposters besides . . ." Who Would Have Thought It? (351).*

Cuando, junto con Isaac, pasamos al otro lado en esta novela [when we cross
along with Isaac to the other side in this novel], the geography shifts entirely:
philosophically, morally, socially, and culturally, Mexico and the United
States speak two different languages. Even their relation under imperialism, a
connection that Ruiz de Burton insists upon and that might tempt contemporary critics to read the two countries as twin sides of the same postnation-
alist coin, does not alter their essential opposition in this novel. The border
has for many Americans been naturalized over the course of the last 150
years, but Ruiz de Burton's chronological intimacy with the forcible geopolitical surgery of 1848 prevented her, and her contemporaries, from taking it
for granted. The language of the "border zone" remains the current lingua
franca of scholarship in American Studies, and as a metaphor for bridging
disciplinary divides, such attention to "border crossing" is very useful. But I

want to argue that we not elide the difference between the easy circulation of transnational theory and the difficult and dangerous paths people are forced to walk as they move from one nation to another. If such political realities are self-evident, they are frequently glossed (crossed) over with a glibness that warrants their reiteration here. The work of writers like Ruiz de Burton, publishing at virtually the moment of geopolitical separation, provides a critical intervention into the border studies of late-twentieth-century transnational theory. The turbulent relationship she describes between Mexico and California—the affiliations that are sustained across countries and the bitter memories that divide—function as a corrective to the cavalier promptness with which contemporary national borders are rhetorically dismantled.

Along with many of her American contemporaries writing in both Spanish and English, Ruiz de Burton's focus is not on the border per se, but on the difficult adjustments people on both sides are forced to make because of it. Her own critical efforts call attention to the unjust treatment of Mexicano citizens of the United States, about whom *El Clamor Público*'s Francisco Ramírez would ask rhetorically in "¡Americanos! ¡Californios!" [Americans! Californians!]: "¿No tenemos todos los mismos derechos iguales a la protección de las leyes?" [Don't we have equal rights under the law?)] and answer in "Los Mexicanos en la Alta California" [Mexicans in Alta California]: "No se les administra justicia, no se les respeta su propiedad, no se les deja libertad en el ejercicio de su industra . . . un ataque flagrante a los principios del derecho de gentes, una triste contradicción con los principios de que hace alarde el gobierno americano." [They do not administer justice to us, they do not respect our property, they do not permit us freedom in the exercise of our industry . . . a flagrant attack on the principles of peoples' rights, a sad contradiction with the principles that the American government boasts of.] Like other Mexicano writers of the mid and late nineteenth century, she also calls attention to the strained relationship between Baja and Alta California both prior to and during the conquest itself. *El Clamor Público* prefaces this critique of the United States ("Son extrangeros [sic] en su propio país. No tienen ninguna voz en este Senado, exceptuando la que ahora tan debilmente está hablando a su favor" [They are foreigners in their own country. They do not have a voice in this Senate, excepting for that which is now very feebly speaking in their interests] with an even more strongly worded picture of the conquered as "los que fueron abandonados y vendidos por México" [those who were abandoned and sold by Mexico]).[21] With equal bitterness, Ruiz de Burton laments Mexico, in this letter to her friend Mariano Guadalupe Vallejo, as having "decayed in such a way that it can only live by leaning on the Anglo Saxon."[22]

This kind of explicit censure is restricted to the writer's personal correspondence, however. In *Who Would Have Thought It?* Ruiz de Burton reaffirms the cultural and political authority of Mexico and slights the United

States for its uncouth behavior. *The Squatter and the Don* recuperates the downward political slide of the gente de razón by insisting upon their moral character, but *Who Would Have Thought It?* literalizes this redress through representation that turns the "contradicciones" of racist discourse on end. "America," in this text parodies Anglo American versions of "Mexico"; it is crude and uncouth, peopled by barbarians who don't care when they miss the spittoon bucket and social climbers whose first contact with high culture sends them into a tailspin of uncontrolled sensuality.[23] In Ruiz de Burton's 1872 novel, aesthetes belong in Mexico while New England houses the vulgar. Isaac's crime is really that he has taste. Like Lola's father, with whom he stays in Mexico, he prefers "Havana cigars to a pipe or a chaw of tobacco, and those miserable sour wines to a good drink of whisky" (73). No less a person than the president is pictured as a meathead who prefers band music to ballroom dancing; when Julian first encounters him, this venerable official is keeping time with the beat of the bass drum by tapping his teeth against "a gold-headed cane, which had just been sent to him by a lady in token of gratitude," whilst his leg, "a ballistic pendulum," "oscillated up and down, and dropped with the emphasis of a pile-driver,—for the foot of the lamented President was not small" (306–7).

But America's chief failing is hypocrisy, that fatal Yankee flaw. According to Ruiz de Burton, Mexicans, if not for the U.S. influence that prevails "with such despotic sway over minds of the leading men of the Hispano-American republics" "would be proud to hail . . . a good and just prince . . . who . . . has some sort of claim to this land, and who will cut us loose from the leading-strings of the United States" (281, 283). Americans, on the other hand, espouse the virtues of liberty without appearing to recognize that they are largely deprived of them. In paragraph after paragraph, Ruiz de Burton satirizes nationalist language, skewering its pretentious homilies as neatly as she censures Hackwell, whose smug sermons eulogizing Pilgrim forefathers are in fact epigrammatic of this lexicon. Democracy in the United States is the rhetorical national umbrella that doesn't keep the rain out. Accordingly, the narrator reflects of Julian, waiting in a storm, that he

> had to submit to the infliction, as everybody else does, will do, and has done. He was drenched and bespattered, with the rest of the traveling community, and, like everybody else, submitted silently, meekly; for in this free country we are the subjects of railroad kings and other princes of monopolies; we obey their wishes, and pay our money (382).

While she indicts American nationalism, she celebrates Mexican patriotism. In a passage that declares her sympathies as decisively as the odes and paeans honoring Mexican military triumphs so numerous in the Spanish language press, Ruiz de Burton suggests that "in some countries certain kinds of evil are impossible" (288).[24] If Mexico were "well governed," it could "avoid the majority of those misfortunes which we now call *unavoidable* human sorrows" (288). Through her description of the Medina household, the author provides readers with a model of such "good government" in microcosm. In keeping with the gendered strategy she develops at the novel's outset, this comparative political commentary is oblique. Anticipating the tone and language of *The Squatter and the Don,* she blames these troubles on "their veritable source . . . our lawgivers," then closes with a conventionally gendered disclaimer whose disingenuousness mocks efforts to keep women out of (literary) politics: "But I am no political philosopher. I am wandering away from my humble path" (288). If she focuses on domestic interiors, however, the comparison between the spacious library and elegant dining room of the Medina country estate and the gilded ostentation of the Norval drawing room is as pointed a critique as any assessment of military maneuvers could be. The Medina rancho, like Mexico generally, is home to "civilized citizens" (278), an aristocracy beleaguered by a "free and independent government" (278) bent on undermining its class privileges, but one that sustains its gentlemanly traditions nevertheless. In Lola's relatives we see Mexico's finest, learned men who, like Ruiz de Burton, are willing to defend Puebla against imperialism but who are nostalgic for monarchy nonetheless; men who read the latest news from Europe in a library replete with "papers, books, reviews, pamphlets, etc" (279), who speak at least three languages and from whose table the newly arrived Isaac enjoys "the best wine he had ever tasted in his life" (286).

Granted, this picture of the sporting life may seem less than inviting to those of us whose civility does not depend on the cooperation of a house full of servants. Abandoning the sustained irony that has characterized her send-up of American manners, she substitutes in its place a celebration of mexicanidad that admits only a select company, relegating the majority to the representational equivalent of no-man's-land. Before we dismiss it as unalterably ideologically compromised, however, we need to read it not only against contemporary theorizing about ethnic, class, and gender differences, but the languages of nationalism and sentimentalism her contemporaries were circulating on both sides of the border. When we begin to do this, we can appreciate how the author uses the drawing room as much to show up American savagery as to show off Mexico's sangre azul; to correct, that is, a literary cartography that fetishized New England and pushed the rest of the Americas off the cultural map altogether. As Rosaura Sánchez and Beatrice Pita argue in their introduction to the novel:

> What is clear is that by 1872, having lived in the United States for about 25 years—about two thirds of her life—she had a highly developed sense of self

as a Latina in opposition to Anglo-dominant society. What particularly concerned her was, on the one hand, the perceived misrepresentations of the United States as regards its democratic and egalitarian principles, and on the other, the subordinate status of Mexicans, especially Californios in the United States, and United States imperialist policies toward Mexico (lvi).

The hospitality Isaac enjoys in Mexico reproaches the hostile treatment Lola suffers in New England, just as the worldliness of the "two Mexican gentlemen" (284) indicts the provincialism of their counterparts in Washington—not to mention the parochialism of American letters.[25]

Polite society in this book is not only an end but a means—a means to indict the barbarism of United States soldiers, the venality of their superiors, and the crass upward groping of people like the Norvals and the Cackles, who could not be polite if their lives depended on it.[26] While it lacks the sardonic edge the novel sustains as a whole, the concluding portion of the novel introduces us to characters equally at home in Sonora ranchos and Washington drawing rooms. Such representation speaks against conventional Anglo American depictions of Mexicanos on both sides of the newly defined border. Their genteel professionalism is as far removed from the slovenly servants of late-nineteenth-century fictions of the Southwest as it is the "sad Indian Queens" and "Aztec pirogues" (*The Century,* 2) who flit across the pages of imperialist romances about Mexico. Their decorous drawing rooms are designed to de-exoticize the "Wild West show" much western Anglo American literature of the late nineteenth-century provides for readers.

And finally, there is Lola, a Mexican child born in California, and therefore an objective correlative for the remapping of the federal polity following the U.S.-Mexican War. In her person she embodies Ruiz de Burton's complex working out of the relation between region and nation, an argument that affirms the cultural integrity of western "natives": not just of California, but of Arizona, Utah, Colorado, New Mexico—that entire land mass once the property of Mexico, ceded only 24 years before the publication of her novel—but insists, at the same time, on their political status as U.S. citizens. In this respect, the 1872 text belongs at the center of a reconstructed Chicana/o canon, a literature that itself, as part of the American literary tradition in its fullest sense, resonates with Ruiz's own political and geographical revisionism. Rather than dismiss the novel because of its sustained classism, or romanticize it as the Movimiento's originary text, such attention clarifies how the novel's rhetorical strategies are dissonant with the discursive practices of its period, encouraging us, in the process, to work toward a more nuanced picture of nineteenth-century Mexican American literature.

# Chapter Four ∼

# "Who would be a Western senator?"

## Californians in "the drawing room of the Republic"

### I: Regional Values and the Western Difference

*Of course there are Senators and Senators. . . . There are the six who are admittedly the first. . . . Then there is the venerable group to which Senator Maxwell also belongs . . . and the fire-eaters, Populists usually; and the hard-working second-rate men, many of them millionaires (western, as a rule) who are accused of having bought their legislatures to get in, but who do good work on Committee. . . . Beyond all, are the nonentities that are in every body.*

—Gertrude Atherton, *Senator North*[1]

*The Honorable Zenus was an example of the possibilities of individual expansion under the rule of popular government. . . . In familiar conversation with intimate friends, it was his habit to fall into the use of ungrammatical phrases, and, in this, one might easily trace the rugged windings of a life of hardship among the great unwashed before success had crowned his labors. . . . He possessed a rare nature: one of those genial men whom the West is constantly sending out to enrich society.*

—Pauline Hopkins, *Hagar's Daughter: A Story of Southern Caste Prejudice*[2]

*"We might love out of our class; would that be a sign of loving worthily?" Belle resented the suggestion of class, and quickly answered, "In the West one is as good as another." Mrs. Payne saw the resentment, and gently replied: "No, dear; I don't mean that. You wouldn't have Mr. Miller marry a squaw, or a negress or a woman all her life a drudge?"*

—Charles Stuart, *Casa Grande*[3]

I n the preceding chapters, I have argued that relying exclusively upon the North-South conflict is not enough to describe the complex network of regional relations that composes the United States. In books like María Amparo Ruiz de Burton's *The Squatter and the Don,* Helen Hunt Jackson's *Ramona,* and Frank Norris's *The Octopus,* the U.S.-Mexican War rather than the Civil War is the flash point for nationalism. Other fictions—Ruiz de Burton's *Who Would Have Thought It?,* for instance—critique federal policy by juxtaposing these upheavals. And despite their own best efforts to dismiss it, narratives like Henry James's *The Bostonians* and *The American Scene* do not make sense without the intervention of the West. This chapter examines Pauline Hopkins's *Hagar's Daughter: A Novel of Southern Caste Prejudice* (1901–02) and Gertrude Atherton's *Senator North* (1900) as novels that explore the traffic between regions from the vantage of Washington, D.C., the federal "switching station." By comparing the projects of different senators from around the country as they are convened in the nation's capitol, they develop a metaphor flexible enough to figure the constantly shifting sectional alignments that produce the United States.

Still, why a western senator? If the drama unfolds as a dispute between North and South, as the titles of both books would have us believe, why mention the West at all? Like a close-mouthed politician, this essay argues, the "other" region carries a cultural weight in excess of its tangential plot value. However politically vexed, *Hagar's Daughter* and *Senator North* complicate the antonymic equation of North and South, whether defined as ethnic or economic difference: Europe over "America," white over black, the leisured classes over laboring people. Just as *Who Would Have Thought It?* requires the intervention of California to critique midcentury American imperialism as the product of northeastern "special interests," Hopkins and Atherton use the West to nuance representations of the turn-of-the-century United States. This region may be geographically peripheral in these Washington novels, but its structural capacity to reconfigure the national space is crucial to the arguments each writer develops about regional relations. In its ability to generate difference by fracturing the national space along several regional axes simultaneously, the figure of the West circumvents the reductive "solutions" produced by the regional "either/or" of the Mason-Dixon line.

Once we invoke a third geographical register, political imperatives that have remained invisible when framed conventionally in two (regional) dimensions begin to take shape. How for example, do class interests help to define continental spaces, and when do they operate across regional divides? In *Senator North,* Atherton defuses class-based anxieties about the nation by exploiting a western senator whose political aims define themselves over and against the "national" interest, where "national" is identified with the patrician New England philosophy of Senator North. Hopkins, on the other hand, interpolates the West in *Hagar's Daughter* in order to embody both gendered possibilities and a set of racially coded values that interrupt and resolve the calcified iconography of the North-South conflict. Born in South Carolina, raised in California, Jewel Bowen is a "western girl" (118). Despite Senator Bowen's southern birth and his extended sojourn in the North, his "Indian" physiognomy also gives him a "decidedly western air" (80). In *Hagar's Daughter,* these hidden regional amalgamations offer a geographical metaphor for the "natural" existence of racial mixtures.

In Hopkins's novel, Washington is the setting for the racial exposure of well placed characters thought to be white. The book's convoluted plot charts the separation and reunification of Hagar and her daughter. Wealthy southerner Hagar marries her neighbor Ellis Enson; after the birth of her daughter, she learns that her own mother was a slave. The family arranges an escape to Europe, which is thwarted by Enson's brother St. Clair and his slave-trading business partner. The first portion of the book closes with the apparent drowning of Hagar and her daughter in the Potomac River; when the scene reopens, we are in the Washington estate of Zenas Bowen, millionaire senator from California. After his daughter Jewel marries New England politician Cuthbert Sumner, she, too, is exposed as black, and we learn that this "western girl" and her mother are actually Hagar and her child. At story's end, Zenas has died (victim of a plot by the same men who have destroyed Hagar's family); Jewel is abandoned by her husband, and a tardily contrite Cuthbert Sumner tries to find his wife, only to learn that she has died abroad of Roman fever.

For Gertrude Atherton as for Pauline Hopkins, Washington is the stage for the resolution of race conflicts fought over the tragic mulatta. While white southerner Betty Madison is falling in love with New England senator North, she learns that she has a black half sister. Counseled by North, Betty reluctantly takes in Harriet, who, passing as white, marries Betty's suitor-cousin Jack Emory. Atherton's novel resolves on a brighter note than *Hagar's Daughter,* but Betty's successful union with North, after a protracted courtship with California senator Robert Burleigh, is enabled not only by the death of North's wife, but by the suicide of Betty's black sister. Harriet's "disgrace" is revealed by Betty's white social-climbing servant Miss Trumbull, who Atherton chastises toward the close of the novel as the wife of upstart western senator George Washington Mudd. Meanwhile, the disclosure of Harriet's race prompts the southern congressman to kill himself; his wife follows suit.

Notwithstanding their different political agendas, both sentimental fictions exploit the relation between domestic dispute and public policy to represent the United States as an imperial nation. They do so, however, not by considering international conflicts head on, but by focusing upon internal violence.[4] Their narratives follow the paths senators take through congress, but they assess political authority by keeping it at home. Atherton's novel invokes Cuba only to nationalize the discussion over war, filtering it through congressional arguments she characterizes as regionally motivated. Like Ruiz de Burton's 1872 novel *Who Would Have Thought It?*, which uses the Civil War as metonymic of the United States's sway over Mexico, Hopkins's novels *Contending Forces* (1899) and *Of One Blood* (1902–3) refract questions of empire through the national political scene. *Hagar's Daughter* also uncovers the imperial economy that enriches Boston abolitionists, much like Hopkins's scathing indictment of New England hypocrisy in "Talma Gordon," published the year before in 1900. But in the novel as in the short fiction, what is more important than revealing "the Future Development of the Anglo-Saxon Throughout the World"[5] is detailing the *regional* coordinates of this expansionist drive in Boston's "old Puritan stock" (6).

If these books confine themselves within national borders, they transgress the domestic genre itself. The tropes of the sentimental novel—romance, marriage, passing—are typically homebound rather than exercised in the House, but in Atherton's and Hopkins's work these events are inseparable from policy decisions, from congressional bills, from presidential veto, from war.[6] Furthering this inextricability of political process and private life is the mise-en-scène itself, which in both novels alternates between senate podium and society ballroom. Even the older generation fulfills "woman's mission" by intervening in political life; Hopkins's Mrs. Bowen makes "her husband's career successful by the exercise of her own intuitive powers. . . . Thanks to her cleverness, he made no mistakes and many hits which no one thought of tracing to his wife's rare talents" (82). Like Ruiz de Burton's championing of Lavinia in the halls of government, or Henry James's lament over the feminization of Boston, these novels exploit the gendered and raced conflation of public and private, political and familial life, national and imperial agenda.

Like the language of blackness in novels by James and Ruiz de Burton, region in *Hagar's Daughter* and *Senator North* speaks for more than one kind of American divide. As in Charles Stuart's *Casa Grande*, the West encodes multiple arguments; Mrs. Payne's efficient racial synthesis ("squaw" equals "negress") also stands in for class distinctions ("squaw" equals "negress" equals "drudge"). Stuart figures national unity by rejecting regional distinctions, and cements regional difference, in turn, through racial division ("In the West one is as good as another. . . . No, dear; I don't mean that. You wouldn't have Mr. Miller marry a squaw, or a negress or a woman all her life a drudge?"). The studied misunderstanding between teacher and student registers the complex interrelation of ethnic differences, race conflicts, and class values that articulate relationships between the "united" states. In effect, the regional metaphors exploited by writers like Stuart, Atherton, and Hopkins invoke rigid oppositions of national myth in order to demonstrate their inadequacy. The persistent appearance of the West in fictions dedicated to the North-South divide, then, demonstrates the lack of fit between bipolar scholarly paradigms for nation and more nuanced literary representations that define federal authority with reference to multiple and shifting terms of engagement.

## II: Regional Common Ground:
## Abolitionism as Social Currency in *Hagar's Daughter*

*Jewel was a Western girl with all the independence that the term implies. She glanced up at her partner, as they whirled away, with a little amused smile slightly sarcastic; "I expected something different from you. Something at least original" (118).*

—Pauline Hopkins, *Hagar's Daughter*

How do we read the political imperatives of abolitionism if we speak from a western space? The responses of self-made California senators Zenas Bowen and Robert Burleigh resonate because they represent alternatives to the political binary figured by conventional geographic mappings of the nation. The racial dramas they negotiate begin traditionally in Washington drawing rooms, however. Here, socially prominent women are exposed as "octaroons," only to be repudiated by aristocrats from both the North and the South. Hopkins allows Hagar, though not Jewel, to escape the tragic end demanded of the mulatta; Atherton's exploitation of Harriet's suicide, on the other hand, does little to expose the political implications of such victimization.[7] But if *Senator North* shores up the distinctions *Hagar's Daughter* begins to unravel, both fictions examine the regional inflections of race relations from the point of view of society's "talented tenth."

In *Contending Forces*, as Hazel Carby has argued, Hopkins "reconstructed a generational history across a century to situate the contemporary reassertion of the doctrine of white supremacy within a framework that demythologized the American story of origins. Democracy was exposed as an imperialist slavocracy."[8] In *Hagar's Daughter*, Hopkins likewise plots revelations about passing across three generations, this time to conflate and collapse the separate but equal policy of wealthy New England-educated Cuthbert Sumner and the Jim Crow sentiments of Jewel's patrician southern father Ellis Enson. While Hopkins parallels these different regional "best societies" in order to subject both to scrutiny, she censures the hypocrisy of the abolitionists most severely. Hagar chastens Charleston slaveholder Ellis

Enson for failing to stand by her (276), but Hopkins ultimately engineers their reunion. By contrast, she withholds authorial forgiveness from Sumner, preventing him from any reconciliation with Jewel. Instead, she consigns him to oblivion in a slight line that speaks volumes: "beyond a certain point his New England philanthropy could not reach" (238).

Readers expect the words "slave" and "servant" to be synonyms for the Charlestonian; more surprising are their correspondences for the Boston merchant. Hopkins argues for the interregional exploitation of black labor by comparing the authority St. Clair Enson exerts over his slave Isaac with the power Cuthbert Sumner enjoys over his servant John. Isaac, who grows up with Enson and consequently shares the "lurking deviltry of a spirit kindred to his master's" (28), returns to his master even after this "kindred spirit" cavalierly wagers him away in a poker game. "Dar's no mon can keep me, I don't keer how much Marse St. Clar sells me; he's my onlies' marser" (43), he affirms proudly to his aunt. Yet Sumner's devoted servant, a "New England colored man who had known him from his youth" (127), expresses his unequivocal attachment with similar hyperbole: "I've been in the Sumner family, boy an' man, for twenty years, an' they're used me white . . . 'Clare, I'd do anyting on yearth for Mr. Cuthbert" (182). In the face of their servants' parallel rhetorical excesses, Hopkins renders moral distinctions between "good" and "bad" masters overly fastidious.

But it is Senator Bowen's disavowal of northern and southern versions of post–Civil War "slavery" that confirms their syntactic equivalence. As a figure for alternate social climes, he allows Hopkins to gesture toward the political common ground northern and southern gentlemen share with respect to racial amalgamation. Bowen's western difference demonstrates that abolitionism, like secessionism, is a social currency circulating to distinguish the "haves" from the "havenots." Hopkins indicts the hypocrisy of the people the plantocracy derisively calls "moonstruck Abolitionists" (17) by juxtaposing the moneyed western senator's refusal to employ a valet with the paternalistic relationships northern and southern aristocrats enjoy over their household help. The South cannot define itself without reference to an Other; it confirms its regional peculiarity by invoking its slaves. The North, be they "greasy mechanics, filthy operatives, small-fisted farmers," or "moonstruck Abolitionists" are alike in that they are "hardly fit for association with a gentleman's slave" (17).

While "society" on both sides of the Mason-Dixon line demonstrates its breeding through the symbiotic attachment of servant and master, the western bronco buster maintains his superior discriminatory powers by rejecting this union. Senator Bowen asserts his distinction by calling attention to the Hegelian relationship between hierarchized self and other. *He* will employ no man, declaring no valley de chamber would boss him around. He'd always been free and didn't propose to end his days in slavery to any slick-pated fashion-plate who didn't know the color of gold from the inside of a brass kettle (89).

As pregnant an assertion as any in this novel, Bowen's insistence that the slave makes the man puns on itself by using a gendered metaphor to suggest that those who depend on servants are themselves unmanly. North and South play the dandies ("any slick-pated fashion-plate") to a conventionally gendered rough-and-ready West, a region, despite its unfamiliarity with high society, where men are born free. While Bowen's homespun metaphors appear to confirm his superior authority, his duping by Walker and St. Clair Enson at the card tables proves the western politician's inability to distinguish dross from gold. Nevertheless, his sustained use of the vernacular marks Bowen's refusal to take up the polished social currencies of North and South, allowing Hopkins to exploit abolitionism as twin tongue to the secessionist southern speeches with which the novel opens. Abolitionism, she argues here, is the real confidence game, a socially separate-but-equal accent that uses class distinctions to preserve the line between the races it ostensibly persuades listeners to cross.

The ambiguities and inconsistencies in Hopkins's own language are more difficult to assess. As Richard Yarborough outlines in his classic introduction to *Contending Forces,* Hopkins's "treatment of racial heredity" is "frustrating" in its "complexity."[9] At times her descriptions of race are predicated upon the conventions of late nineteenth-century scientific writing whose axioms of phrenological difference and racial heredity run counter to her own political agenda. At other instances, Hopkins describes race as produced by culture. Sustained attention to what Kevin Gaines aptly calls the "protean" (444) nature of Hopkins's writings on race focuses upon the ideological ambivalences opened up by her work. The following passage, for instance, invokes biology but ultimately turns not upon "blood" but the transformation such "exposure" implies: "Here was a woman . . . possessed of all the Christian virtues . . . her blood mingling with the best blood of the country if untoward circumstances had not exposed her ancestry. But the one drop of black blood neutralized all her virtues, and she *became,* from the moment of exposure, an unclean thing" (emphasis added, 62).

Like other writers of her era, Hopkins made use of the languages available to her. Sui Sin Far exploits what to modern eyes reads as a confused vocabulary to represent the autobiographical Chinese American heroine of "Leaves from the Mental Portfolio of an Eurasian." Mixed race characters are doubled and divided here through the metaphor of blood. A childhood fight the central character and her brother have after they are taunted with racist insults highlights turn-of-the-century languages of racial amalgamation:

"They pull my hair, they tear my clothes, they scratch my face, and all but lame my brother, but the white blood in our veins fights valiantly for the Chinese half of us."[10] My own sense of the complexities of Hopkins's prose in particular has been catalyzed by the work of scholars like Yarborough and Gaines, whose astute appraisals forestall any simple conclusions about her writing. I am less interested here in refocusing attention on its ideological murkiness, however, than on tracing the relationships between racial definition, class position, regional location, and national identity this rhetoric evokes. Following the meandering cultural paths Hopkins develops opens a rich associative landscape in which race and other markers of identity are contextualized against the horizon line of U.S. nationalism.

Notwithstanding its politically opaque character, then, racial definition in *Hagar's Daughter* is also an index for preserving class distinctions—which explains why the blueblood Bostonian and the aristocratic Charlestonian behave identically once their wives become "colored." Sumner's response to the racial exposure of wife (Jewel) and former lover (Aurelia) seems to confirm race as a biological fact that makes the discriminations of the social scale irrelevant. While he disparages Aurelia by telling her: "If you were as pure as snow, and I loved you as my other self, I would never wed with one of colored blood, an octaroon!" he repudiates Jewel, his "white angel of purity" as quickly as this "gorgeous tropical flower" (238, 103).[11] But if we compare Sumner's crumbling resolve toward his wife with the strategical two-step of his regional antithesis Ellis Enson, we see that both are guided by similar class-based prejudices. Once again, Hopkins invokes the regional third term in order to further this complicated assessment of tropes for racial difference. Unlike the waffling aristocratic scruples of North and South, the self-made man from the West never wavers. The sterling character of Senator Bowen's affection for Hagar and Jewel, the unfaltering loyalty he demonstrates for his adopted daughter (and which he would have shown his wife, Hopkins asserts through Hagar), calls attention to the unsteady steps of abolitionist and southern planter.

If the distinction between Senator Bowen and his congressional colleagues is regionalized in *Hagar's Daughter,* it is classed as well. The California senator's difference is a social one; Hopkins stresses his poverty-stricken origins in Mississippi in the biography she provides for him. Like references to blackness, regional inflections speak over and through the geographical boundaries they delimit, allowing Hopkins to insist upon the classed registers of her characters' statements about racial mixing. The failure of Hagar, Jewel, and Aurelia to pass once they learn of their "black blood" is simultaneously a pointed affirmation of social values. Throughout the novel, in fact, authorial focus upon the effects of interracial contact remains fixed upon the social "fountain head." Elise Bradford clarifies this register of Hopkins's argument when she tells Sumner that he cannot distance himself from amalgamation: "black blood is everywhere . . . we cannot feel assured that it has not filtered into the most exclusive families" (160). Elise warns that "caste" (159) is corrosive for North and South alike; as the journalistic voice that scripts the moral reminds us at novel's end, this expression has everything to do with "the best society":

> This story, showing as it does, the ease with which beautiful halfbreeds may enter our best society without detection, is a source of anxiety to the citizens of our country. At this rate the effects of slavery can never be eradicated, and our most distinguished families are not immune from contact with this mongrel race. Mrs. Bowen has our sympathy, but we cannot, even for such a leader as she has been, unlock the gates of caste and bid her enter" (266–67).

### III: "I was not always so fine as I am now": Class, Race, and Regional Difference in *Senator North*

*Democracy is a great institution in spite of its nuisances. Still, I admire Hamilton more than Jefferson (163).*

—Gertrude Atherton, *Senator North*

Like Hopkins, Atherton exploits the raced registers of region to plot the effects "beautiful halfbreeds" have on "our best society." But where Hopkins demonstrates the inevitability of amalgamation by confirming how interracial relations provide the foundation for the federal building, Atherton admits no such Jeffersonian mixing. Just as James allays his worries about the proliferation of "mongrel race[s]" by confining race relations to the social "basement,"[12] Atherton defends against successful passing in the Washington ballroom (and by implication, the national polity itself), by restricting racial exchange to the kitchen. Stage-managing interracial exchange through social segregation, Atherton plays out interracial bonding in the friendship between protagonist Betty Madison's social-climbing white housekeeper and her black sister, Harriet, only to punish both for their liberties before the close of the novel.

Both writers mourn the sin of blood ties by pathologizing mixed marriage. Plot undercuts argument in *Hagar's Daughter* when readers watch Elise Bradford's child play upon the lawn of St. Clair's southern house at the novel's close, recognizing him as "the last representative of the Enson family" (284). By preventing mixed-race couples like Jewel and Sumner from producing heirs, Hopkins questions Bradford's faith in the inevitability of racial amalgamation. Likewise, Atherton's insistence that the southern "line will die undishonored" (217) forestalls identifying mixed race children as anything other than "the unfortunate result of coupled races" (*The Californians,* 8). Yet if Hopkins frames this misfortune as the result of the political circumstances exerted upon a resisting family circle, Atherton's vituperative language conclusively shores up the "natural" distinctions between black and white when Harriet internalizes this stricture. The "world . . . condemn[s]" Aurelia (238), but Harriet condemns herself. She refuses to have children, to ensure that "the curse I had been forced to inherit should not poison another generation" (215).

Like all such rhetoric, Atherton's racist language is vapid. Worth considering, however, is the extent to which even an apparently "pure" register of racial difference cannot extricate itself from arguments about class positioning. The novel's feminine "intellectual," Betty Madison's southern compatriot Sally Carter, expresses some of its most grotesque statements. Her language is scored along a social grid, however, so that its inflections shift depending upon the class positioning of her target. Sentimentally condescending to poor blacks ("I love the dear old darkies in the country" [194]), coldly patronizing to the middle class ("even the prosperous colored people are tolerable so long as they don't presume" [194]), Sally is at her melodramatic best when she scorns the well-placed Harriet, a woman, "so hideously unnatural, so repulsive, so accursed" (194).[13] Like James's own brush with melodrama in *The Bostonians,* Atherton's linguistic excesses are reserved for those who pass—socially. Harriet, who lunches with the upper echelons of Washington society at the home of her half sister and who marries southern senator Jack Emory, demonstrates the extent to which color and class are synonyms. In Atherton's fiction, biology is the daughter of social condition, which makes the following conceptually murky statement plausible: "Black blood is loathsome, horrible!—and the less there is of it the worse it is" (194).

Atherton circulates the trope of blackness more indiscriminately than her discriminatory prose appears to warrant: anxiety over *inter*racial social presumption describes *intra*racial horrors with equal facility. The "racial" disgust Betty is stricken with debilitates her most severely when its object is other whites. One of the most interesting relationships in the novel is that which binds Betty to her overfamiliar housekeeper Miss Trumbull. A vulgar shadow figure who follows in the wake of Betty's educational trajectory, the housekeeper is the classic Freudian alter ego, embodying a repressed self-disgust that perpetually returns to try her mistress. As the agent of revelations, moral indictments, and registers of class mobility, this white servant occupies the ideological heart of the novel: she reveals Harriet's marriage to Jack Carter, calls into question Betty's relationship with North, and embodies the corruption of the nation's political life when she resurfaces at a government social function, newly espoused to a crude congressional upstart from the West. Interestingly, Atherton uses a gendered metaphor to plot the tensions in this relationship. Miss Trumbull's pleasantries function, in effect, as the

feminine counterpart to the blandishments of the gentleman suitor: suc-
cumb, and you will be (socially) ravished. Notwithstanding her rebukes and
rudeness, Betty plays the feminine part to this seduction, for she persists in
her intimacy with the housekeeper, surprising her in her dressing room, re-
lenting from her sangfroid long enough to make her the gift of her own
clothes, and finally, forcing herself to recognize her as an equal at congres-
sionally-sponsored social functions.

Atherton distinguishes between Miss Trumbull's easy alliance with Harriet and her presumptive familiarity with Betty, but in her proximity to both
sisters, this "average American" mediates the relation between black and
white at the same time as she defines it. Harriet's encouragement of the
housekeeper's friendliness invokes the twin threats of class mobility and
racial instability, reminding Betty that the housekeeper, like the half sister,
has the capacity to change her station. "[Y]ou must remember that I was not
always so fine as I am now, and Miss Trumbull does not seem so much of an
inferior to me as she does to you" (160), Harriet explains to Betty. More
than anything else, this acknowledgement of the porous quality of social
boundaries seals the tragic mulatta's fate. Like her peripatetic frissons over
Harriet's "drop of black blood," Betty's resistance to Miss Trumbull's over-
tures shores up constantly deteriorating boundaries between white and
black, servant and lady. Paradoxically, the very effort required to maintain
distinction attests to its impermanence. Social backsliding, like racial regression, remains a constant threat throughout the novel.

As well as the inextricability of these identifications: Atherton's narrative
worry over grades of color and caste demonstrates their mutuality. The ex-
haustion of fending off Miss Trumbull never ceases—Betty dismisses her
from the house only to hear footsteps behind her in the halls of government,
where, as the wife of western senator George Washington Mudd, the former
servant has gained entrance. With her usual lack of subtlety, Atherton ma-
ligns "Mrs. Mudd" through a name that plays on color and caste. Such character defamation clarifies the cultural work this figure provides the writer,
for Betty's shadowing by Miss Trumbull simultaneously doubles and dis-
rupts her shadowing by Harriet. Atherton thus insists on the thematic link
between class slippage and racial elision, duplicating it with language that
calls attention to the alliance. Betty uses the same vocabulary to admonish
Harriet for her familiarity with Miss Trumbull that she circulates to distance
herself from her half sister. "You cannot give them an inch," she warns Harriet. "If you treat them consistently as upper servants when they are in your
employ, and ignore them if they are not, they will keep their place and give
you no annoyance; but treat them with something more than common de-
cency and they leap at once for equality" (160). Compare this "leap . . . for
equality"—a figure that simultaneously registers concern about "the colored

race in its enfranchised state" (16)—with Betty's "southern" insistence on keeping upwardly mobile blacks in their place: "To her the entire race were first slaves, then servants, entitled to all kindness so long as they kept their place, but to be stepped on the moment they presumed . . . Senator Burleigh? He would laugh impatiently at her prejudices, and tell her that she ought to go out and live in the free fresh air of the West" (79–80). The white servant's steady move toward respectability is the price the writer has to pay for erasing the interracial relationship she has introduced at the outset of the novel. But it is also the reminder; for if her half sister conveniently destroys herself, her housekeeper, like Hopkins's Hagar, reinvents herself and meets Betty on her own ground. Mrs. Mudd thus carries with her the traces of white anxiety during Reconstruction about the social status of blacks.

"The free fresh air of the West": in the class-bound figures of Atherton's narratives this formulation celebrates democracy, the national value conceived to this day as having a regional birth. But in *Senator North*, the expression is ironized, since, as in Ruiz de Burton's *Who Would Have Thought It?*, democracy is not a Jeffersonian pluralism, but a Hamiltonian distinction that acknowledges "ordinary people" only insofar as they redefine themselves as genteel. That Betty finds this air only temporarily bracing indicates Atherton's inability to hold to that definition of nation that invents Americanness as open and middle-class over and against the calcified grid of social values adhered to in Europe. In her California novels, as historian Kevin Starr notes, Atherton portrays "the Old Californios as an embattled élite welcoming annexation by the U.S. and hence the direct ancestors of the upper classes of contemporary California."[14] Just so, Washington D.C. becomes a ballroom where only the crème de la crème mingle. When Betty rejects young western senator Robert Burleigh in favor of senior statesman Senator North, Atherton unconsciously chooses an anachronistic, "old-fashioned" definition of nation that relies upon social parameters associated with the northeastern region. Yet in the world of the novel, Senator North's regionally marked profile is central to the workings of the federal government in Washington D.C. Notwithstanding such classed descriptions of region, Atherton will find herself duty-bound, like other writers at the turn of the century, to search for a national definition that transcends geographically defined sections.

### IV: Reconstructing Reconstruction:
### Interpolating the West in *Hagar's Daughter*

*"Are you pleased with Washington?" "Oh, yes, but I miss the freedom of the ranch, the wild flight at dawn over the prairie in the saddle, and many other things" (119).*

—Pauline Hopkins, *Hagar's Daughter*

Even today, the American West is an icon for democratic values, for the "quality" rather than the "equality" Owen Wister's Virginian—an aristocrat in cowboy clothing—speaks against. Just as Ivan Doig's 1987 *Dancing at the Rascal Fair* claims Montana as leveling space (even the title alludes to social inclusion, for the rascal fair embraces everyone: "devils and angels all were there,/ heel and toe, pair by pair,/ dancing at the rascal fair"), so at the turn of the century, too, writers like Wister, Hopkins, and Atherton exploit the wide open spaces of the West to experiment with social mobility.[15] *The Virginian* (1902) decides uncompromisingly in favor of calcified class values; in a rhetorical sleight of hand worthy of late twentieth-century politicos, the Virginian assures us that "It was through the Declaration of Independence that we Americans acknowledged the eternal inequality of man" (101).[16] But for women writers like Hopkins and Atherton as well, the "free fresh air of the West" proves too indiscriminate a value to become an authoritative icon for national identity.

Granted, the former confers political energy and social presence on the working class, qualities Atherton unhesitatingly refuses even her middlebrow figures. The enterprising Venus of *Hagar's Daughter* dresses up as a man in order to rescue her grandmother and Jewel from southern captivity. When we consider the punitive measures historically enacted against cross-dressing white women and women of color in the nineteenth century, the author's exploitation of costume changes potentially acknowledges working black women as a political force. In "Drag's a Life: Women, Gender, and Cross-Dressing in the Nineteenth-Century West," Evelyn Schlatter notes that punishment typically included fines, jail time, or incarceration in asylums.[17] Within this context, Venus's intervention is not fun loving, but courageous. Just as the working-class foils Hopkins juxtaposes with her stenographer-heroine Sappho of *Contending Forces* provide a cross-generational, interclass link with the light-skinned femininity sanctioned by the black sentimental novel at the turn of the century, so Venus suggests alternate possibilities for feminine action.[18] If they are lampooned, these ex-slaves nonetheless, as Sandra Gunning suggests, rewrite "traditional modes of morality to combat their own victimization" (102).

Still, undermining every Venus is a minstrel figure like Marthy, whose "frank, fun-loving countenance, with its soft brown tint, its dazzling eyes and teeth" and "soft crinkly hair" hid by a "towel tied turban-fashion" returns readers to the stylized and unaccommodating rhetoric of conventional representations of rural blacks.[19] Coupled with Hopkins's refusal to invest any but the social élite with the status of heroine, such minstrel figures prevent the writer from developing a sustained class-based critique. Instead, they demonstrate a fundamental and unresolved ambivalence about middle-class authority.[20]

Despite this inability to unreservedly dignify the black middle class, the self-made man of the open range (a millionaire, granted, but risen from humble beginnings) wedges himself into the close congressional anterooms of *Hagar's Daughter* the same way his western colleagues blockade *Senator North*. Why? Precisely because he lacks the aristocratic glamour of "fashionable Washington" (*HD*, 112), Senator Bowen calls attention to the open space—or rather, the incomplete overlay—between a central government geographically and ideologically located in the Northeast and a federal authority that *must* signify in excess of particular regional values. In the process of distinguishing classed values and providing them with regional coordinates, Hopkins clarifies both sets of dividing lines. Once the classed contours of the West come into relief, the social altitudes of New England's topography resolve themselves as well, preventing us from conflating its parameters with the borders of the nation.

If, on the one hand, Hopkins censures the racial distinctions Atherton celebrates in her efforts to develop a patriotic language, both Washington novels represent the federal government as peopled by southern champions of the Lost Cause and the northeastern manufacturers who have profited from their collapse. Unlike the colorful grizzly hunter from California, the northern and southern social élite is predictably bland. Hopkins indicts "fashionable Washington" by telling us how it "greeted its world and congratulated itself on being here, discussed the host and hostess, admired the arrangements for dancing just as the dear five hundred always have done and always will do" (112). The cynicism encoded in this paean to vanilla sameness articulates Hopkins' pessimism about the efficacy of Reconstruction.

At the same time, her cheerless attitude about the possibility of political change gestures toward the collapse of the North-South opposition. The mercenary schemes the southern gentlemen develop—significantly enough, to plunder the wealth of the newly moneyed western Senator Bowen—are as venal as Sumner's political work is upright. Nevertheless, juxtaposing this description of the northern heir apparent with the urbane dissolution of the disappointed South demonstrates a fundamental similarity of tone. Sumner is "an only child of New England ancestry favored by fortune. . . . His father, a wealthy manufacturer, was the owner of a business that had been in the Sumner family for many generations. His mother had died while he was yet a lad. It was a dull home" (83). No one would accuse the family of vulgarity, but its dullness resonates with the weariness of the "dear five hundred" to whom Sumner belongs. Compared with the uncompromising political freshness of Senator Bowen, the resentment of defeated southerners and the irritation of victorious northerners sounds the same enervated note.

Benson cynically exploits his position in the treasury to limn his own pockets: "The country owes me a fortune," he avows, "and I'm bound to have it" (79). This lack of interest in furthering the goals of an ostensibly re-defined nation characterizes Cuthbert Sumner's retreat as federal worker as well. Once denied Jewel, he tenders his resignation to the treasury and scut-tles back into the privacy of his Washington house in a move Hopkins uses as spatial metaphor for provincialism. Only a lack of energy prevents him from literalizing this desire by fulfilling his servant John's wish to "leave Washington and return to Massachusetts and the family home" (127). Through this inability to reshape local affiliations in the national interest, Hopkins locates the North and the South as structurally equivalent, while evacuating their political geographies of sociopolitical distinction.

Hopkins deconstructs the North-South divide not only through struc-tural and tonal parallels but through lexical means as well. By transporting chivalry across enemy lines, she levels quintessential regional demarcations. Within the space of a few pages, she conflates detective Henson (southern plantation owner Ellis Enson) and Cuthbert Sumner (Boston abolitionist). The abduction of Jewel Bowen reveals Henson's southern origins by pro-voking his "innate chivalry" (222), but Hopkins scripts Sumner's response to Mrs. Bowen's racial origins using the same regionally marked vocabulary of gentle birth. The opening phrases of this portrait of the Bostonian introduce him in a manner befitting the Carolinian; Sumner, she tells us, "was born with a noble nature. . . . Chivalrous, generous-hearted—a manly man in the fullest meaning of the term" (265).

An even more striking regional borrowing occurs in this biographical vi-gnette of Jewel's husband, where Hopkins associates not only Sumner, but abolitionism itself with the peculiar institution:

> Modern pessimist [sic] are fond of crying that love, as well as *chivalry*, has died out of our practical world. If this were true, then Sumner lived after his cen-tury, for his belief in higher and better things was intense. He had a desire to worship purity in any shape, to champion the weak, and carve a pathway to honor that was characteristic of the *chivalrous* days of old (126, emphasis added).

Like Henry James's Basil Ransom, whose penchant for writing pro-slavery political essays in the post–Civil War period is framed as a backward-think-ing filial act, Hopkins's Sumner is a walking anachronism, busy on his "po-litical treatise" in order to "please his father" by making "a stir in the literary world" (126). The passage ostensibly participates in these "days of old" by celebrating them over and against contemporary life, but when we set this juxtaposition of the "practical" with the "chivalrous" alongside Elise Brad-ford's clear-eyed assessment of the inevitability of race mixing ("black blood is everywhere. . . . We try to stem the tide but I believe it is a hopeless task"

[160]), its elision carries an ironical edge.[21] Elise's inferior social position makes her practical; Sumner's protected status encourages him to enjoy his own noble nature. Add to this our knowledge of the readiness with which he casts off wife and mother-in-law once their racial identity is revealed, and his steadfast faith in chivalry begins to look not so much old-fashioned as moth-eaten.

The dis-ease that characters like St. Clair Enson and Sumner demonstrate toward the Reconstructed nation pushes both regionally defined figures equally beyond the pale of federalism. Benson's disappointment over the "disastrous" end of the war prompts a temporary exile in Europe and the recognition that he is "almost a foreigner" in the United States (120). Sumner's inability to acknowledge social contacts with blacks marks a similar alienation from a political reality, however grudgingly admitted by the "dear five hundred." The point, however, is not to censure the failings of a few but to dismantle specious structural divisions altogether.[22] Hence Hopkins's interest in redefining the national as a category that is more than the sum of the North-South dyad. The writer may be less hopeful than is Jewel about the possibilities for a new nation, but she reevaluates the efficacy of the regional polarity when she affirms, in a phrase that echoes Atherton's celebration of Betty Madison as the "American Beauty Rose" that "ours is a united country once more. And you are mistaken, too, in your judgement: we have no foreigners here. We have effaced the word by assimilation; so, too, we have no Southerners—we are Americans" (121).

Appropriately enough, it is neither southern planter nor northern abolitionist who makes this assertion, but the novel's "western girl" (210). As in Atherton's Washington romance, the West speaks for a complex of values that register, on the most abstract structural level, difference itself. When gendered, the West gives the lie to the separate spheres argument; when classed, it redefines the North-South divide as the expression of one monochromatic social value; when raced, it recontours the geography of the United States in a way that demonstrates the flat inflexibility of black and white descriptions of the country's racial politics. Born on a southern plantation, bred on a western ranch, educated in a northern school, Jewel Bowen embodies Hopkins's revisionary regional dialectic. Through this "western girl" Hopkins comments upon genre as well as gender: Jewel plays upon the dime novel, a literary form produced out of the New England publishing establishment that remains to this day in the critical literature virtually synonymous with western writing.[23] When she is abducted by Benson's men, she defends herself as vigorously as Annie Oakley:

She had been brought up upon a ranch; one of her early habits remained fixed, and even in Washington she was never unarmed when without male escort. The jeweled toy she carried was a present from her father, and he had taught her to use it with deadly effect. Many a day they had hunted together, the young girl bringing down her game in true sportsmanlike style (210–11).

While this portrait of independent femininity is compromised by Jewel's inability to fire, as well as the association of her "toy" weapon with paternal authority, the story blurs the overly schematic distinctions Hazel Carby draws between Jewel, the "mere victim" and Aurelia the "fighter"(148). In fact, the novel provides both women with "fire and life," and Hopkins's description of Jewel's penchant for "diablerie" (114) in effect opens the door of the lady's drawing room to the outer world. This "western" energy and activity undermines the spiritless trope of the tragic mulatta by investing her with an agency she is conventionally bereft of. In one stroke, Hopkins enlivens the pale portrait of the mulatta, and, by framing Jewel's "fire" as a regional rather than a raced characteristic, avoids recirculating disabling representations of women of color as licentious.[24]

Regional difference furthers two arguments simultaneously, by defying conventionally sexualized representations of black women and censuring circumscribed gendered boundaries. Consider Venus' central position in the release of Jewel. While her "cleverness" and talents flourish when she is dressed as a young man, Hopkins assigns her a hyperbolically feminine name to underscore her interest in the gendered registers of character. And if Jewel ultimately fades from the text in what Carby calls "an awkward authorial dispatch" (153), this "western girl" at least calls attention to the narrow parameters feminine Washington is restricted to operating within. Mrs. Bowen develops her talents by speaking through her husband's career; Hopkins attributes the senator's rise to his wife's "cleverness . . . which no one thought of tracing to his wife's rare talents," then defends her in a passage that rings with asperity at the limitations imposed upon femininity. Mrs. Bowen, she announces, "had simply fulfilled woman's mission in making her husband's career successful by the exercise of her own intuitive powers" (82). Daughter Jewel, on the other hand, escapes the "calm routine" of "housekeeping and churchgoing" only to find herself embroiled in a sinister plot of political machinations and personal vendettas.

Hopkins scripts Jewel's enforced journey to the South as transgressive, but only insofar as it provides her with a loophole of retreat when she finds an escape route through the subterranean tunnels of the plantation house where she has been incarcerated.[25] If her journey through the "dark passage" (215) is a geographical and spatial metaphor for her transformed racial identity, her acknowledgement of her blackness ends not with social triumph but death. Like Ruiz de Burton, whose aristocratic Mexican heroine journeys east but is denied access to the public sphere, Hopkins's genteel black heroine cannot leave the perimeter of the plantation house until her maid Venus leads her out of bondage.[26] Such upper-class heroines gesture toward openings that only their working-class counterparts can widen. What makes the lady's limited defiance possible at all, however, is *regional* difference. As westerners living in the East, Lola and Jewel can flash "fire and life" without endangering their social position. Jewel's cowgirl costume may appear incongruous in this Washingtonian "Story of Southern Caste Prejudice," but her western apparel is central to it. Even her name registers this regional difference, for it resonates with the striking image of her holstered "jeweled toy," the gun that is a gift from Senator Bowen, the novel's other western value.

By insisting that the cultural work of the novel requires the interpolation of the West, I do not wish to privilege this space itself: such a theoretical move, I would argue, merely reinstates a model of regionalism that leads to a kind of renewed provincialism. To read the West as the text's argumentative pivot does not mean that we should simply substitute its sectional perimeters in place of the Mason-Dixon line. This kind of interpretive move leaves intact the conventional map of the nation. On the contrary, regional distinctions are in Hopkins never represented as absolute values. Nor are differences between them furthered in the service of separatism. Instead, as the author clarifies from the opening secessionist speeches of *Hagar's Daughter,* regional "character" is always defined to advance a grander project. Her southern hopefuls are not intent on protecting their regional island in a national sea; instead, they look forward to the time when their "principles . . . have been triumphantly established over the entire country—North, South, West" (17). As Ruiz de Burton's critique of the "blue Presbyterians" in *Who Would Have Thought It?* demonstrates, this imperial aspiration is the goal of northern and southern business interests alike. Like the northern manufacturers who win the war, the southern aim is to make its peculiar institution over as a (multi)national corporation. On the textual level, we can see the interplay of regional inflections as a competition over which particular local language will be circulated as the national currency. What has prevented us from seeing the correspondences here is, simply, power: the North's economic and representational preeminence. The North's victory, in other words, has enabled it to assume the mantle of the national character; its distinct regional parameters have come to look synonymous with the outlines of nation. This conflation, in turn, condemns other regional tropes as regional precisely because they do not enjoy the same transformative capability.

By invoking the western "accent," Hopkins tunes our ears to hear a wider band of regional frequencies. I have argued in the introduction of this book that we gloss the movements across regions rather than focus our attention on a fixed regional point of departure, and it is this dialectic that Hopkins embodies in Jewel and her senatorial father. Just as Ruiz de Burton uses Lola's trip east to construct California in relation to the "blue Presbyterians," Hopkins invokes Senator Bowen's "decidedly Western air" (76) in the stifling atmosphere of Washington politics (76) to question the integrity of the sociopolitical divide constructed between North and South. The West, in this novel, demarcates a political rather than a geographical space. Like his stepdaughter, the senator is an icon for transcontinental relations; born in Mississippi but come of age in California, his energetic "ungrammatical phrases" show up both the nerveless quietism of northern politicians and the enervated dissolution of southern statesmen. As I have suggested earlier, Hopkins uses the nouveau-riche western senator to highlight the class-based parallels between Boston-bred manufacturing heir Cuthbert Sumner and the prodigal St. Clair Enson, who stands to inherit the spoils of his Charleston planter-father's estate. Bowen's vernacular underscores the divide between such "dumb-headed aristocrats," who enjoy the fruits of inherited wealth, and himself as a "rugged" (82), bronco-busting veteran who must make his own name. A foil for the well-connected sons of North and South alike, he voices his disgust with the Byzantine ethics of the capitol:

> It's worth while getting rich just to see how money can change the complexion of things. . . . Well, Mrs. Senator, I've fit the enemy, tackled grizzlies, starved, been locked up in the pens of Libby Prison, and I've come out first best every time, but this thing you call society beats me (87–88).

In fact money really does "change the complexion of things," for if Senator Bowen's vernacular explicitly calls attention to "society," it articulates a coded argument about race as well. From the outset, Hopkins's descriptions of the western senator register his "dark complexion" together with his wealth.[27] She develops this relation between racial difference and social distance in the description of Bowen that follows, the novel's most deliberate act of portraiture:

> The Honorable Zenas was an example of the possibilities of individual expansion under the rule of popular government. Every character of his was of the self-made pattern. In familiar conversation with intimate friends, it was his habit to fall into the use of ungrammatical phrases, and, in this, one might easily trace the rugged windings of a life of hardship among the great unwashed before success had crowned his labors. . . . He possessed a rare nature: one of those genial men whom the West is constantly sending out to enrich society. He had begun life as a mate on a Mississippi steamboat. When the Civil War broke out, he joined the Federal forces. . . . His wife dying . . . he took his child, Jewel, and journeyed to California, invested his small savings in mining property in the Black Hills. His profits were fabulous; he counted his pile way up in the million. His appearance was peculiar. Middle height,

lank and graceless. He had the hair and skin of an Indian, but his eyes were a shrewd and steely gray.... There was no denying his awkwardness; no amount of polish could make him otherwise (80).

The argument is a complicated one. Bowen's regional otherness is a product of racial difference, Hopkins insists, first by accentuating difference itself (Bowen's nature is "rare," his appearance "peculiar," his profits "fabulous"), next by insinuating allegiances to the black South (why else would one join Federal forces during the Civil War if born in Mississippi?), and finally by explicitly figuring the senator as an Indian. Unlike his black wife and daughter, the senator is never able to pass. Instead, there is no denying his "awkwardness," no remedy, financial or cultural, that can transform the blurred edges of his vernacular speech into the clipped accents of the patrician, no garment that can cloak his lack of "polish."

Nonetheless, his regional travels become a metaphor for the crossing of racial boundaries. As a northern-identified Mississippi steamboat mate, the California senator gestures toward a place where mixing can be tolerated. No surprise, then, that Bowen does not harbor prejudices about amalgamation. "Next to her God she placed this man," Hagar says upon her second husband's death, "whom she knew instinctively would never have forsaken her" (275–6). While the admission of blackness is an obstacle for northern abolitionist and southern planter alike, the western senator, Hopkins insists through Hagar's celebratory eulogy, would "never for one instant . . . have wavered from his constancy to her. . . . Ellis had come back to her; yes, but although love forgave . . . love could not blot out the bitter memory of the time when he had failed her" (276).

Yet political ambiguity remains the keynote of the portrait Hopkins draws of the senator. Bowen's faith in Hagar is neither put to the test through revelation (it is her own unswerving constancy to this western man/ideal Hopkins emphasizes), nor demonstrated through the material fact of a child (Jewel is his adopted daughter, and he does not have a child with Hagar). Instead, his portrait is shot through with contradictions. Bowen is wealthy but of "the great unwashed," a Federal officer from the South, a man of "stern" character but "mild" disposition, a "dark" skinned man with "Indian" hair but "gray" eyes. This series of oppositions, fused in one skin, speaks for the North-South polarity Hopkins undermines throughout the narrative. It also gestures toward the relationship between regionalism and the colonizing projects of the United States. Bowen's senatorial seat in California, after all, is enabled by the profit he makes in a mining venture in the Indian Territory of the Black Hills. The "profits" that provide him entrance into the closed ranks of Washington policy makers are thus racially marked by Hopkins in a sentence that traces the wealth of the nation (that is, of Bowen as a U.S. senator) back to the exploitation of a subjected population. Granted, the originary appropriation of native land is located only obliquely here, but it is available to readers. Hopkins explicitly acknowledges "expansion" when she introduces the "Honorable Zenus" in markedly ironic language as a cliché of Manifest Destiny, "the example of the possibilities of individual expansion, under the rule of popular government."[28] And she marks the racial site of colonization when she insists on the "Indianness" of Bowen's physiognomy. When the bamboozled senator's fortune is partially recuperated by the South (the Carolinian General Benson induces him to gamble large sums in addition to faking a will in his own favor), "justice" may not be done, but its derailment is indicated. In this sense, however "honorable," we see the fortunes of the open space of the West implicated in the same policies that have brought the North and South to conflict.

Ultimately, the fate of "good" and "bad" characters alike bears out Hopkins's insistence that we gloss individual inequities as illustrations of regional problems. As her portrait of Senator Bowen indicates, what appears idiosyncratic is actually a register of systemic failure—which is why the senator from California can be simultaneously "peculiar" and an "example . . . of the self made pattern" (80). In this way, affiliations between people—more specifically, between the individual character of distinct senators and the congressional social body of which they are a part—gesture metaphorically toward relationships between region and nation. Authorial censure of federal policy attests to what keeps the states united. Put another way: "[t]he sin is the nation's" (283), as Sumner finally realizes at the close of the novel. Like María Amparo Ruiz de Burton's indictments of congressional policy in *The Squatter and the Don* and *Who Would Have Thought It?*, what makes the nation greater than the sum of its (regional) parts in *Hagar's Daughter* is precisely the federally authored policies that enforce and sustain inequities felt (and felt differentially) as regional conflicts and local injuries.

## V: "without a touch of provincialism":
## Sacrificing the West to Nationalism in *Senator North*

*Jack was the son of a Virginian who had been a Rebel to his death. . . . His Southern accent and intonation were nearly as broad as a negro's. Betty had almost lost hers; she retained just enough to enrich and individualize without a touch of provincialism. She belonged to that small class of Americans whose ear-mark is the absence of all Americanisms (29–31).*

—Gertrude Atherton, *Senator North*

*Washington is certainly the headquarters of democracy. Here every American really does feel that he is as good as every other American; I wish to heaven he didn't (26).*

—*Senator North*

Zenas Bowen's "ungrammatical phrases" mark his political distinction; in *Senator North*, "broad" "accents" are incommensurate with patriotism. Where the Boston-bred writer uses the language of region to explore the democratic center of the United States (the growing middle class) as a conflicted venue, the Californian exploits the regional metaphor to insist that only a "small class of Americans" can rightfully occupy the national space. Like the ostensibly uninflected tongue of contemporary network television, *Senator North* rejects regional values as too broadly accented to stand in for the federal polity. Instead, it is characters like Betty Madison, gifted with the aristocratic education that effaces local speech, who are properly entitled to be circulated as "American" rather than "southern" commodities on the Union's marriage market. Ultimately, *Senator North* uses the protracted courtship between Betty and her fiancé to argue for a wedding of regions that is not a democratic leveling of regional differences, but monarchical. Through Betty's romance, Atherton argues that the South must be convinced to submit its local patrician values to the better judgement of the aristocratic North.

To argue that an iconography indigenous to New England best speaks for the national character is conventional for Anglo American nationalist discourse of the last half of the nineteenth century.[29] Nevertheless, the troubled nature of the relationship between Senator North and Betty Madison forces a marriage between region and nation that bears the traces of the effort involved in managing this relationship. Like *Hagar's Daughter*, *Senator North* requires the presence of the western senator in the Washington drawing room, and so demonstrates the insufficiency of the Mason-Dixon line to map the borders between region, nation, and empire.

For Atherton as for the other writers of this study, region is an acronym encoding a complex knot of political issues. In *Senator North*, the writer signifies the reduced authority of those regions framed as exotic (compared with the familiar literary topography of New England as national "center"), through social station and racial difference. Atherton's attention to the "intonations" of Jack Emory's "Southern accent" resonates with James's description of Basil Ransom, the southern protagonist of *The Bostonians*, whose "discourse was pervaded by something sultry and vast, something almost African in its rich basking tone, something that suggested the teeming expanse of the cotton-field."[30] Both the Californian and the Bostonian render the socially disenfranchised status of southerners in the North through the trope of blackness.[31] Like Ruiz de Burton, Atherton argues that those who guide the Union must share the interests of their class. She lampoons the senatorial hopefuls who circulate the language of democracy as a substitute for social elevation in a manner that recalls the class-inflected critique of national authority her fellow Californian develops in *Who Would Have*

*Thought It?* Where Ruiz de Burton turns the regional social scale on its head, however, exposing the "blue Presbyterians" themselves (55) as an ungainly mass of nouveau-riche social climbers, Atherton identifies the "newly settled community of adventurers out West" (33) as soiling (muddying) the limpid stream of Washington's blue-blooded aristocracy with their plebeian consanguinity. Educated in the arid cultural climes of "the colleges of their State" rather than "the big Universities" of the North, these western senators transform what should be a green "oasis" into a "social Sahara" (290). She exploits the image of "spittoons and toothpicks" (12)—the very same objective correlatives Ruiz de Burton uses to expose Bostonian natives as culturally impoverished—to ridicule the self-made men of "those dreadful Western States" (34).

It is not only Betty Madison's provincial southern relatives who define these congressional upstarts from the West as out of their class in Washington. More worldly intimates of senatorial circles are quick to confirm the conventional social hierarchy of region. The Washington scene, it turns out, is as striated by social differences as an Arizona mesa is with iron ore. The unimpeachable Lady Mary confirms Jack Emory's dismissive assumption that western senators are "bound to be corrupt" (33) when she provides this tepid corrective:

> The hard-working second-rate men, many of them millionaires (Western, as a rule) who are accused of having bought their legislatures to get in, but who do good work on Committee, whether or not they came under the delusion that they had bought an honor with nothing beneath it (27).

Even Betty herself, whose voice most closely approximates Atherton's own, defines the best of western senators—Robert Burleigh, who is "brilliant, ambitious, and honorable"—as second-rate when she playfully "coquet(s)" with him, while Senator North "was exalted [by her] to the vacant pedestal reserved for ideals" (51). Through Betty Madison, Atherton honors the senator from the East using the same language with which Pauline Hopkins celebrates the congressman from the West. Hagar discards her habitual reserve for Senator Bowen alone, whom she reveres: "Next to her God she placed this man" (275), we are told after his death. Likewise, Betty drops her sardonic demeanor in front of Senator North, whom she literally "worship[s]" (51).

The regional parameters assigned to romantic "worship" in both novels indicates how each senator stands in for authorial ideas about the nation's political geography. As a western senator, Bowen occupies not so much a *place* as a *space;* he is a focal point for the possibility of political opportunities and regional relations unimaginable under the linear terms of the North-South opposition. Atherton's Senator North too is the expression of a historical ideal who "might at any moment hold the destinies of the United States in his hands." His sterling character is the national coin; over and over again, Atherton frames Betty's relationship with him as an affiliation with the public sphere itself. When her cousin Jack Emory lavishes praise upon her as a provincial ornament—"the last rose on the old Southern tree"— Betty corrects him by identifying herself as belonging "to the whole country" (35). While western suitor Burleigh patronizingly characterizes women as bereft of "the national sense" (68), Atherton styles Betty's infatuation with North as a patriotic affair. He appeals to her "through the powerful medium of patriotic pride" (51), a phrase that clarifies his regional identity as a synecdoche for national authority. "She felt almost as much at home in this family section of the Senate Gallery as in her own room with a copy of the Congressional Record in her hand" (104), we are told at one point, and at another, that marrying Burleigh would be to bury herself in the West whereas to unite herself with North would transform her into an "American beauty rose" (121). The project of falling in love with him is thus the agenda of nationalism; if we were to add a subtitle to the narrative, we might call it "Senator North, or, How I Began to Love the Union."

Like paper money, the national coin needs backing to assert its worth. Just as Hopkins exploits Senator Bowen to show up the twin failings of North and South, Atherton uses the moneyed social climbers of the western states to shore up the unimpeachability of New England as a synecdoche for the "values" she designates as national. Like Hopkins, then, her own version of the Mason-Dixon difference cannot be maintained without invoking the West. Once again, the specter of Miss Trumbull becomes useful, for in marrying a western senator (the ironically named George Washington Mudd), this "'I'm-as-good-as-you-are' American" (151) reflects the vulgarity of a democratic discourse affiliated in *Senator North* with western "adventurers." As I have suggested above, class status is the glue that cements the "national sense." In marrying North, Betty transforms herself from southern belle into American beauty. Mrs. Mudd, on the contrary, merely shifts her vernacular to the common language of the West Coast.

But it is not only Miss Trumbull who is a foil for northern values. Bowen, the California senator of *Hagar's Daughter,* is the focal point for Hopkins's exploration of a regionally mapped nation that exerts imperial claims. Burleigh, the California senator of *Senator North,* identifies vilified domestic policies and imperial desires as western in origin, defusing them by disassociating them from the New England region that stands in for the national character. In an American twist on English descriptions of colonial Australia, Atherton ships all the potentially damaging by-products of Manifest Destiny to the (western) provinces in a move that keeps "the center" clean. "Who would be a Western Senator?" Burleigh asks rhetorically, bracketing this region as essentially foreign:

My colleague and I received a document to-day, signed by two thousand of our constituents . . . in which we were ordered to acknowledge the belligerency of the Cubans at once or expect to be tarred and feathered upon our return. The climate of my State is excellent for consumption, but bad for nerves. Doubtless most of these men come of good New England stock, whose relatives "back East" would never think of doing such a thing; but the intoxicating climate they have been inhaling for half a generation, to say nothing of the raw conditions, makes them want to fight creation (275–6).

Anticipating Willa Cather's European and Anglo American expatriates, drunk on ozone in New Mexico, Atherton censures the West as an exotic lotus land whose despoiled Mexican and Native American inhabitants have catalyzed their own dispossession. María Amparo Ruiz de Burton presciently lampoons this fantasy by parodying her life in Monterey as somnambulistic (in an 1852 letter to Mariano Vallejo she parodies Yankee industry through a cleverly hyperbolic comparison: "Ningunas noticias interesantes hay que comunicarle . . . casi he llegado á persuadirme de que dormimos eternamente y que andamos y venimos [como] zonambulos . . . nosotoros los montereyanos no somos como esa gente ambiciosa de por allá arriba que no tiene mas deseo que atesoran dinero" [No interesting news to tell you . . . I have almost persuaded myself that we are in an eternal sleep and that we come and go like somnambulists . . . we the montereyans are not like this ambitious people up there who have no desire other than to hoard money].[32] For Owen Wister, the "huge, delicious indifference" the West casts upon men can be withstood only by the strong; this is what distinguishes the admiring but effete narrator, who glories "No lotus land ever cast its spell upon a man's heart more than Wyoming had enchanted mine" (62) from the more unyielding Virginian. For Atherton, however, this lack of interest in accumulating wealth at all costs that the expansive geology of the West fosters is itself a condition to be fought against. In her books, the origins of American imperial violence are displaced from "good New England stock" to the "raw conditions" and "intoxicating climate" of the West, which, when inhaled, turns men of reason into savages who "want to fight creation." In Cather's work, as I will argue in the following chapter, this racial substitution finds its full expression.

# Chapter Five ∿

# All in the Family?

## Willa Cather's Imperial Housekeeping in the Southwest

### I: The Frontier, Civilization, and its Discontents

*On the first day of September Fred Ottenburg and Thea Kronborg left Flagstaff by the east-bound express. As the bright morning advanced, they sat alone on the rear platform of the observation car, watching the yellow miles unfold and disappear. With complete content they saw the brilliant, empty country flash by. They were tired of the desert and the dead races, of a world without change or ideas. Fred said he was glad to sit back and let the Santa Fe do the work for a while.*

—Willa Cather, *The Song of the Lark*[1]

*With Louie, Lillian seemed to be launching into a new career, and Godfrey began to think that he understood his own wife very little. He would have said that she would feel about Louie just as he did; would have cultivated him as a stranger in the town, because he was so unusual and exotic, but without in the least wishing to adopt anyone so foreign into the family circle.*

—Willa Cather, *The Professor's House*[2]

*"They weren't mine to sell—nor yours! . . . You've gone and sold your country's secrets, like Dreyfus. . . . I'm not so poor that I have to sell the pots and pans that belonged to my poor grandmothers a thousand years ago" (242–3).*

Who is admitted to the American family, and who defines its borders by being cast out as "unusual," "exotic," a "stranger"? The political seizure of the Southwest officially ends with the Treaty of Guadalupe-Hidalgo, but the imaginative appropriation of this land is harder to manage. The project of late-nineteenth-century narratives of California is to authorize cultural title to the state, but adjudicating such claims means placing the West in relation to the nation's "family circle." As Godfrey's musings on his son-in-law's "adoption" suggest, this undertaking bleeds over into the twentieth century as well. In this chapter, I consider how Willa Cather's southwestern fictions attempt to resolve these questions. Like Helen Hunt Jackson, Gertrude Atherton, Owen Wister, Zane Grey, and other turn-of-the-century sentimental writers who locate the West at a temporal and cultural remove from the nation as a whole, the raced representations of region Cather publishes two decades into the new century push the "desert and the dead races" back to antiquity and position the "brilliant, empty country" at the apex of a cultural hierarchy that assigns people distinct steps on the evolutionary ladder of history. Just as Henry James's modernist reflections on the Pullman allow him to contemplate "'the general conquest of nature and space'" in *The American Scene*,[3] Cather invokes the railroad to remind us that "Westward the course of empire takes its way."[4] And like the naturalist writings of Frank Norris, Cather assigns the "dead races" of the Southwest a fate as biologically determined as the "violent, uncurbed passions" of their physiognomy.[5]

Because they blur boundaries between nineteenth-century sentimentalism, turn-of-the-century naturalism, and twentieth-century modernism that scholars prefer to think of as fixed, Cather's western landscapes have provocative implications for literary periodizing. Conventional literary cataloguing balks at connecting high modernists like Cather with pulp fiction writers like Zane Grey and Owen Wister, but a comparative review clarifies the shared arguments and common rhetorical figures in the desert landscapes of both kinds of writers. If the Pullman resonates throughout James's *The American Scene* (a novelist Cather honors by invoking in *The Professor's House*), the railroad car is equally central to his protégé Owen Wister, whose famous novel *The Virginian* opens with a scene identical to Cather's image of the "east-bound express" with which I opened this chapter: "Some notable sight was drawing the passengers, both men and women, to the window. . . . Through the windowglass of our Pullman, the thud of their mischievous hoofs reached us" (11). Like his literary descendents Thea Kronborg and Fred Ottenburg, Wister's narrator is as foreign to the western landscape he surveys as is Frank Norris's Presley to the agricultural valleys of California depicted in *The Octopus*. By implication, the reader is similarly framed as voyeur in *The Virginian,* ensconced in the comfort of "our Pullman," watching the rodeo scene below from the safe distance of a window seat. Cather's exploration of native ruins in the Southwest—and their relation to expressions of U.S. nationalism—is also anticipated by Zane Grey in *Riders of the Purple Sage*.[6] But the striking resemblance between Cather's Tom Outland and Grey's own Bern Venters is uncanny only to our own critical eyes, accustomed as we are to distinguishing the modern novel from the western as the literary equivalent of haute cuisine from fast food. In fact, the timeline constructed by contemporary literary periodizing remains resolutely ahistorical; a cursory attention to the shared discursive context within which both Grey and Cather wrote dictates connections in their narrative lexicons.

But given the extent to which her Southwest, and not his, remains the nation's—her novels are still the most popular guidebooks for tourists surveying the region—Cather's intricate arguments about race, region, nation, and empire demand close attention.[7] The process in which relics of particular cultures become the property of the country at large (the way the "pots and pans" Tom Outland stumbles over on the mesa in New Mexico become his), registers the aesthetics of appropriation at the moment when western territories are being admitted into statehood.[8] As such, Cather participates in the work of writers like Mary Austin and Fray Antonio Chavez, who self-consciously labored to supplement a narrowly regional expression of the American aesthetic by establishing a national art native to the West.

I wish to reconsider the relationship between art, culture, and nationalism I opened with in the preface to this volume by looking closely at the way Cather drafts this equation. Cather, I will argue here, uses a series of raced substitutions and displacements to connect empire with sexual difference. At the heart of this intersection she places the effeminized figure of the Jew, the domesticated but "exotic" "stranger" who cannot be adopted into the nation's "family circle." Just as the conquest of Mexican land is rewritten as a domestic "annexation," Cather cements this relationship through the metaphor of home (consider, for instance, the title of *The Professor's House*). She uses domesticity as civilizing force, that is, to simultaneously justify *and* cover over imperial relationships. Like other gendered metaphors that encode relations of power, Cather's figure shows up the differences in authority upon which imperial relationships are based. In *The Professor's House* the writer articulates this civilizing influence by equating the masculine "housekeeping"/"excavating" of Tom, Roddy, and Henry in the Cliff City ruins with the Jewish cupidity she argues underwrites this archaeology. We can trace "consent" to conquest in her work through the servility the domesticated muster for their superiors. Henry's fawning acquiescence in Tom's domestic scheme makes him a geriatric contradiction in terms: "He was a wonderful cook and a good housekeeper. He kept that cabin shining like a playhouse. . . . And he was such a polite, mannerly old boy; simple and kind as a child" (197).

But it is Jewish obsequiousness that takes the fall for the "annexation" of Native American artifact that provides Cather, along with many nineteenth- and twentieth-century writers, with her sustaining metaphor for American culture. Loretta Wasserman tracks "Cather's Semitism" through characters like the half-Jewish Merryweather of "Behind the Singer Tower," whose "villainy" is the product of what the writer calls his "racial characteristics." While Wasser-man highlights the pressure exerted upon such characters, describing Cather as "an especially painful case" in the list of modernists who use "dismissive stereotypes," she ultimately recuperates the novelist's racist portraits. If she ac-knowledges the "venomous portrait" of Merryweather, whose "servility . . . made him swallow, toadlike, any rebuff," she reads the slavishness of Cather's Jewish characters as "forbearance." [9] Where I identify Louie's meek acceptance of his brother-in-law's blackballing of him at the Arts and Letters Club as servile,[10] Wasserman argues that Cather admires such humility in the face of anti-Semitism as an example of "patient forgiveness (Christian, we might say)" (17). Precisely: as a positive quality, such forgiveness cannot be Jewish. Nonetheless, whether one reads approbation or disgust in Cather's portrait of Louie Marsellus, her exploitation of him and other Jewish figures furthers her arguments about American cultural and social life. Considered more closely, Cather's sexualizing of imperial appropriation provides opportunities for ex-amining relationships between sectional conflict, nationalism, and imperial designs.

## II: "Of savage Sinai": Cather's Orientalist Literary Precursors

> My dark-browed daughter of the sun,
> Dear Bedouin of the desert sands,
> Sad daughter of the ravished lands,
> Of savage Sinai, Babylon,—
> O Egypt-eyed, thou art to me
> A God-encompassed mystery!
>
> I see sad Hagar in thine eyes.
> The obelisks, the pyramids,
> Lie hid beneath thy drooping lids.
> The tawny Nile of Moses lies
> Portrayed in thy strange people's force
> And solemn mystery of source.
>
> The black abundance of thy hair
> Falls like some twilight sad of June
> Above the dying afternoon,
> And mourns thy people's mute despair.
> The large solemnity of night,
> O Israel, is in thy sight!
>
> Then come where stars of freedom spill
> Their splendor, Jewess. In this land,
> The same broad hollow of God's hand

That held you ever, outholds still.
And whether you be right or nay,
'Tis God's, not Russia's, here to say.

—from "Jewess," Joaquin Miller [11]

Writing conquest as seduction rather than rape is nothing new. As I have suggested in the previous chapter, Gertrude Atherton makes her living from this kind of "romance." In fact, from Joaquin Miller to Helen Hunt Jackson to Robert Louis Stevenson, discursive history anticipates Cather's own constellation of immigrant and native-born raced figures.[12] While western literary narratives invoke a Jewish presence with regularity (we could add the names of Guadalupe Vallejo and Cather's own contemporary, María Cristina Mena, to the writers listed above),[13] western histories have until recently imagined the territories west of New York as beyond the pale of Jewish settlement.[14] U.S. orientalism is a complement to language that celebrates the "frontier" as the border dividing the savage from the civilized: it sanctifies Anglo American possession by backdating prior claims on land, fixing native inhabitants as hoary mystics congenitally unsuited to living with the technological marvels that advance the work of the nineteenth-century "American" farmer. Just as the Jewish "stranger" inhabiting *The Professor's House* stands in a peculiar relation to the Native American artifacts Cather dusts off as material "title" to the Southwest, orientalist language at the turn of the century links Native Americans, Mexicans, and Jews using a geographically distanced and distancing metaphor of racial strangeness and displacement.

Such iconography distinguishes American populations not only politically but metaphysically, shoring up the integrity of raced definitions of "self" and "other" that perennially threaten integration. Where writers such as Josephine Clifford McCrackin and María Amparo Ruiz de Burton authorize landowners by satirically compacting the dispossessed at the bottom of the social hierarchy, orientalism simply obliterates history, depriving people of agency and cutting them off from the mundane activities of social life and political process. This deracination is more complete than overt political critique: rather than deny people the right to contest authority, it renders their claims irrelevant. Longtime residents of California are swathed in a romantic mist that smoothes over the gritty realities of their daily lives and renders their material presence insubstantial. German Jews who emigrated to Santa Fé, New Mexico, long before Joaquin Miller made his way west, Russian immigrants whose New York-born children could not speak, let alone spell words like "Sinai"; these are the "dark-browed daughter[s]" and sons mythified and mystified and thus made (psychically) foreign to U.S. soil. The same language that supports travel writers to Mexico (*The Century Magazine* characterizes Mexico City as populated by "strange figures" of whom it can be said "'There is nothing stranger out of Egypt'")[15] relocates Southern California within the vicinity of Jerusalem's Old-Town *shuk* (bazaar) in Helen Hunt Jackson's documentary essay "The Present Condition of the Mission Indians in Southern California." Published in *The Century Magazine,* this piece disguises Indians, like the "Bedouin" "Jewess" of Miller's poem, as Middle Eastern nomads. Such a rhetorical solution to the political problem of native land tenure lengthens decades into ages, representing the authority of centuries of tribal existence in California in the persons of centenarians who belong not to a contentious present but to the state's harmonious (and of course irretrievable) past. In this manner writers translate a potentially threatening legal claim into a curiosity more appropriate for the circus than the courtroom.[16]

Jackson repeatedly pays tribute to the state's elders using language that anticipates the calcifying iconography Cather will use in books like *Death Comes for the Archbishop,* language that, as Genaro Padilla writes in *My History, Not Yours: The Formation of Mexican American Autobiography,* "sediment[ed] . . . cultural practices in a kind of deanthropromorphization."[17] One group of older women is statues, silent and "motionless. . . . As if they were dead."[18] Like Cather's Tom Outland, who stares in wonder at the Indian mummy preserved in the Cliff City of *The Professor's House,* Jackson avows: "If I had been told that Benjamina was a three-thousand-year-old Nile mummy, resuscitated by some mysterious process, I should not have demurred much at the tale" (525). Imagined as an "old Bedouin sheik" (525), this woman who has resided in California for 117 years becomes in Jackson's account a museum artifact indigenous to the Middle East.

When we compare this orientalist iconography with Miller's "Jewess" published in *The Century Magazine* some ten months prior to "The Present Condition of the Mission Indians," the raced inflections of Jackson's essay come into sharper focus. On the one hand, the poem is a conventional celebration of U.S. liberty (a land " . . . where stars of freedom spill/ Their splendor") in the face of the tyrannies of the Old Country (" . . . whether you be right or nay,/ 'Tis God's, not Russia's *here* to say"). On the other hand, the invitation beckoning Jewish immigrants to American shores is confined to the closing verse, while the three stanzas that precede it catalogue the eroticized figure of the "dark-browed daughter of the sun" who is the object of the poet's gaze—not as Ellis Island hopeful but only as embodiment of " . . . the ravished lands,/ Of savage Sinai, Babylon." Helen Hunt Jackson uses Egypt to stage the despoliation of Native Americans in California as an Israelite captivity and native people as contemporary wandering Jews in " . . . immediate danger of being driven out from their last foot-holds of refuge, 'homeless wanderers in a desert'" (529). Likewise, Miller describes modern day Jewish exiles as "tawny" "savage[s]" to develop a myth of American origins ("the solemn mystery of source"), which in effect folds over the national map until the New York shore abuts the desert Southwest. The lexical parallels are striking. Both writers represent their subjects as Bedouins, both repeatedly refer to the "savage" heat of "desert sands" ("Jewess"), both represent "un-American" femininity using the figure of Hagar, and both—perhaps this is merely the offhand ethnography of the non-Semite?—conflate the Jewish slave with the Egyptian overseers who directed the building of "the obelisks" and "the pyramids." Miller's "Jewess" is "Egypt-eyed," and Jackson's Indian mother has "a mouth like an Egyptian priestess" (523).

Why does the Jew continue to wander through this western landscape? What accounts for the peripatetic but stubborn persistence of the Diaspora in writings about California and the Southwest? One solution is to see the Israelite "mystery" as a racial substitution: as archetype of exile, the Jew provides Anglo writers of the West with a safe metaphor for invoking the sociopolitical disturbances of more familiar territory. The generic character of this metaphor for victimization (what Miller refers to luridly as "thy people's mute despair") keeps its referent evacuated of historical content, while its hazy romanticism wards off the grimly prosaic spectacle of homelessness it is meant to acknowledge. Geographically and generically distanced from the language of social critique, the romantic image of the "dark-browed" Jew is a comfortable euphemism for the people currently beyond the pale in the Southwest—the other black-haired residents displaced by railroad magnates and forty-niners. More significantly, the millenial wandering of the Jewish people—their sustained rootlessness—provides a convenient way to argue for a similar inclination on the part of the forcibly disenfranchised people for whom the Jews substitute. Just as European figures of anti-Semitism have long equated the Jews with gypsies, arguing tautologically that sojourners cannot enjoy the rights of citizens because they "choose" to wander, American anti-Semitic images yank the rug from under the feet of residents assumed to be incompetent to quash their own inbred "wanderlust."

Such a process of substitution is undeniably at work, but it does not fully account for the complex web of regional and racial representation in such nineteenth-century American texts. Like Carolyn Porter, who suggests in "What We Know that We Don't Know: Remapping American Literary Studies" that "the aim would be to see one story in relation to the other," I am arguing that we not separate regional "stories."[19] More specifically, investigating the literary presence of Jews in western literature confirms the fact that the U.S. cannot adequately be mapped as a jigsaw of differently colored regional pieces. Just as California in *The Squatter and the Don* is irreversibly the product of federal design, interregional commerce and competition, and transcontinental social agendas, so the literary presence of

Jews in western literature points to numerous interconnected stress fractures in American political life. Expose one stress point (the waves of Jewish immigration to the eastern seaboard that peak at the turn of the century) and watch as this hairline break runs and splits, breaking into different channels, connecting up with other divides only to be carved deeper in its turn: the heavy incursion of nonnative Californians in the wake of the railroad and the Gold Rush, the difficulty of defining what constitutes the nation with "foreigners" on two different coasts, the pressure of movements for suffrage and labor, the economic transition to what the nineteenth-century called "speculation," to name some of the concerns that figure in María Amparo Ruiz de Burton's 1885 novel alone. In the section that follows I return to Cather's work to illuminate some of the ways this complicated network of pressure points shapes the system of regional relationships that produce the nation.

### III: "That feeling of empire": Cather's Raced Iconography of the Southwest

*There is no claim to brotherhood with aliens in the first grossness of their alienism (92).*

—Henry James, *The American Scene*

*"I happen to know, Louie, that Scott blackballed you for the Arts and Letters. . . . Do you happen to have read a novel of Henry James,* The American? *There's a rather nice scene in it, in which a young Frenchman, hurt in a duel, apologizes for the behaviour of his family. I'd like to do something of the sort. I apologize to you for Rosamund, and for Scott, if he has done such a mean thing. Louie's downcast face brightened at once. He squeezed the Professor's arm warmly. "Oh,* that's *all right, sir! As for Scott, I can understand. He was the first son of the family, and he was the whole thing. Then I came along, a stranger, and carried off Rosie" (168, 169–70).*

—Willa Cather, *The Professor's House*

The raced patterns of regional and national life characteristic of western narratives at the turn of the century are no less tangled in Willa Cather's fictions several decades later. Two different but interrelated rhetorics describe the symbolic space of her desert Southwest. One language pictures the West as a remote vastness: this is the "brilliant empty country" around Flagstaff that I cited at the opening of this chapter, and which Thea and Otto, "tired of the desert and the dead races," watch "flash by" (408) from their railroad car at the end of *The Song of the Lark*. Another narrates how the West was won precisely by peopling it with vanquished "natives": the "Ramas boys" who dance "so well" (290) with Thea in the Mexican quarter of Moonstone, and the "cooking-smoke of the Ancient People" she dreams of in Panther Canyon (375). Considered in relation to a nationalist agenda, these distinct regional topographies reconcile to a single vanishing point, fulfilling the federal mandate "Westward the course of Empire takes its way" (*SL*, 69), which Thea sees Ray Kennedy as embodying in his travels as train operator.

To invoke this catchphrase is to locate us in a politicized critical space we are habituated to at the close of the millennium. But familiarity need not breed contempt. As Paul Gilroy argues in *The Black Atlantic: Modernity and Double Consciousness*, such

> important enquiries into the contiguity of racialised reason and unreasonable racism [should not] be dismissed as trivial matters. These issues go to the heart of contemporary debates about what constitutes the canon of western civilisation and how this precious legacy should be taught. In these embattled circumstances, it is regrettable that questions of "race" and representation have been so regularly banished from orthodox histories of western aesthetic judgement, taste, and cultural value.[20]

In suggesting that the nationalist paradigm Cather plays out in the Southwest is a conventional one, I wish neither to dismiss it nor to gloat over it. The appeal of her doubled and divided discourse of empire remains compelling: we have only to thumb the pages of a contemporary novel of the frontier region to see Cather's stereoscopic vision replicated in prose that plots the perimeters of the Blackfeet reservation in the same breath as it affirms "that there's land and more land and then more of more, just for the taking here in Montana."[21] If her recovery of the West is more conservative than is Walter Benn Michaels's when he celebrates *The Professor's House* as developing a form of "cultural citizenship . . . compatible with a certain critique of racism," it enables a play with sexual conventions difficult under the discursive terms of Cather's era.[22] Eve Sedgwick and Judith Butler have outlined two distinct versions of homosocial domesticity.[23] What both of these critics leave out, however, and what Michaels's non-committal "cultural" reading of the novel dismisses, is the racially striated social world that enables them. Aesthetic possession and cultural achievement are developed in the Cather canon, but at the cost of ethnic scapegoating.

A closer look at a particular southwestern landmark—Ácoma, "the rock" that inspires Father Latour in *Death Comes for the Archbishop*—reveals the mechanics of this social space and resolves the dissonance produced by the different languages Cather uses to map it.[24] In *Death Comes for the Archbishop*, Ácoma is both an absolute value (a "wilderness at the end of the world" [281]), and so thick with people that the bishop's unabstemious predecessor Fray Baltazar is crowded off its edge, "dropped . . . in mid-air" (113) by the Indians whose work has sustained his hospitality. As a "wilderness," Ácoma is an icon for the westward move across a continent labeled as American. As a city, and the origin for the "Legend of Fray Baltazar," Ácoma *also* celebrates the Anglo takeover, for it is a parable for the (transient) success of the Spanish conquest that predates the signing of the Treaty of Guadalupe-Hidalgo. Both the Father's sensuality and the "tyranny" (106) he exerts over the neophytes resurface in his "descendents," Mexicano priests like Latour's enemy Padre Martínez, whose face mirrors this "lawless . . . power": his eyes "brilliant yellow," his "shoulders like a bull buffalo's," his mouth "the very assertion of violent, uncurbed passions and tyrannical self-will; the full lips thrust out and taut, like the flesh of animals distended by fear or desire" (140–1).[25] Here as elsewhere in American literature, such racist figures distinguish the "civilized" races from the "savage" ones.[26] Where Cather honors the bronze face of the statue of bishop Lamy (Latour) as revealing "something 'fearless and fine and very, very well-bred—something that spoke of race,'"[27] Martínez, in a remake of Ovidian metamorphosis, is "terrifying"—at one instance-shape shifting into a "buffalo" (32), at another less personable than the goats who are "light and elegant" and whose faces, "supercilious and sardonic" as a Van Dyke portrait with their "mocking, humanly intelligent smile[s]," are more European than his own (30–31). Like the bison killed off by Anglo American encroachment, Martínez is the last of a dying breed, "hat[ing] the Americans" whose "occupation meant the end of men like himself" (153).

What Padilla calls deanthropromorphization—which discredits the Spanish Conquest as a contradiction in terms—is an aesthetic tool Cather often exploits. Mountains and deserts exert a human agency: Northern New Mexico is murderous in *Death Comes for the Archbishop* (able to "drink up youth and strength" [9]) and brooding in *The Professor's House* ("muttering and making noises" [193]). But the people who live there are quite literally "sediment[ed] . . . at every turn."[28] In Mexican Town, for instance, Thea wonders how a young man reclining in the sand can "flatten himself into the ground like that" (*SL,* 295). Six years after the 1927 publication of *Death Comes for the Archbishop,* Frank Dobie will say of the "country inhabited by the Cogat tribe" that it is "a withering, saline country, filled with biting dust and strewn with the crumbling shells of mussels and snails that had been stranded in some immemorial time by the recession of the sea."[29] Cather herself concatenates the Laguna of Ácoma with the mesa they live upon: "rock-turtles on their rock," they are animated fossils, "fixed," "reptilian" (103), "hardened" and "shut within their shells . . . types of life so old" they not only predate "the sacrifice on Calvary" (100) but all of human history itself.

If Cather turns the natives of the Southwest to stone and refuses them the "dreams" that constitute civilization (even the sympathetic Father Latour finds "no way [to] . . . transfer his own memories of European civilization into the Indian mind" [*D*, 92]), Jewish foreigners are likewise reduced to beasts (100, 103). The Shylockian figures who compete for attention in this Circean corral of racial types, a ring where Mexicans lumber like buffalo and Indians skitter swift as antelope, are truly mythical creatures: Banker Sigmund Stein of "Scandal " has "a voice like a crow's" (*Collected Stories,* 163) together with a "horse-like face" (162). Pianist Miletus Poppas of "The Diamond Mine" recalls an even less savory bird: he is "a vulture of the vulture race, and he had the beak of one."[30] Even "the finest kind of Jews" (*SL*, 343) the wealthy Nathanmeyers who, inassimilable themselves, help Thea to transform her talent, are differentiated from "the white-skinned races" who possess finer "qualities of feeling" (344). Like other tribal people, they exist as anachronisms. With her "swarthy complexion . . . eagle nose, and sharp, glittering eyes," Mrs. Nathanmeyer is "powerful," but in the primitive, precultural sense of an Aztec God or the sculptured visage of an Egyptian monument (346).

Biologically differentiated like the Indian and the Mexican, the Jew is subjected throughout Cather's work to the pressures of early-twentieth-century anti-immigrant discourses. Walter Benn Michaels rather glibly describes American culture as readily "available . . . to Jews about whom there is 'nothing Semitic' but their noses" (238). (But, what noses.) In fact, like the other "others" of Cather's fiction, Jews are constitutionally unable to accept such a legacy. A "wannabe" without pathos, the banker of "Scandal" could be borrowed wholesale from any number of frankly racist tracts, like Professor John R. Commons's much reprinted compendium *Races and Immigrants in America.*[31] In an infelicitous parody of biblical imagery, Cather describes Stein as an Austrian "beggar . . . of many-coloured ambitions" who is marked by the characteristic "long nose" as well as "flat cheeks, yellow as a Mongolian's, tiny, black eyes . . . and dingy, dead-looking hair [that] looks as if it were glued on" (162–3). Jews in the short fictions as well as *The Professor's House* are economically rapacious and sexually predatory, but they lack any easy entrée into culture. [32] The racially defined eroticism of Cather's Jewish, Mexicano, and Native American characters has as much to do with disquietude about social border crossings as sexual mestizaje. Significantly, the immigrant Jew's coercive sexuality aligns him with people typed as indigenous to the Southwest—the licentious Padre Martínez of *Death Comes for the Archbishop* or the bloodthirsty Aztecs of "Coming, Aphrodite!"—not, as Michaels suggests, with Anglo American aspirants like Tom Outland.[33] Perennially "exotic" (*PH*, 78), the Jews are the conventional strangers in a strange land who help immigrants like Father Latour of *Death Comes for the Archbishop* and Mrs. Kronborg of *The Song of the Lark* appear at home in America.

From this vantage, the parameters of contemporary Western culture—one not buried in Panther Canyon or the Blue Mesa—look narrow. Notwithstanding critical efforts to distinguish modernist fiction from its sentimental precursors, the regional politics of Cather's fiction reiterate turn-of-the-century texts (Norris's *The Octopus,* Helen Hunt Jackson's *Ramona,* a host of short fictions about the Southwest published in *Harper's, The Over-land Monthly,* and *The Atlantic Monthly.*) Like these earlier narratives that celebrate the "Spanish" Southwest as a feudal golden age, Cather is nostalgic for the Indian labor that testifies to a more settled class system. Father La-tour's residence has adobe walls "finished on the inside by the deft palms of Indian women" (*D,* 33) while the church in which he worships is a monu-ment to political order as well as spiritual grace: "Powerful men they must have been, those Spanish Fathers, to draft Indian labour. . . . Every stone in that structure, every handful of earth in those many thousand pounds of adobe, was carried up the trail on the backs of men and boys and women" (*D,* 101). Like James, Cather frames the Southwest through a series of es-sentially European-derived encounters: we are often reminded that Thea is Swedish, that Fathers Latour and Vaillant are French, and that Professor St. Peter is of French Canadian as well as American stock. Like James's *Hawthorne,* Cather suggests that American civilization west of New England remains postulated rather than proven. The finest citizen of Moonstone, apart from Thea herself, is Doctor Archie, who the narrator casually slights together with the state of Colorado ("He was a distinguished-looking man, for that part of the world, at least" [4]), and whose penchant for Robert Burns aligns him with sentimental songs, not the German arias he will hear Thea sing so brilliantly. Thea, on the other hand, whose Swedish intonations promise a cosmopolitan career, is more often framed against her birthplace than native to it. Herr Wunsch first sets her apart from the landscape when he wonders: "What was it about the child that one believed in? Was it her dogged industry, so unusual in this free-and-easy country?" (122).

Indeed, "free and easy," whether in its Mexican, Anglo, or Indian versions, characterizes the West, rendering it both romantic and second-rate. Ray's painless surrender of his dreams is cut short when he is literally broken up by the railroad upon which he has traversed the western expanse, but not, like Doctor Archie, made good.[34] Rather than "'master nature'" (*D,* 233), this railroad man, "deeply sentimental, like most railroad men" has been mastered by it, and by "the adventurous life he had led in Mexico and the Southwest" (*SL,* 57–8). Instead of developing the frontier, he, like the Mexicans for whom he has such fondness, drifts across borders.[35] In his ambitionless self-sufficiency he rivals the Indian communities of Cather's later novel of New

Mexico, who reveal to Father Latour "the simple story of their lives. They had here all they needed to make them happy. They spun and wove from the fleece of their flocks, raised their own corn and wheat and tobacco, dried their plums and apricots for winter" (26). Like similar treatments of the Southwest in the work of travelers who glorified it before her, such as D. H. Lawrence, Mary Austin, and Charles Lummis, this ethnographic fantasy is most objectionable when it tries to be kind. The patent condescension with which the Father describes the art of the santeros (santos which in the contemporary marketplace fetch thousands of dollars for nonnative collectors) is difficult to ignore: "These poor Mexicans, he reflected, were not the first to pour out their love in this simple fashion" (*D*, 255).

### IV: "Set back your watches," or, "There are almost a thousand years of history in this soup": Western Civilization and Regional Time

*It takes an endless amount of history to make even a little tradition, and an endless amount of tradition to make even a little taste (127).*

—Henry James, *The American Scene*

*"It's Scott's dinner to-night. Your tastes are so different, I can't compromise. And this is his, from the cream soup to the frozen pudding." "But who said I didn't like cream soup and frozen pudding?" Louie held out his hands to show their guiltlessness. "And are there* haricots verts *in cream sauce? I thought so! And I like those, too. The truth is . . . that I like all Scott's dinners, it's he who doesn't like mine! He's the intolerant one.*

—Willa Cather, *The Professor's House* (109)

*"in travelling towards the frontier, the decreasing scale of civilization and improvement exhibits an accurate illustration of inverted history."*

—Timothy Flint, *Francis Berrian*[36]

Having documented it, I am not interested in belaboring the racism that relegates western "natives" to a secondary cultural and social stratum—this kind of writing is at once conventional and uninteresting. Instead, I wish to look more closely at the links Cather develops between racial and sexual difference, links that allow her to structure arguments about regional difference and national self-definition. How does she race region in her fictions? How should we read the transcontinental pilgrimages characters like Thea Kronborg, Tom Outland, Professor St. Peter, and Father Latour make to the Southwest? The view we obtain of this region often looks as flattened by speed as if it were flashing by the window of Thea and Otto's railroad car. Mountains, mesas, arroyos, and canyons mass indistinctly under the murky light of the setting sun. The distilled blue of the New Mexican sky, the crepuscular red of Arizona sandstone, the yellow rock of Colorado mesas lose clarity as their edges blur in the dusk. Like Ray himself, a likeable character who nevertheless gets left behind, Cather's vocabulary yearns for a simpler past removed from the driven present. In this way, the very sentimentality that Cather connects with regional cultural production (dismissed as artifact rather than art) informs the larger textual world of the author's western novels.

I argued earlier in this chapter that that two languages inform Cather's work, one celebratory of the desert, another dismissive. Walter Benn Michaels gestures toward the ambivalence inherent in this bifocal perspective when he argues of Tom Outland's cliff dwellers that it is precisely their "disappearance as a people that made possible their arrival as a culture" (234). But when he identifies the artifacts preserved "miraculously" in the domestic spaces of the Cliff City as containing a form of "cultural purity" that can be repossessed by "citizens" of Cather's Southwest—citizens like Tom Outland—he simultaneously overestimates Cather's valuation of the bequest and underestimates the difficulties involved in the "transfer" of ownership.[37] Michaels sustains his gloss of "cultural citizenship" by interpolating it exclusively from *The Professor's House,* but we can obtain a more conclusive reading when, like Tom in his railroad car, we travel the breadth of the Cather canon. Cather's characteristic literary recycling (an efficiency characteristic of authors generally but of Cather particularly) means that the cliff dwellers appear in multiple textual incarnations. Like Outland, who is the descendent of *The Song of the Lark's* Ray Kennedy, the "pots and pans" (*PH,* 243) of the Blue Mesa are relatives of the "potsherds" (*SL,* 380) Thea recovers in Panther Canyon. From this broader lookout, the cultures of the Southwest are as aesthetically compromised as James's golden bowl. I write "cultures," for indeed, any assessment of indigenous art must include not only the Indian cliff dwellers whom Michaels distinguishes as "the originators of American culture" in *The Professor's House,* but the "Spanish explorers" he dismisses as irrelevant but who Cather invokes throughout *The Song of the Lark* and *Death Comes for the Archbishop.*

Before returning to the cliff dwellers themselves, let me take the case of the mestizo descendents Michaels ignores. On the one hand, the Mexicanos of Cather's fictions are neither petty nor provincial. In contradistinction to the lacquered finish of Anglo ladies, Mexican women achieve grace without "constraint" (*SL,* 289). As Ray Kennedy notes, there was something more attractive in ease of manner than in absent-minded concern about hairpins and dabs of lace . . . the way a woman stood, moved, sat in her chair, looked at you, was more important than the absence of wrinkles from her skirt (*SL*, 144).

The men demonstrate a similar "natural harmony" of movement (*SL*, 289), but their *cultural* production, as distinct from their *biological* form, is rudimentary. This distinction is crucial to Cather's aesthetic economy, and clarified, as Eric Peterson reminds me, in the "sentimental but strangely cruel scene" she orchestrates in which Spanish Johnny listens to Thea's sublime performance.[38] Johnny's musicality is homely as a quavering soprano heard from an upstairs window, sentimental as a Burns lullaby crooned to a child, and far removed from the disciplined passion that drives Thea to perfect her vocal brilliance and to showcase it throughout the opera houses of Europe.

*Death Comes for the Archbishop* extends this critique of regional culture to the plastic arts. Father Latour appreciates the santos he comes across in "the poorest Mexican houses," favoring their unpretentious integrity over the "factory-made plaster images in his mission churches in Ohio" (27). He opens a space for a working-class aesthetic when he likens them to "the homely stone carvings on the font of old parish churches in Auvergne" (28). But, as in *The Song of the Lark* and *The Professor's House* before it, this possibility is contained. Like southwestern artifacts more generally, Cather locates the craft of the santero at a firm remove from the art of the cathedral sculpture (hence the need for a "modern" Church to take the place of those already existing in Santa Fé) as a distant relative on the cultural family tree. Geographical distance—region—is translated as temporal distance. Like the rude dwellings they grace, the products of the American Southwest are timeless, not because, like European art, they speak to the ages, but because they *precede* history altogether.

Cather outlines this cultural teleology most adroitly through a comparison of culinary techniques. Father Latour exerts his civilizing influence not only through the bon mot but the bon gout, turning his Mexican congregations away from "*chili colorado* and mutton fat" (114), reeducating them in the virtues of modern nutritional science. He grows "such fruit as was hardly to be found even in the old orchards of California," and urges "the new priests to plant fruit trees wherever they went, and to encourage the Mexicans to add fruit to their starchy diet" (265). To possess cultivation is literalized in this book, so that to be "well satisfied with beans and jerked meat" is to be "a native Mexican, of unpretentious tastes" (114). To be French, on the other hand—not provincial like the natives of the American West—is to have a *cuisine*. In passage after passage Cather describes the bond between the two missionaries, distinguishing their refined enjoyment from the cruder

appetites of priests like Father Martínez by detailing their shared appreciation of European food specialties and their efforts to recreate such dishes in
the New World.

The edible measure of culture is equally important to the narrative logic
of *Death Comes for the Archbishop,* where Cather takes pains to elaborate it
in the following gloss. The soup Father Joseph reproduces for his colleague
to savor "is not the work of one man," as the bishop insists, but "the result
of a constantly refined tradition. There are almost a thousand years of history in this soup" (*D,* 38).[39] Through this thousand-year-old soup and its
recreation in the American Southwest, Cather develops the chronology of
her cultural topography. The demarcation of region in books like *Death
Comes for the Archbishop* has everything to do with political arguments
framed as Darwinian shortcomings, what Cather calls in *The Song of the
Lark* "a natural law" (156) and what the aesthetic hierarchy in all of her fictions documents. Like the terraced rock of desert canyons, the potsherds
Thea and Tom recover do not conflate historical periods in order to develop
a "cultural model" shared by all Americans.[40] Instead, they mark the distance
some Americans have traveled from their humble origins.[41]

And so back to the Indian bones disinterred by the narrative anthropol-
ogy of *The Professor's House, The Song of the Lark,* and *Death Comes for the
Archbishop.* Native American artistry illustrates the racial scale upon which
Cather projects cultural value. The cliff dwellers, as Ray asserts in *The Song of
the Lark,* "were clever at most everything but metals; and that one failure kept
them from getting across. It was the quicksand that swallowed 'em up, as a
race. I guess civilization proper began when man mastered metals" (*SL,* 146).
Cather repeatedly defines civilization as "mastery" and locates its origins, like
Father Latour himself, in Europe: "[The Indian] conception of decoration
did not extend to the landscape," he muses in *Death Comes for the Archbishop.*
"They seemed to have none of the European's desire to 'master' nature, to
arrange and re-create" (233). A contemporary reading might incline toward
irony, but the writer affirms "arranging" and "recreating" here as producing
art; it is precisely this "master" work that defines Thea's vocal excellence.

Archaeological observation furthers an American identity constructed by
racial long division, not the accretitive amalgamation of the melting pot. As
Thea says of the Panther Canyon artists: "In their own way," she muses,
"those people had felt the beginnings of what was to come. These potsherds
were like fetters that bound one to a long chain of human endeavor" (380).
"[C]hain" affirms affiliation and entrapment simultaneously. Combined
with "fetters" and the sense of being "bound," the verbal texture suggests
how reluctantly Thea, objective correlative for the flowering of civilization,
admits the beginnings of culture in "prehistory." The potsherds mark the dividing line between articulated expressions of civilization and the mute

blood impulses that connect people to a common human tribe, what Cather in "The Best Years" calls "the clan feeling, which meant life or death for the blood, not for the individual."[42] Like the feminine artifacts Tom recovers in the cliff city ("the pots and pans that belonged to my poor grandmothers"), Cather distinguishes the shards from high art (the German operas Thea sings) through the metaphor of gender.[43] As (female) raw material, the ancient shards are more "sensation" than "idea" (373) and must be left behind like the desert "world" they come from, "the brilliant, empty country . . . without change or ideas" (408) that flashes by Thea and Otto as they move east in their railroad car. Art is the flowering of imperialism; the racial line of descent must be acknowledged, but it must also be attenuated, not too closely held lest it compromise.

## V: Playing Indians: A Boy's Life

Cather's texts shore up distinctions between art and artifact, between sentimental lullaby and German aria, but if we read her southwestern novels closely, we can locate the traces of the effort that is involved in "beating back the past."[44] Violence is managed in these texts through a series of homoerotic displacements that romanticize as well as contain its ill effects. In "The Enchanted Bluff," first published in *Harper's* in 1909, Cather develops the desert trope central to the ideas she works out in her later novels. As in *The Virginian,* where the West as a "romance of American adventure," is the "great playground of young men" (51), Cather's story is a "Boy's Life," a rewriting of Tom Sawyer's idyll that opens with a circle of Nebraska farm boys convened on an island in late summer around the "last watch-fire of the year"[45] in order to honor the high water mark of their adolescence. The narrator, from across the divide of adulthood, is nostalgic for that youthful desire, unalloyed because unacted upon, that is embodied in Arthur Adams, the precursor for the series of ambiguously gendered young men who go in search of desert adventure. With his "fine hazel eyes that were almost too reflective and sympathetic for a boy" (413), Arthur recalls rail workers like Ray Kennedy ("the bride" of the industry who is "as fussy about his car as an old maid about her bird-cage" [*SL,* 139]) and Tom Outland (once a call boy for the Santa Fé). Both figures are "often" seen but never compromised by the company of "gambler's sons" and "old Spanish Fanny's boy" (413). The intense same-sex attachments they enjoy signal homoerotic possibilities that can be represented only because the class and race differences Cather invokes to contain them make such relationships unacceptable and therefore "unthinkable."

Arthur's swashbuckling tale anticipates Professor St. Peter's own wistfulness for youth, a nostalgia that finds expression in his monumental history of the "*Spanish Adventurers in North America*" (*PH,* 25) and that in the less scholarly light of the Nebraska campfire recalls *Golden Days*' characterization of Aztecs who "used to sacrifice their prisoners on the temple top," and the conquistadores who tried to make this metaphor literal; as Arthur notes, "Some of the Spaniards thought there was gold up here somewhere" (415). Sexual expression here as elsewhere in Cather's canon is ineluctably fused with imperial "mastery." Cather frames desire (the professor's attraction for Tom Outland, the narrator's longing to enter the shared intimacy of same-sex attachments in "The Enchanted Bluff") against the backdrop of a Southwest constructed as a fantasy past, an imperial "Adventureland" that Amy Kaplan aptly labels "perpetual boyhood."[46] Kaplan very deftly describes this discursive field, peopled by westerners like Hamlin Garland, Edward Eggleston, Edgar Watson Howe, and Joseph Kirkland; Cather's novels can be situated in this field as well. Their literature develops a "sense of the region as a space where a collective childhood can be recovered . . . where gangs of boys do little but play cowboys and Indians" (255).

The relationship between this imperial romance of the Southwest and covert desire is never more plainly expressed than near the close of *The Professor's House:*

> Just when the morning brightness of the world was wearing off for him, along came Outland and brought him a kind of second youth. . . . He had not spent his youth in the great dazzling Southwest country which was the scene of his explorers' adventures. By the time he had got as far as the third volume, into his house walked a boy who had grown up there, a boy with imagination, with the training and insight resulting from a very curious experience, who had in his pocket the secrets which old trails and stones and water-courses tell only to adolescence (258–9).

I wish to look more closely at these "secrets" in the "old trails and stones and water-courses" of "The Enchanted Bluff" and in the cliff cities of the later novels: *The Song of the Lark*'s Panther Canyon, the Blue Mesa of *The Professor's House,* and the Enchanted Mesa described by Jacinto in *Death Comes for the Archbishop.* In the short story, this "monument" testifies to the conflict Cather stages between "prehistory" and "American history"; between "a peaceful tribe that made cloth and pottery" who "went up there to get out of the wars," and the "war party from the north" (417) who obliterates them. I want to read Cather's retelling of the "dolorous legend" (417) as a primordial scene, as central to Cather's conception of the Southwest as the Enchanted Mesa is to the oral narratives and written texts of the Laguna who continue to make their home on the Ácoma mesa nearby.[47] For Cather, this New Mexican place, solitary "because no white man has ever been on top of it," yet simultaneously peopled by "The tribe that lived there . . . before the Spaniards came" (416), preempts the Nebraska landscape where the boys establish their campfire, just as Tom Outland's Blue Mesa displaces the midwestern university town in which the professor's daughters listen, enthralled with stories of Tom's "free-lance childhood as a gay adventure they would gladly have shared" (*PH*, 123).[48]

Before exploring the implications of the novel's "gay adventure," I would like to quote in full Cather's first version of the legend in "The Enchanted Bluff:"

There's a big red rock there that goes right up out of the sand for about nine hundred feet. . . . like a monument. . . . The tribe that lived there had some sort of steps, made out of wood and bark, hung down over the face of the bluff, and the braves went down to hunt and carried water up in big jars swung on their backs. They kept a big supply of water and dried meat up there, and never went down except to hunt. They were a peaceful tribe that made cloth and pottery, and they went up there to get out of the wars. You see, they could pick off any war party that tried to get up their little steps. The Indians say they were a handsome people, and they had some sort of queer religion. Uncle Bill thinks they were Cliff-Dwellers who had got into trouble and left home. They weren't fighters, anyhow. One time the braves were down hunting and an awful storm came up—a kind of waterspout—and when they got back to their rock they found their little staircase had been all broken to pieces, and only a few steps were left hanging away up in the air. While they were camped at the foot of the rock, wondering what to do, a war party from the north came along and massacred 'em to a man, with all the old folks and women looking on from the rock. Then the war party went on south and left the village to get down the best way they could. Of course they never got down. They starved to death up there, and when the war party came back on their way north, they could hear the children crying from the edge of the bluff where they had crawled out, but they didn't see a sign of a grown Indian, and nobody has ever been up there since (416–7).

Like the Indian tribes of *The Song of the Lark,* what the people of the Enchanted Bluff lack, what as in Ray's story proves their undoing, is technology. The cliff dwellers, remember, "were clever at most everything but metals; and that one failure kept them from getting across" (*SL*, 146). Likewise, the steps so carefully hung from the precipice that Arthur recalls for the circle of listening adolescents are made of "wood and bark"; indigenous *to* rather than an improvement *upon* nature, they result in the village's mass destruction. Like the cliff dwellers of Panther Canyon, the tribe that builds on top of the high red rock is immeasurably higher up the cultural family tree than the war party on the bottom; they weave cloth and fashion pottery, the same pottery that Thea acknowledges as the "fetters that bound one to a long chain human endeavor" (*SL*, 380). But they "have none of the European's desire to 'master' nature" (*SL*, 233). Arthur clarifies this picture of civilization as the composite of aesthetic achievement, on the one hand, and imperial mastery, on the other, when he says: "They weren't fighters" (417). So despite their graceful living arrangements, their demise is at the hands of a war party whose more conventional barbarism—an Aztec-like refusal to extend mercy to their victims—aligns them with the "savages" of Western Anglo American literature.

This political parable justifies European incursions not only "down in New Mexico somewheres" where "There aren't no railroads or anything" (416), but into Arizona, Colorado, Utah, California—the entire Mexican landmass surrendered to the United States just 60 years before Cather begins reconfiguring it in "The Enchanted Bluff." Cather repeatedly uses the railroad as icon for the conflict between western interests she defines as pretechnological and the national project that cuts across the grain of the landscape as remorselessly as the train breaks apart Ray Kennedy, himself linked with "adventurous . . . Mexico and the southwest" (*SL*, 58). The conflict of interest between the insistent vocabulary of region and the sweeping language of nationalism is concisely embodied in Arthur's offhanded reference to New Mexico. Only from the chronological remove of the 1927 publication of *Death Comes for the Archbishop* are Ácoma and the Enchanted Mesa, 60 minutes west of Albuquerque on Interstate 80, named and historically particularized. But in 1909, as in 1915 (*The Song of the Lark*) and 1925 (*The Professor's House*), the Land of Enchantment is not locatable. The mesa looks real, but as you approach this "rock at the end of the world" its outline breaks up with the heat. A literary mirage, this landscape is not a geographical space—a blue sky sounded by clouds—but rather the symbolic zero point by which civilization measures itself.

The enchanted bluff marks a cultural divide in the broadest sense; a paean to the romantic companionship the boys enjoy before their masculine camaraderie is attenuated through marriage, the mesa divides Indian village from European civilization, and so marks the point at which history distinguishes itself from the primitive. Cather's thesis about culture collapses space in favor of time; figured by means of a regional metaphor, her representations allow temporal and racial distinctions to speak for one another. Just as time, measured by the progress of civilization, encodes racial difference, so the Southwest's timelessness uses geographic coordinates to define racial axes. This contact allows the aging French archbishop in New Mexico to stay "a young man"—or at least, to wake like one every morning (*D*, 272). Intimacy with a harsh landscape is proximity to a savage culture, a culture that the Father himself insists, at the close of the book and the close of his life, will transcend ("I do not believe, as I once did, that the Indian will perish. I believe that God will preserve him" [*D, 296*]).

## VI: Making a House a Home:
## Mother Eve and the Rationalization of Imperial Scavenging

*Of course they never got down. They starved to death up there, and when the war party came back on their way north, they could hear the children crying from the edge of the bluff where they had crawled out, but they didn't see a sign of a grown Indian, and nobody has ever been up there since*— "The Enchanted Bluff," *(217).*

*"Louie's a good host. First-rate cigars, and plenty of them," Scott tapped his breast-pocket. "We had poor Tom served up again"*—The Professor's House, *(111).*

The nostalgic longing for a masculine company at the edge of dissolution that infuses "The Enchanted Bluff," and the savagery that characterizes the rock point to another coordinate of this divide: a homoerotic desire that Cather speaks as a form of cultural—not sexual—crossing over.[49] The homosocial world that the boys of "The Enchanted Bluff" occupy, that makes Tom Outland and his friend Roddy and their cook a "family"; that allows Archbishop Latour to recall his long-time companion Father Vaillant home from Tucson—these social spaces are opened by the author's play with racial difference.[50] Cather's Anglo Americans enjoy a proximity to indigenous America that is non-threatening because it is contained. In flirting with the native other—and the immigrant "stranger" whose disembarcation too closely recalls their own arrivals—they enjoy a liminality that momentarily transgresses borders, reminding participants of their limits in a manner that shores up Anglo American authority.[51] The boys who tell stories of New Mexico by a Nebraska campfire not only *talk* about Indians, they *look* like them. Crucial here, however, is the simile: "'Suppose there ever was any gold hid away in this old river?' Fritz asked. He lay *like* a little brown Indian, close to the fire, his chin on his hand and his bare feet in the air" (415, emphasis added). Tom Outland appropriates Native American artifacts as the property of his own ancestors, becoming, as Walter Benn Michaels aptly states, an "*imaginary* Indian" (222, emphasis added). Even the archbishop experiences a kind of distasteful cross-cultural epiphany in the ceremonial cave in the mountains outside of Pecos, a cave the Indian Jacinto takes him into for shelter (127) and which he associates with stories of human sacrifices.

The affectionate fetishism Euro-Americans hold for Indian relics across Cather's Southwest not only plays with racial boundaries, but flirts with gender crossings as well. In the later novels, she assigns archaeological labor and its objects a sex. Collecting and surveying native artifacts is typically framed as feminine work, performed, with the important exception of Thea Kronborg, by men. Michaels analyzes the implications of Roddy's "betrayal" of Tom Outland in *The Professor's House* to consider how it constitutes American culture, citing the contrast between Roddy's assessment of the artifacts as "no different than anything a fellow might run on to: a gold mine or a pocket of turquoise," and Tom's idea of them "as a collection of family heirlooms, the 'pots and pans that belonged to my poor grandmothers a thousand years ago'"(quoted in Michaels, 220). But he misses the most curious and important character of this passage: the decisive gendering Cather assigns to excavating. Roddy attests to this himself when he defines archaeology as a masculine sphere by describing the find as "no different than anything a fellow might run on to." Like looking for gold or mining for turquoise, Tom's artifacts testify for Blake to the masculine work of prospecting, the western world of forty-niners and frontiersmen. For Tom himself, by contrast, they are "family heirlooms" that belong to women: "pots and pans" passed down in a line of descent that extends not from grand*father* to father to son, but from grand*mother* to grand*son*.

Why is Tom as "imaginary Indian" related to Native American women rather than Indian "braves"? We can respond to this question by considering the archaeological process in relation to empire; more precisely, by examining how Cather assigns differently placed males (he who is served versus he who "once had been served" and "who now served cheerfully") opposite genders. The citation is from Charles Stuart's 1906 novel *Casa Grande: A California Pastoral,* but the gendered relation this sentimental novel posits between served and server at the turn of the century is echoed in Cather's modernist novels.[52] Stuart's Manuel ("the old Mexican cook, trim and soldierly, was mixing bread" [44]) is a mirror to feminized characters like Roddy Blake and Ray Kennedy. The following description of Manuel resonates note for note with Ray's bride-like space on the train: "Neat and methodical himself, the house was an expression of his character. The orderliness of the place was hardly feminine, although there was a deep vein of femininity in the Mexican's make-up" (Stuart, 16–17). Of course gender, here as in Cather, is the language of imperial history: because they have been conquered, Mexican men (like 50-year-old black "boys" in the South) are in these novels "feminine."[53] If Cather refutes Roddy's overeager masculinizing of the excavating work that undergirds empire, she describes Tom's work digging out the Cliff City as a domestic labor. Mrs. St. Peter questions him "about the Indian pueblos": "He was reticent at first, but he presently warmed up in defense of Indian housewifery" (118). Like his successor Louie Marsellus, the Jewish "adventurer"(138) who marries Tom's fiancée Rosamund St. Peter, Cather frames Tom's affinity with the cliff dwellers as an empathy with the feminine arts. Just as Mother Eve is an eroticized figure for the simultaneous attraction and repulsion of racial "opposites," so their shared bride momentarily joins Tom and Louie.

Mother Eve's feminine corporeality bears mute witness not only to the ethnographic crime scene played out directly in "The Enchanted Bluff" (the mesa marks the location of the grisly mass murder of a peaceful tribe by the "savage" warriors who starve them to death), but to the oblique restaging of this contest in Louie's blasphemous cannibalization of Tom, (a parody of the Last Supper in which Louie is referred to as the "host" and Tom is "served up" to the apostles). Like the intimacy of Christ's betrayal by Judas, Tom's attractiveness and Louie's unpleasantness are twined, contingent upon the same gendered phenomenon. Recall that it is Louie who dresses his wife, Louie who oversees the archetypally feminine activity of home furnishing, and Louie who transforms the masculine preserve of the "vein of turquoise" into a feminine adornment, a gendered alchemy the novel's epigraph (a "quotation" from Louie himself) is dedicated to proving: "'A turquoise set in silver, wasn't it? . . . Yes, a turquoise set in dull silver" (frontispiece).[54] Just so does Tom insist less on colonizing the wilderness than on feminizing it. Along with the remainder of his "happy family" (198), Roddy and Henry, the latter is "a wonderful cook and a good housekeeper," who "kept that cabin shining like a playhouse," dressing "it all out with piñon boughs" and trimming the "kitchen shelves with newspapers cut in fancy patterns" (197).[55] The archaeological dig and the "cabin built on top of the mesa" make "excavating" and "housekeeping" parallel verbs. As Tom and family are building their own house, that is, they are digging up the houses of the "Ancient People": "We brought old Henry up by the new horse-trail and began housekeeping. We were now ready for what we called excavating" (211).

Housekeeping, then, is complicated in this book. Domesticity enshrines Tom's ménage on the Blue Mesa just as it encircles the professor's claustrophobic entrapment in his own house. Both forms of domestication are implicitly linked with Louie Marsellus's occupation of the Outland house, and to Louie himself, whose pilfering of Tom's pecuniary inheritance mirrors the theft of his Indian "inheritance" on the mesa. The beautification of the mesa depends on the symbiosis of two kinds of domesticity: "domestic" as a political expression of internal policy over and against international affairs, and "domestic" as an articulation of a privatized space, the familial home we set in opposition to the public sphere. Both kinds of domesticity function allegorically in *The Professor's House*, however, for what is called domestic *policy* is really imperialism disguised (Tom's defense of Indian housewifery is actually imperial looting), and what is called domestic *behavior* is really sexual difference translated (the "family" on the mesa signals homoerotic attachments, not paternal relations). Using a complicated process of substitution, Cather allows Tom to enjoy a more refined proprietorship of the Southwest than the racial dominion exerted by his predecessor Ray Kennedy, who in thinking "the Southwest really belonged to him" possesses "that feeling of empire" (*SL*, 277). Zane Grey censures the Mormons in *Riders of the Purple Sage* for the evils of conquest, who are demonized as "the mind behind it all . . . an empire builder" (145); Cather displaces responsibility onto the unfortunate Roddy. Significantly, it is only following his censure of Roddy that Tom, alone again, makes the cliff dwellers his: "Something had happened in me that made it possible for me to co-ordinate and simplify. . . . It was possession. . . . For me the mesa was no longer an adventure, but a religious emotion" (250–1). Like Grey's Venters, who "had come, in a way, to be a cliff-dweller himself," Tom "inherits" a native legacy, the "haunting memory . . . of something past" (*Riders of the Purple Sage*, 97). That "something" that purifies imperialism for Outland, transforming it from "an adventure" into "a religious emotion," is not one but two expendable bodies, the eroticized figure of Roddy, Tom's mate, and the racialized form of Louie, inheritor of Rosamund, the crass capitalist who converts Tom's pure designs into cash. In sabotaging his "happy family," Tom transfers censure for the sale of his "country's secrets" to Roddy. But Blake's betrayal of Tom's interests is *itself* a substitution for a betrayal by Jewish interests. Recall that in naming Roddy as a traitor to the nationalist agenda, Tom likens him to Dreyfus, a comparison Blake himself cements when he insists, as Tom tells us, "'That man was innocent. It was a frame-up' . . . It was a point he would never pass up" (243). Like the wandering Jew, Roddy is both outcast and cast out, the medium through which the Jew-as-banker speaks: "he'd always supposed I meant to 'realize' on them," Tom explains, "just as he did, and that it would come to money in the end. 'Everything does'" (243).

Precisely, and if narrative energy is devoted here to covering over the ugly side effects of progress through a bodily substitution that splits the desire for technology down the middle, distinguishing Tom's "chivalry" from Louie's vulgar seductions, the narrative is relaxed enough at one point to acknowledge the apparently "quixotic" (172) origin of such American alchemy. Kathleen St. Peter mourns the inevitable by-product of capitalization when she laments the end of "romantic dream[s]" of desert adventure in Tom's conversion: "now he's all turned out chemicals and dollars and cents" (131–2). Like the peaceful tribe of the Enchanted Bluff, left to starve to death by the warriors who sever their link with the rest of the world, Louie's cannibalism ("serving up") of Tom is another way of lamenting technological rape. Louie, the inassimilable "stranger" who tries unsuccessfully for incorporation into the American body politic (and is rejected by the "little group of fellows" of the "Arts and Letters" [80]) enjoys a peculiar revenge as the agent for another melting pot plot that reduces Tom's "sentimental superstitions" into "dollars and cents." Or, to historicize this iconography,

Louie catalyzes the transformation by which primitive America (the tribal "superstitions" of the Blue Mesa) is made over into a more European image.[56] Just so, guilt over conquest—recall the seduced and murdered Mother Eve—is assuaged.

Tom's attachment to the mesa (a locale that resonates with "prehistoric" Old Testament iconography when he likens it to "the hanging gardens of Babylon" [192]) is accordingly justified as a "quixotic" refusal of Roddy and Louie's crass masculine conversion of culture into cash. Tom's sympathy, his finer "quality of feeling" for "Indian housewifery," distinguishes his affection from that of these parallel, rejected figures of imperial desire, and makes his own interest in the domestic lives of the cliff dwellers morally palatable. But ultimately, whether it be for the benefit of the Smithsonian or a private German collector, what Tom, Roddy, and Henry are all doing is invading the cliff dwellers' village and appropriating its artifacts for their own use. Cather undermines her own best efforts to sanitize "looting" (*SL,* 148) when she insists in both *The Song of the Lark* and *The Professor's House* on uncovering not just shards of pottery vessels, but the bodies of the "grandmothers" themselves. The former novel provides this version of the mesa story:

> I was going to tell you about the handsomest thing we ever looted out of those burial mounds. It was on a woman, too, I regret to say. She was preserved as perfect as any mummy that ever came out of the pyramids. She had a big string of turquoises around her neck, and she was wrapped in a fox-fur cloak, lined with yellow feathers that must have come off wild canaries. Can you beat that now? The fellow that claimed it sold it to a Boston man for a hundred and fifty dollars (*SL,* 148).

This is a stripped-down burial site, racially speaking, but from it we can excavate the traces of ideas Cather will develop more fully in *The Professor's House:* the "string of turquoises" anticipates Louie's "turquoise set in silver," for instance, and the "fox-fur cloak" prefigures the fur coat he will provide for Rosamund. If Ray is blithe about his excavations and Thea's answer echoes his own in tone, her later refusal in Panther Canon to disturb the artifacts she finds suggests that on some level Cather identifies this work as grave-robbing. As rescripted in *The Professor's House,* the story of the "mummy" reverberates with German archaeologist Heinrich Schliemann's famous excavations in Crete, and the ransacking of Egyptian tombs by European and American imperial powers in the teens in the service of their own national collections.

The parallels between Cather's southwestern landscapes of the twenties, strewn with potsherds and fragments of bone, and the Victorian fascination with archaeology (what Anne McClintock in *Imperial Leather* lists as a "middle class . . . fixation with origins, with genesis narratives . . . with skulls, skeletons and fossils" and aptly calls "the imperial bric-a-brac of the archaic") suggests, once again, that the cataloguing impulse behind periodization works in the service of political as much as literary distinctions.[57] McClintock's astute thesis about "the dilemma" facing British colonials, that "ruins and skeletons" were "allegorical reminders of the failure of a single narrative of origins" (31) explains equally cogently Gertrude Atherton's obsession with skulls in *The Splendid Idle Forties:*

> Detached skulls lay in heaps, grinning derisively. Stark digits pointed threateningly, as if the old warriors still guarded their domain. Other frames lay face downward, as though the broken teeth had bitten the dust in battle. Slender forms lay prone, their arms encircling cooking utensils, beautiful in form and colour. Great bowls and urns . . . wrought with a lost art . . . were placed at the head and feet of skeletons more lofty in stature than their fellows.[58]

If Atherton's skeletons are dutifully compliant with turn-of-the-century social norms (only the "lofty" are graced with potsherds), they also resonate strikingly with the human remains strewn across Cather's own modernist southwestern landscapes. In *The Professor's House,* Cather describes the "dried human body" Tom, Blake, and Henry find:

> At last we came upon one of the original inhabitants—not a skeleton, but a dried human body, a woman—we thought she had been murdered; there was a great wound in her side, the ribs stuck out through the dried flesh. Her mouth was open as if she were screaming, and her face, through all those years, had kept a look of terrible agony. Part of the nose was gone, but she had plenty of teeth, not one missing, and a great deal of coarse black hair. Her teeth were even and white, and so little worn that we thought she must have been a young woman (214).

More curious here than the subliminal invocation of the Egyptian "mummy's curse" that testifies to the "happy family's" guilt (everyone associated with finding her suffers a tragic end, as does Ray in the earlier novel after looting a similar body) is the insistence on physicality, an interest so prolonged and minutely observed it can only be described as sustaining a kind of erotic energy. On the one hand this sexualization of the "woman" and her brutal end accord with Cather's representations of "savage" cultures as early as "The Enchanted Bluff" and "Coming, Aphrodite!" and as late as *Death Comes for the Archbishop.* On the other hand, once it is revealed as punishment for unlawful sexual expression, her murder aligns her more closely with Tom, the "second infatuation" of Professor St. Peter, who keeps his dead pupil's horse blanket because it still smells "like his skin" (130)[59] and whose friendship Mrs. St. Peter is "fiercely jealous of" (49).[60]

When he describes his attachment to Tom as outside the (hetero)social ("'Your bond with him was social,' he tells his daughter Rosamund, 'and it follows the laws of society. . . . Mine wasn't'" [63]), the professor points to this congruence, and the way in which the ancient Native American woman ventriloquizes the unlicensed desire that drives the narrative. Judith Butler argues of Cather that "substitutability is a condition for this sexuality,"[61] but it is not a substitution of the gendered name, this scene makes evident, as of a raced body. What Butler refers to as that "unspeakable desire" is pantomimed here; recall the focus on the woman's "mouth . . . open as if she were screaming" (214). The narrator's portrait of Tom remains, throughout, the text's romantic point of origin. Stilled at the age of compromise, Tom embodies that youthful desire celebrated in "The Enchanted Bluff," desire expressed both as erotic possibility (in Cather's fiction, the unconfined celebration of a homosocial bond severed at adulthood, either by being physically cut or emotionally hedged), and in its widest definition as the untrammeled fullness of heart that comes from being too young to see that one's desires will inevitably pattern themselves after experience and circumstance. What keeps this picture from corroding like *The Picture of Dorian Grey* is not the absence of self-disgust or mixed feelings about homosexuality—the stresses exerted on homoeroticism in Cather's oeuvre are marked—but a kind of transference to an other who is sufficiently racially displaced to bear the brunt of violence without fear of self-censure.[62] Or again, a series of others, for the bond between Tom Outland and Professor St. Peter is cemented both by their shared nostalgia for (pre)history (indigenous and "Spanish" America), and the social (the shared community effected by the exclusion of the Jewish "stranger" who marries the professor's daughter but who remains outside the cultural consanguinity).

The brutal voyeurism of the "Mother Eve" scene bears witness to these substitutions and exclusions, just as a more dreamlike eroticism in the following scene from *Death Comes for the Archbishop* shores up Father Latour:

> The banjo always remained a foreign instrument to Father Latour; he found it more than a little savage. When this strange yellow boy [Pablo] played it, there was softness and languor in the wire strings—but there was also a kind of madness; the recklessness, the call of wild countries . . . the bent head and crouching shoulders of the banjo player, and his seesawing yellow hand, which sometimes lost all form and became a mere whirl of matter in motion, like a patch of sand-storm" (182).

Ultimately, "Cather's fiction enacts" a lot more than "a certain gender trespass in order to facilitate an otherwise unspeakable desire."[63] What stabilizes social, sexual, and political authority in *The Professor's House*—as well as in *The Song of the Lark* and *Death Comes for the Archbishop*—is the appropriation and transformation of a racial other. Given the extent to which explicitly raced characters—Native Americans, Mexicans, and Jews—are sexualized in Cather, being Anglo American but looking for all the world "like a brown little Indian" is a metaphorical displacement that allows for the "safe" exercise of desire—both prohibited sexual desire and that "desire for empire" ideologically furthered and institutionally established by the popular literature of the turn-of-the-century to which Cather's own iconography is indebted. Sexual passing stands in for political passing, that desire for empire (the conquest of the Southwest) masked as a domestic "annexation."

The threat posed by this psychosexual dynamic is further deflected by a kind of Vesuvian miracle: a stilling of human movement Cather's novels of the Southwest enact repeatedly, where not just agency but change itself is bracketed as a function of "European man and his glorious history of desire and dreams" (*D*, 103). The "silence and stillness and repose" of the cliff dwellers, "preserved" as Tom Outland says, "like a fly in amber" (*PH*, 201–2) is what makes the "sweep" and "charge" of the railroad "over the great Western land" in Cather's 1948 story "The Best Years" so powerful. These unchanging sunset vistas, never the color "of living blood" but, like Mother Eve, "the dried blood of saints and martyrs preserved in old churches in Rome" (*D*, 270), "mean power, conquest, triumph."[64]

Through such comparisons, Cather finds a way to express the relation between civilization and history, or, more specifically, civilization *as* history, an aesthetic problem that interested her throughout her career. History is not so much the marking of time—the striated colors of Arizona canyons offer this much—as the ever more sophisticated mastering of it. This is why the railroad, as Doctor Archie tells Thea, "is the one real fact" in a country that is "like the sand . . . blow[ing] north one day and south the next" (*SL*, 103), because its purposeful linearity imposes a teleology on a landscape that doesn't *go* anywhere.[65] Or why throwaway comments like this one about Mrs. Nathanmeyer ("Her standards have nothing to do with Chicago. Her perceptions—or her grandmother's, which is the same thing—were keen when all this was an Indian village" [*SL*, 344]) are indispensable in exposing the cultural logic of the later novels. Time passes, but natural selection does not operate; like the Native American relics Tom Outland uncovers, Jewish physiognomy is immutable, its "perceptions" impervious to the Darwinian innovations that enable progress. Such dismissive assessments reveal the biological framing device upon which Cather's historical template for American expansionism depends, a template that celebrates modernity and maintains not its cultural purity, as Michaels argues, but its *racial* backbone.

Given the "post"-everything world-weariness that characterizes our own critical moment, my efforts to relocate Cather's regional narratives in relation to a nationalist agenda of "power, conquest, triumph" run the risk of being dismissed as—worst of sins in a sophisticated age—politically earnest. In other words: been there, done that. But state-of-the-art comments by Judith Butler and Walter Benn Michaels, while provocative, suggest we rethink such a position. However deft, the critical commentary both scholars develop remains single-minded, their considerations hampered because they reduce the numerous faultlines of Cather's literary landscapes to a single stress point. Before we dismiss the phrase "class, race, sex, and gender" as a critical cliché, then, we need more seriously to investigate the complicated relationships that give meaning to its constituent parts. The doubled and divided role the mapping of ethnicity plays in Cather's later novels demands we nuance our ways of reading culture. The parallel ways she positions indigenous others and exogenous strangers suggests we not divorce theorizing about Jewishness—now in the process of being translated "west" from Near Eastern Studies departments to the cultural caché of Cultural Studies—from long-standing efforts to authorize Ethnic Studies. If they do nothing else, Cather's deanthropromorphized figures challenge critical cartographies that refuse to locate emerging formulations of Jewish Cultural Studies and current formulations of Ethnic Studies like transnationalism and border studies on the same cultural map. The relation between Jewish Studies and Ethnic Studies has historically been fraught, yes, but characters like Louie and Eusabio, Sigmund Stein and Padre Martínez remind us of our common interests.

# Epilogue

*For as long as our records go back, we have held these two things dear, landscape and memory. . . . To keep landscapes intact and the memory of them, our history in them, alive, seems . . . imperative (142–43).*

—Barry Lopez, "The American Geographies," *About This Life*

Any museum-goer is familiar both with admonishments not to touch the objects on display and the pressing desire to do so. To place a cheek against the cool imperviousness of a marbled frieze from a building toppled 25 centuries before, to run our fingertips over the sand-gritted surface of a thousand-year-old pot, to pocket a fragment of stone from a roofless house lived in 700 years ago—which of us has not at some point hoped that in extending our hand we will encounter the grace of connection with the long dead?

In the previous chapter I explored these questions as Cather represents them in her southwestern fictions. Investigating the nature of history and the quality of our relationship with the landscape and its inhabitants allows Cather to develop an American aesthetic that is regionally distinct but suffused with the epic grandeur of empire. The "discovery" of Indian artifacts as the narrative prompt for sanctifying claims on the region is hardly unique to Cather, however. Instead, it might be called American literature's primal scene: Philip Freneau finds "The Indian Burying Ground," Thoreau stumbles on arrowheads while walking near Walden Pond, Hawthorne acknowledges the prior Indian land deed that haunts the Pyncheon family in *The House of the Seven Gables*. In New England writings, this scene is often submerged under layers of colonial history and argument, but western narratives more frequently foreground such ruins as a central concern. The early-twentieth-century novels of Zane Grey and Willa Cather and the late-twentieth-century musings of essayist Barry Lopez focus upon native artifacts to establish new claims to "native ground." Like all archaeological endeavors, their descriptions of burial grounds and cooking sites evoke the chronology of empire, the rise and fall of civilizations now pithily com-pacted in layers of stone and dirt. Just as Edward Gibbon's voluminous *The Decline and Fall of the Roman Empire* chronicles the collapse of the British empire, and William Prescott's *The History of the Conquest of Mexico* details the story of the United States, twentieth-century writers invoke a usable past as a frame for their investigations of contemporary struggles over contested territory.

Like Cather's Tom Outland, Zane Grey's Bern Venters plays out his west-ern adventure against the backdrop of the cliff dwellers' homes. Both narra-tives (the story of Bess and Venters occupies the protracted middle portion of *Riders of the Purple Sage* in structural parallel to Tom Outland's story in *The Professor's House*) allow outlaws—Verner explicitly, Tom in (sur)name—a domestic life on the mesa in the childish role-play that is seen as a rehearsal for adult life. Outland's happy family on the mesa is male; Venter's own ob-ject of desire (the mysterious masked rider whom he shoots and then nurses back to health) is cross-dressed. For both writers, however, the desert is (tem-porarily) Edenic in a fantasy of origination that confers upon the Anglos who have "invaded" (*RPS*, 97) the ruins the spiritual sanctity to possess it authoritatively.

For Cather as for Grey, the ruins are a kind of deed enabling the transfer of western property to its rightful heirs. Just as Tom comes upon the city of an extinct civilization "preserved in the dry air . . . like a fly in amber" (*PH*, 201–2), its rooms full of water jars and unbroken bowls, grinding stones and clay ovens, so Venters stumbles upon a "stupendous tomb," houses where "the smoke-hearths, the stone hatchets; and stone pestles and mealing-stones lay beside round holes polished by years of grinding maize—lay there as if they had been carelessly dropped yesterday" (107). Cather's city of "immor-tal repose" and Grey's "stupendous tomb" resonate in an era that witnesses federal efforts to divide native land bases through the Allotment Act whilst the European powers "discover" the burial grounds of the Minoans in Crete and the tombs of Egyptian rulers at Luxor. As I have argued in chapter 2, such temporal metaphors distinguish between the interests of different peo-ples in the West by assigning them distinct locations within a chronological "zoning" of regional territory. Just as Tom finds himself in sole possession of the mesa, so Venters "had come, in a way, to be a cliff-dweller himself," con-vinced "he was the only white man who had ever walked . . . down into that wonderful valley" (97).

Both writers, Cather in "The Enchanted Bluff" and Grey in *Riders of the Purple Sage,* envision a prior contest between a domestic people and a war-like one that concludes with the disappearance of the civil but less aggressive tribe. Like the wood and bark staircase Arthur finds as testimony of a van-ished people in "The Enchanted Bluff," the cunningly fashioned steps "cut in the solid stone" of a "precipitous" granite incline that Venters admires prompt his reflections on the disappeared cliff dwellers (83, 84). In this way, Cather and Grey script the contest between Mayan and Aztec peoples as an indigenous conflict, writing out the presence of the Spanish Conquest and its Mexican descendents in order to leave the unpeopled territory free and clear to Anglo cliff dwellers. The records of the dead testify to the vigor of the empire that discovers them in precise measure as they are silent about what has destroyed them. If this silence ostensibly marks the enigma of past devastation, it also stands in place of any articulation of the destruction that follows upon the more contemporary Anglo settlement of the West.

As if in implicit contradiction of the Puritan "Errand" that defines the West as a barbarous place only settlers can make into a garden, the desert wildness in these western narratives has been domesticated long before the arrival of Anglo Americans. While Grey's narrative is less troubled than Cather's, revealing none of the traces of guilt over appropriation that her own novels witness, the artifacts of the lost tribe in his novel make the wilderness a home for its recent Anglo inhabitants just as they do for Tom on the mesa; Venter gathers up "an armful of pottery . . . strong enough and suitable for his own use" (108). [1]

I would like to close this book by looking briefly at a more contemporary reworking of resettlement, one that more squarely faces the questions Cather raises but forecloses upon in the 1920s. In his 1998 essay "Theft," Barry Lopez foregrounds the question of cultural appropriation that remains a central problem in writing of and about the West, exploring in the process that "regeneration through violence" that remains the primary mythos of the American "frontier" in both history and literature.[2] The use contemporary "discoverers" make of native artifacts is clearly a way to work out how we justify our own presence in the landscape, but it is equally clearly a means to explore what Carl Gutiérrez-Jones calls "trauma"—the persistence of violence as the conventional "theme of American mythology."[3] Cather and Grey exploit the cliff cities in order to sanctify Anglo occupation; Lopez as clearly indicts this fantasy of possession, but all three writers register the violence that accompanies empire. All three also on some level identify archaeology's voyeurism as a fantasy of power that must ultimately cede to other handlings of conflict.

Cather's ambivalence to the limits she must set upon frontier adventure are reflected in her doubled and divided narrative: in *The Professor's House,* youthful fantasy and mature resignation are figured in the persons of Tom Outland and Professor St. Peter. A professor graces the pages of Lopez's essay as well, but the central division of this essay is not corporeal but temporal: the writer gives us his reflections on a youthful "misdemeanor" at 12 and follows and breaks this memory with a kind of coda that re-presents the narrator exactly "[t]wenty-five years after that day on the Flint River" (269). If the two writers play out the same scene, they draw different lessons from it. Nonetheless, the parallels are striking: just as Cather gives us characters who play at being Indian, Lopez tells us that along the way to the archaeological dig on Georgia's Flint River his uncle "began to speak of Indians" (264). The same glamorization of violence in the contest between farming peoples (Mixtecs and Mayans) and predatory sun worshippers animates the boyish fantasies of Cather's Arthur and of Lopez's youthful self, and the same essentially classed conflict over what constitutes the past—whether to preserve the artifacts or to dispense with them in the service of goals deemed less enlightened by the writers—reveals itself in both narratives.

While Cather and Lopez establish links between the histories of prior civilizations and the lives of those occupying their ruins, however, they assess the wake of conquest differently. The young Lopez is as drawn to the legend of the Aztecs as is Arthur, as enamored of their "predatory" legacy and as sure of his own "ownership" of their history as Tom Outland is of the mesa that hides the Cliff City, but while Cather condones and spiritualizes this "power" in *The Professor's House,* Lopez undermines it from the outset of his essay (264). He accomplishes this self-critique by providing readers with two distinct interpretations of the Macon County landscape, one a symbolic "empire of geography" (the 12-year-old realizes his Aztec fantasy by visualizing a country that "seethed with the threat of violence from small animals" [266] and a river that is "fierce, predatory" [267]), the other a "specific geographical understanding" that reflects "local expertise" and "an intimacy with place."[4] At the same time that the young Lopez is creating a romantic landscape in which he occupies the position of adventurer-discoverer (with the fragments of two potsherds in his shorts pocket, he begins to imagine "how I would explain what I'd found to my brother, tell him how I, myself, had located this obscure site, had discovered what once had belonged to Aztecs" [267]), the adult Lopez is evoking for us a "specific American geography" (132) that does not collude with the "wild West" scenes of Indian savagery playing themselves out in the boy's imagining. In the following thick description, Lopez interweaves the concrete particulars of locale and the particular history of the Creek tribes to offer a supple account of the landscape that links the lives of past and present through shared agricultural practice:

> The Creeks, [Gordon] was saying, were a confederacy of tribes, the most powerful of which were the Muskogee. The ceremonies of a farming people held them to the earth, in particular *boskita,* an eight-day celebration built around the ripening of the last corn plants. (We drove a macadam network of back-country roads . . . passing isolated clapboard shacks elevated on stone pilings

and weathered gray, passing the spindle-lattice of picked cotton fields and fields thick with sorghum and ripening corn, passing Herefords slow-grazing pastures in the awakening light.) (264).


Lopez writes his uncle's recitation of the Indian past in a different key from his own remembered mystical point of connection with prior civilizations. Like a fugue, Gordon's precise naming of local tribes and the care with which he distinguishes their histories ("I knew no one else in Georgia who referred to local Indians. He lined out their histories with the same knowledge and authority he brought to discussions of what he called the War Between the States" [264]) counterpoints the romantic reverie of his nephew, who sees in his river trip a "confluence" that "was preordained" and a "cabalistic power" connecting him with the lurid legends of the Aztecs in language that expertly mirrors the portentous vocabulary of Manifest Destiny.

"Indians," "Aztecs," "Spaniards," the same blank ciphers for conquest that saturate Cather's southwestern fictions find their way into Lopez's youthful daydreams, but Lopez signals their function as imperial icons through Gordon's dry reminder that this self interested gloss of history "could be a mistake" (265), and through his own insistence on their incantatory power. Finding potsherds he sees as material reminders of Aztec "notoriety" and "horror" (264), he brings his "fingers hesitantly into contact with their gritty edges protruding from the soil. *Aztecs.*" (266). As metonym for the fantasy of a fallen empire, this murmured word and the clay fragments the child pockets ("What Aztecs had once held, I now held" [267]) in defiance of his uncle's interdiction gesture toward the romance of power, a vision his uncle efficiently dispels both when he offers an alternative interpretation for the site ("On the way home Gordon said . . . he believed the pieces of pottery . . . would prove to be Mayan" [268]) and when he obliquely acknowledges the childish theft of the pottery:

These are all theories. . . . in another time they will talk about us, about what we did, or what we might have believed. We make sense of ourselves as a people through history. That is why we should make no modifications in records of the past, you see, but only speculate (268).

This is an alternative history lesson. Where conventional chronicles plot the relationship between past civilization and present empire as one of object and subject (the past as "object" of study for acting "subjects" in the present), this view scales down our own lives as merely another layer in the thick texture of historical record offered by the landscape. In the process, Lopez critiques the legacy of American exceptionalism that continues to inform even contemporary accounts of U.S. history. In Ivan Doig's 1987 novel of pioneer settlement, for instance, the parceling of Montana lands is likened to "the boustrophedon pattern a farmer makes as he plows back and forth the furrows of his field, or, indeed, of the alternate directions in which earliest Greek is written! Thus . . . the American experiment, the ready granting of land to those industrious enough to seek it" (*Dancing at the Rascal Fair,* 90). By contrast, the "stylized patterns resembling the impression of leaf fronds" (266) incised on the red and gray shards of pottery 12-year-old Barry Lopez picks up in "Theft" resist definitive interpretive gloss and refuse to work in the service of metaphors for self distinction. Rather than removing us from the rise and fall of civilizations as interpretive gods paring our fingernails, this insistence on the virtues of interpretive suspension implicates us in a historical record, connecting us with the people who have come before us.

Like *The Professor's House,* which witnesses the death of Tom Outland, Lopez's essay closes with the figurative demise of its youthful make-believe Indian. His uncle's history lesson provokes the young Lopez to reject "the power that had been undeniable" and to distance himself, like Cather's Professor St. Peter, from the seductions of outlaws ("the boyish fascination with a notoriety that makes being any kind of outlaw attractive was gone now" [268]). In the coda to his recollection of the Macon County trip, Lopez substitutes in place of his chastened 12-year-old self a 37-year-old narrator who writes out his youthful mistakes when he insists, in the context of another archaeological dig at an Anasazi site in Marble Canyon, Arizona, "I haven't picked up anything on these sites. I just want to tell you that plainly. I don't do that" (270). Like the stories of assimilated immigrants who distance themselves from their European pasts by writing of them in the third person, Lopez's own breach between youth and age divides the young discoverer from mature historian as cleanly as Cather divides western epic hero from midwestern chronicler.

More importantly, by insisting that this second group of "shards formed part of a historical record, that they should be left for some other mind to come upon and to interpret after we are gone" (269), the adult Lopez relinquishes the role of "discoverer," and the glamorization of violence that accompanies this legacy. Making of himself a subject of study rather than musing like the hero-discoverers of *The Professor's House* on what "catastrophe" had "overwhelmed" the cliff dwellers (213), or wondering with Verners in *Riders of the Purple Sage,* "Had an enemy destroyed them? Had disease destroyed them, or only that greatest destroyer—time?" (107), the narrator of "Theft" realizes that a proprietary interest in the ruins is impossible. Like the elderly santero of Antonio Chavez's story "The Angel's New Wings," whose "mind limped back right away to the more even ground of the past," the 37-year-old Lopez recognizes that life and the landscape—memory and topography—are indissoluble.[5] Professor St. Peter's mistake—and Cather's with him—is to belittle his own desires as a pale substitute for the lives of the western adventurers he studies. What "Theft" suggests, by contrast, is that we cannot possess the past because we are implicated in it. In honoring this simple fact—that it is really our own relationships we look for in the strata of history—the professor-teachers of Lopez's "Theft" gesture toward a richer kind of scholarship.

# Notes

### Preface

1. Playwright Anna Deavere Smith, for instance, suggests that we "are slow to articulate the twists and turns of an America which is more complicated than black and white," seeing in California's politics an opportunity to nuance American identity: "It seems to me that the riot, the O.J. Simpson verdict, and the Million Man March are all part of a bigger sweep." Anna Deavere Smith, "The Shades of Loss," Berkeley Repertory Theatre Stagebill, 12. *Twilight: LA, 1992* from *On the Road: A Search for American Character,* Sharon Ott, Director. Marines Memorial Theatre, January 26-March 16, 1996.

2. Barry Lopez, "The American Geographies," *About This Life: Journeys on the Threshold of Memory* (New York: Vintage Books, 1998), 136. Further citations to this essay collection will appear in the text.

3. Willa Cather, *My Ántonia* (1918; New York: Houghton Mifflin Company, 1977), 245; Owen Wister, *The Virginian* (1902; New York: Oxford University Press, 1998), 15; Jane Tompkins, *West of Everything: The Inner Life of Westerns* (New York: Oxford University Press, 1992), 44; J.S. Holliday, *Rush for Riches: Gold Fever and the Making of California* (Berkeley: Oakland Museum of California/University of California Press, 1999). Holliday characterizes Mexican California using the same patronizing tones as does Hubert Howe Bancroft, one of his major (and hardly disinterested) sources. Before 1848, "California drifted," her "scruffy pueblos" (16) and "recalcitrant Indians" (23) the home of the "crude but ebullient Spanish-Mexican society" (21). "Easygoing, comfortably oblivious to their backwardness, the Californios had no vehicles more modern than cumbersome, creaking ox-drawn carts with wheels of solid rounds sawed from tree trunks. And no roads or bridges. No school, library, or hospital. No newspapers or books other than those delivered by the traders. And no post office. Most Californios were illiterate; they knew only how to scrawl a mark in place of signature. But they also knew how to show the Americans there was more to life than work. Like dancing, feasting, and singing in celebration of three-day weddings and religious holidays. To be condemned but also envied by many a Yankee" (27). Such "crude," "comfortable," careless history-making does little to enrich our understanding of the western region. Further references to these works will be cited within the text.

4. Sui Sin Far, "Leaves from the Mental Portfolio of an Eurasian" in *The Big Ai-iieeeee! An Anthology of Chinese American and Japanese American Literature,* eds. Jeffery Paul Chan, Frank Chin, Lawson Fusao Inada, and Shawn Wong (New York: Meridian, 1991), 117.

5. While I do not think we can ever really "recover" local geography in narrative, as Barry Lopez suggests in "American Geographies," his critique of American natural history as a national geography of so many "constituent" and "interchangeable parts" that "can be treated as commodities" is a very useful one. This "homogenized . . . geography" that "appears in ads, as a background in movies, and in patriotic calendars" (136), Lopez argues, belies historical understandings of American land: "All local geographies, as they were defined by hundreds of separate, independent native traditions, were denied in the beginning in favor of an imported and unifying vision of America's natural history. The country, the landscape itself, was eventually defined according to dictates of Progress like Manifest Destiny, and laws like the Homestead Act which reflected a poor understanding of the physical lay of the land" (137).

6. Steven Tatum, "The Problem of the 'Popular' in the New Western History," in Forrest G. Robinson, ed., *The New Western History: The Territory Ahead* (Tucson: The University of Arizona Press, 1997), 164.

7. José David Saldívar, *Border Matters: Remapping American Cultural Studies* (Berkeley: University of California Press, 1997), ix.

8. Correspondence with the author. My own work has been informed by the nuanced model of political and cultural self location Padilla develops in *My History, Not Yours: The Formation of Mexican American Autobiography* (Madison: University of Wisconsin Press, 1993).

9. At this point I am a little tired of continued eastern gibes about the West as a satire-free zone. Apparently it is only east of the Mississippi River that people possess sufficient critical acumen to discern irony, existing exclusively upon Greek tragedy as they do, while we westerners ruminate in tone-deaf splendor on a rhetorical diet of pulp fictions!

10. Forrest G. Robinson, "Clio Bereft of Calliope: Literature and the New Western History," in Robinson, ed., *The New Western History,* 90.

11. There are, of course, significant and thought-provoking exceptions to this rule, including Lisbeth Haas's important revisionary history of California, *Conquests and Historical Identities in California, 1769–1936* (Berkeley: University of California Press, 1996), and Blake Allmendinger's innovative redefinition of western texts, *Ten Most Wanted: The New Western Literature* (New York: Routledge, 1988).

12. *Blood Meridian, or The Evening Redness in the West* (1985; New York, 1992). Emily Wortis Leider's rich biography of Gertrude Atherton implicitly underscores the nature of this (continued) sexualized representation of the West as region when she describes the turn in Atherton's work away from the Europe and the eastern United States and toward California: "In her contempt for 'effete' dandies and 'morbid' novelists and poets likes the hint of a

shift in Gertrude's loyalties . . . toward conservative morality and 'virile' pos-
tures. Aesthetic languors clashed head-on with American dynamism, particularly the dynamism of California and the American West" (*California's
Daughter: Gertrude Atherton and Her Times* [Stanford, California: Stanford
University Press, 1991], 102.)

13. Pauline Hopkins, *Hagar's Daughter: A Story of Southern Caste Prejudice* in
*The Magazine Novels of Pauline Hopkins* (1901–2; New York: Oxford Uni-
versity Press, 1988), 210. Apologies to Américo Paredes's classic study of the
Tejano corrido, "*With His Pistol in His Hand": A Border Ballad and Its Hero*
(Austin: University of Texas Press, 1958).

14. Willa Cather, *The Song of the Lark* (1915; Boston: Houghton Mifflin Company, 1956), 69.

15. Willa Cather, *The Professor's House* (1925; New York: Vintage Classics,
1973), 78.

## Introduction

1. Eric Lott, *Love and Theft: Blackface Minstrelsy and the American Working
Class* (New York: Oxford University Press, 1993), 171. Further references
will be cited in the text.

2. Michael Rogin, *Blackface, White Noise: Jewish Immigrants in the Hollywood
Melting Pot* (Berkeley: University of California Press, 1996), 25, 12.

3. Frank Dobie, *San Francisco: A Pageant* (New York: D. Appleton-Century
Company, 1933), 133. Further references will appear in the text.

4. José David Saldívar, *Border Matters: Remapping American Cultural Studies*
(Berkeley: University of California Press, 1997), xiv. Further references will
be cited within the text.

5. In fact, both scholarly and popular studies of the "wild West" are frequently
as highly colored as the rosy southwestern mesas that frame contemporary
magazine and television advertisements for "American" cars and trucks.

6. The persistent circulation of words like "geographies" in the titles of recent
Modern Language Association and American Studies Association convention sessions confirms the primacy of this metaphor.

7. Consider contemporary discussions about immigration, for instance, which
frequently appear to have a regional character but speak to ideas and conflicts about the nation.

8. Jesús Velasco-Márquez, panel discussion on "The U.S.-Mexican War
(1846–1848)," a television documentary series premiering on PBS, Fall
1998, Conference on California History from 1848–1998, University of
Southern California, February 7, 1998.

9. Feminist scholars like Annette Kolodny and Jane Tompkins, whose work has
critiqued the exploitation of regionalism as a gendered stand-in for provincialism and urged a rethinking of the feminization of "local color," have also
informed my thinking. If such writers have only cursorily considered the

racial inflections of region, their work, combined with the long-standing recovery efforts of scholars in Mexicano and Chicano studies, opens a space
for reading the writers featured in this study "regionally" without belittling
them for working on a provincial canvas.

10. Note the relatively high number of job openings that are defined by field
and literary tradition compared with the paucity of advertisements for work
on comparative cultural study, the contents of even "special issue" offerings
in the most prestigious academic journals, the field- and discipline-specific
patterns of institutional support in the form of grant offerings and endowed
chairs, representation on MLA committees and boards, etc.

11. Donald E. Pease, "National Identities, Postmodern Artifacts, and Postnational Identities," in Donald Pease, ed., *National Identities and Post-Americanist Narratives* (Durham: Duke University Press, 1994), 1–2. Pease
celebrates an ongoing paradigm shift in American Studies that has already
involved "a complete overhauling" of the field's "ruling assumptions."

12. See Patricia Limerick, *The Legacy of Conquest: The Unbroken Past of the
American West* (New York: W.W. Norton, 1987). Further references to this
book will appear in the text. For literary models, see: Philip Fisher, ed., *The
New American Studies: Essays from Representations* (Berkeley: University of
California Press, 1991); Amy Kaplan, "Nation, Region, and Empire," in
Emory Elliott, ed., *Columbia History of the American Novel* (New York: Co-
lumbia University Press, 1991); Pease, ed., *National Identities and Post-Amer-
icanist Narratives;* Carolyn Porter, "What We Know that We Don't Know:
Remapping American Literary Studies," *American Literary History* 6:3 (Fall
1994); and Amy Kaplan and Donald Pease, eds., *Cultures of United States
Imperialism* (Durham: Duke University Press, 1993). Additional citations to
these studies will appear in the text.

13. Paul Gilroy, *The Black Atlantic: Modernity and Double Consciousness* (Cambridge: Harvard University Press, 1993), 5. Additional citations will appear
in the text.

14. Alok Yadav, "Nationalism and Contemporaneity: Political Economy of a
Discourse," in *Cultural Critique* 26 (Winter 1993–94), 210. Further citations will appear in the text.

15. Lott is discussing the raced character of American cultures here ("A peculiarly American structure of racial feeling"), but his assessment speaks to the
need to develop more historically responsible models for American Studies,
I would argue.

16. This definition is Alok Yadav's, who argues that we distinguish between "'official' nationalisms (enforced from the top down, through the state appara-
tuses, repressive and ideological) and 'insurgent' nationalisms (directed
against structures of domination, both intranational and international)"
(200). I would argue that in practice this opposition may be less easy to enforce; nonetheless, I am indebted to Yadav's essay for his clear and uncompromising critique of the cultural work nationalism—what I can only call
the "N" word!—provides for progressives in the Academy.

17. When they focus upon the railroad as an image for region and nation, scholars like Sara Blair point to this critical dissatisfaction with insufficiently dynamic critical models. See Blair's 1996 study *Henry James and the Writing of Race and Nation* (New York: Cambridge University Press) and in particular "Documenting the Alien: Racial Theater in *The American Scene*," which explores the racial registers of the Pullman railroad car.

18. Caren Kaplan, *Questions of Travel: Postmodern Discourses of Displacement* (Durham: Duke University Press, 1996), 144. Further citations will appear in the text.

19. Henry Nash Smith, *Virgin Land* (Cambridge: Harvard University Press, 1950). Additional references will appear in the text.

20. See for instance Smith on Beadle: "What Beadle contributed was . . . the perception that Boston was yielding first place as a publishing center to New York" (90). *Virgin Land*'s bibliography reflects this overdependence on both eastern publishing centers.

21. Frank Norris, *The Octopus: A Story of California* (1901; New York: Viking Penguin, 1986).

22. Thanks to Genaro Padilla for help with this argument. Although Jonathan Arac fails to discuss the implications of identifying Hawthorne as a regionalist writer in his critique of "hyper-canonization" in American literary historiography, he opens a space for recontextualizing this author when he identifies him as a "northeastern moralist" (16). See his "Nationalism, Hypercanonization, and Huckleberry Finn," in Pease, ed., *National Identities and Post-Americanist Narratives*.

23. Arlik Dirlik in Rob Wilson and Wimal Dissanayake, eds., *Global/Local: Cultural Production and the Transnational Imaginary* (Durham: Duke University Press, 1996), 42. Further references to essays in this volume will appear in the text.

24. See for instance Steinbeck's *The Pastures of Heaven, Tortilla Flat,* and *Cannery Row;* Baca's *Martín & Meditations on the South Valley;* Cervantes' *Emplumada;* Cary's *Black Ice;* Soto's *Living up the Street;* and Lopez's *About this Life: Journeys on the Threshold of Memory.*

25. Or consider the following, a rhetorical moebius strip that leads nowhere: "The local as I use it here has meaning only in as much as it is a product of the conjuncture of structures located in the same temporality but with different spatialities, which is what gives rise to the problem of spatiality and, therefore, of the local, in the first place" (Dirlik, 39).

26. And see Porter's very useful remapping of regionalism according to Fisher: "When [the term] is extended finally to include 'the regionalism of gender and race,' its elasticity becomes quite miraculous. . . . 'Regionalism' is an . . . odd label, whether applied to what is better known as the identity politics in the larger cultural arena or to the academic development of fields such as African-American studies" (482–83).

27. See "The Making of California," *The Century,* 26:1 (November 1890): "*The Century* begins a systematic record of some of the chief features of the

Anglo-Saxon movement to California, a part of the national life which has no parallel either in our own history or in that of any other country. We say 'a part of the national life,' for though the immediate scene of the search for gold and of the foundation of one of our greatest commonwealths was a narrow strip of Pacific Coast, the lines of sympathy and interest about that day reached to every quarter of the country. . . . Nothing more characteristically American than this movement has been exhibited in our one hundred years. The material conquest of California is not only important in itself, but as having set the pitch for the winning of the nearer West" (151).

28. Ivan Doig, *Dancing at the Rascal Fair* (New York: Harper & Row, 1987), 171.

29. Witness this 1884 illustration, for instance, in which the U.S.-born Felipe of Helen Hunt Jackson's *Ramona* begins "to yearn for Mexico,—or Mexico, which he had never seen, yet yearned for like an exile" (359).

30. In *Imperial Leather: Race, Gender and Sexuality in the Colonial Contest* (New York: Routledge, 1995), Anne McClintock makes a corollary point in order to critique the temporal logic of the "postcolonial": "A good deal of post-colonial studies has set itself against the imperial idea of linear time. Yet the term postcolonial, like the exhibit, is haunted by the very figure of linear development that it sets out to dismantle. Metaphorically, the term postcolonialism marks history as a series of stages along an epochal road from 'the precolonial,' to 'the colonial,' to 'the post-colonial'—an unbidden, if disavowed, commitment to linear time and the idea of development . . . so the singular category 'postcolonial' may too readily license a panoptic tendency to view the globe through generic abstractions void of political nuance. The arcing panorama of the horizon becomes thereby so expansive that international imbalances in power remain effectively blurred" (10–11). Additional citations will appear in the text.

31. José David Saldívar, *The Dialectics of Our America: Genealogy, Cultural Critique, and Literary History* (Durham, NC: Duke University Press, 1991).

32. In this respect, literary theory follows along in the wake of electronic mass marketing. Paeans to the "World Wide Web" are uttered with the same expansive cheerfulness as is the announcement of the dissolution of national borders. But if the Web stretches across the globe, it originates in a very tiny area of it: Northern California's Silicon Valley. See David Kaplan's *The Silicon Boys and Their Valley of Dreams* (New York: Morrow, 1999) for a geographically and economically historicized account of the genesis of the electronic age and its continued dominance by the corporations and venture capitalists of the South Bay, as well as Lisa Nakamura's trenchant critique of the raced parameters of cyberspace in "Race," in Thomas Swiss, ed., *Key Terms for the World Wide Web and Culture,* (New York: New York University Press, forthcoming 2000).

33. In all fairness, some of its most eloquent proponents acknowledge the dangers of an inadequately historicized transnationalism. Carolyn Porter, for instance, cites Vera Kutzinski's "'cautionary tale'" and suggests that "Kutzinski is clearly right when she says that [Lawrence] Buell underestimates 'the

specificity of significantly different historical situations'" (516). I would argue that this one-sentence concession does not constitute a sufficient exploration of the problems Kutzinski raises, however.

34. It hardly needs acknowledgment to affirm that for most television viewers, the virtual travel glamorized by such visual collages is the only form of globetrotting they are in a position to enjoy. What does bear repeating, however, is that the kinds of travel advertised by postcolonial theorists as anodyne for the dangers of nationalism are equally inaccessible to people without the financial resources to become "cosmopolitans." Despite efforts in American Studies to rethink the European imperial etymology of poststructuralism's travel metaphors, surprisingly little attention is paid to scholars whose work surveys conditions on the American continent. While the United States has become a primary site for the discussion of cultural studies, the field remains defined by theorists whose critical points of reference are elsewhere. While I do not wish to dismiss the groundbreaking work of postcolonial critics like Edward Said, Homi Bhaba, Gayatri Spivak, and Benedict Anderson, I do suggest we situate them more fully before we appropriate their analyses for considerations of American contexts. Transnationalist celebrations of the global may describe travel freely undertaken by scholars who move between Bombay and London, for instance, but how useful are its paradigms for understanding the migrations forced by economic circumstance and political necessity: of the poor in Tijuana who work in Los Angeles, of Laotian refugees farming California's Central Valley, of Vietnamese immigrants opening up small businesses in San José? When we shift from *the* local to *a* local*e*, the practice of using models of exile and nomadic dispersal characteristic of "diaspora studies" to explain immigration patterns in the United States becomes vexed. Despite announcements of its Independence, American Studies remains in many cases subordinated to a postcolonial model framed as normative, and perennially under obligation to a model of "high theory" that includes few works by scholars working on the American continent. In light of this continued inferiority complex, it is not surprising that discussions of nationalism in the United States take their cues from British and European scholars.

In addition, performing a postmortem on nationalism is overly hasty given the vigor of the patient. Despite the alacrity with which critics celebrate the dissolution of national boundaries (in languages that bleed over from the advertising campaigns of multinational corporations currently hailing themselves as utopic global systems), nationalism remains, as Alok Yadav insists, "a hegemonic articulation of identity in our present world" (203). Theorists advertise the advent of global capital, distinguishing between the multinational corporation (in the words of Masao Miyoshi "one that is headquartered in a nation") and the transnational corporation (a conglomerate that "might no longer be tied to its nation of origin but is adrift and mobile, ready to settle anywhere and exploit any state including its own" [86–87]). But a "truly transnational corporation (Miyoshi in *Global/Local,* 86), I would argue, is really a theoretical projection—an intellectual distopia, if you will—that can never, given its definition as wholly nationless in its affiliations, become a reality. Moreover, as Yadav argues, if we invest the transnational corporation with omniscient authority, we ignore fundamental questions of class. More precisely: it is control over work upon which, Yadav notes, "the centrality of the nation-state rests." Even if we grant the "huge increase in the magnitude of migrant labor . . . all such movements remain under the control of governmental bodies. Establishing the general terms and conditions of work and providing for the reproduction of the labor pool . . . remain largely in government hands" (214). Ultimately, he insists, the argument for the erosion of nationalism "turns out to be more a wish than a reflection of anything we have seen happen in the past quarter century" (213–14). Notwithstanding such fantasies (that it "*should be* irrelevant because it is anachronistic, because it is repellant, because it does not make sense for the multicultural state"), nationalism is "in fact, alive and well, in the United States as elsewhere" (204). We cannot merely wish national borders away, even if some of us regularly traverse them to give paid talks about global capital.

So why do theorists "in the United States as elsewhere" continue to turn a benevolent eye upon the emperor who has no clothes? With Yadav, who suggests that definitions of nationalism are themselves a function of critical location ("the overwhelming focus on the dangers of nationalism [are] . . . drawn from European experience, but *applied* to the non-European world" [210]), I would argue that the "no borders school" is developed largely out of discrete, geographically specific economic and political formations; most obviously, the recent reinvigoration of the European Economic Community in general or the history of a united Germany in specific. If we look to other parts of the globe, the foothold that global capital has seems more precarious. Nor is it surprising that those nations who have the most invested in the World Bank should be the ones to grant it global authority. Countries whose savings accounts are less substantial may not be as quick to speak to the advantages of transnational capital.

35. In a note, Porter cites Genaro Padilla and Gerald Vizenor to acknowledge the "dangers of fetishizing 'the border' as icon" (523), but this brief aside does not adequately put such dangers to rest.

36. Brian W. Dippie, "American Wests: Historiographical Perspectives," in Patricia Limerick, Clyde A. Milner II, and Charles E. Rankin, eds., *Trails: Toward a New Western History* (Lawrence: University Press of Kansas, 1991), 135. Additional citations will appear in the text.

37. Richard White, *It's Your Misfortune and None of My Own: A New History of the American West* (Norman: University of Oklahoma Press, 1991), 89, 58. Additional references will appear in the text.

38. Kevin Starr, *Material Dreams: Southern California Through the 1920s* (New York: Oxford University Press, 1990), 176.

39. Jerome Frisk and Forrest G. Robinson implicitly gesture toward this reliance on a New England template when they suggest the New Western History's

debt to Sacvan Bercovitch: "As Michael Malone notes, the New Western History is 'in large part . . . the predictable result of mainstreaming the western subdiscipline by applying to it trends in the broader field of American history and American Studies.' More specifically, revisionist interpretive methods and agendas are at intervals in striking alignment with the widely influential writings of Sacvan Bercovitch, Fredric Jameson, and Edward Said" (6).

40. In fact such revisionary claims echo the language of the New Western historians. Unconsciously recirculating the stirring language of Manifest Destiny, Patricia Limerick's 1991 essay "What on Earth Is the New Western History?" and its pointedly critical recapitulation in Frisk and Robinson are both saturated with expressions that recall the pioneer advancing across the continent: "'nobody had ever done this before'; critical histories of colonial conquest and environmental plunder were being written 'for the first time' . . . For it is above all else their claim to originality that separates the *New* Western Historians from those who have gone before them, and it is the bold newness of the revisionist narrative that holds the attention of contemporary workers in the field" (2). It might be worthwhile to consider all such stirring paeans to a new critical world order, whether in history, literature, or elsewhere, as the narrative equivalent of "Fanfare for the Common Man," composer Aaron Copeland's nationalistic tribute to American democratic values—that is, indebted to the very idea of American exceptionalism they are designed to critique.

41. Priscilla Wald, *Constituting Americans: Cultural Anxiety and Narrative Form* (Durham: Duke University Press, 1995), 47.

## Chapter 1

1. Henry James, *The American Scene* (1907; Middlesex, England: Penguin Modern Classics, 1994) 172. Further references will be cited within the text.

2. María Amparo Ruiz de Burton, *Who Would Have Thought It?,* Rosaura Sánchez and Beatrice Pita, eds. (1872; Houston: Arte Público Press, 1995), 8. Further citations will appear in the text.

3. Henry James, *The Bostonians* (1886; Middlesex, England: Penguin Modern Classics, 1978), 157. Further citations will appear in the text.

4. Amy Kaplan, "Nation, Region, and Empire," in Emory Elliott, ed., *Columbia History of the American Novel* (New York: Columbia University Press, 1991), 252. Additional references will be cited in the text.

5. See Amy Kaplan's trenchant assessment of literary nostalgia in this essay. "The regions painted with 'local color' are traversed by the forgotten history of racial conflict with prior regional inhabitants, and are ultimately produced and engulfed by the centralized capitalist economy that generates the desire for retreat" (256). Further references will be cited within the text.

In *Question of Travel: Postmodern Discourses of Displacement* (Durham: Duke University Press, 1996), Caren Kaplan considers the economic coordinates of this relationship between "region" and "center": "The peripheries in such configurations provide immigrants and exiles but are never the sites of modernist cultural production themselves; that is, they provide the raw materials to be synthesized in the generative locations of the modern, Western metropolis or they offer opportunities for spatial exploration on the part of metropolitans in search of metaphysical displacement" (32).

6. Compare this portrait of Concord rusticity with St. Augustine's "Spanish antiquity." Both are regional vignettes, but there is a tonal difference between contemplating Puritan "remains" and Spanish ruins—one mourns the fragmented state of the former, which cry out for resurrection, and "delights" in the crumbling "gateways and ramparts of the latter, "crowned with the sweetness of slow decay" (*The American Scene,* 336).

7. While I am not interested in belaboring this point, it seems important (in the interests not only of nineteenth-century literary studies but also to reflect upon continuities with contemporary anti-immigrant activity) to refuse the consolations of euphemism in discussions of racial formations in literature, canonical or otherwise. To characterize James's difficulties with "tatterdemalion darkies" and "the Hebrew conquest of New York" in *The American Scene* as "racial uncertainties," for instance, (in Sara Blair's *Henry James and the Writing of Race and Nation* [Cambridge: Cambridge University Press, 1996], 161), or to frame his representations of Jews in New York (" . . . multiplication, multiplication of everything, was the dominant note, at the bottom of some vast sallow aquarium in which innumerable fish, of overdeveloped proboscis, were to bump together. . . . The children swarmed above all. . . . This, I think, makes the individual Jew more of a concentrated person, savingly possessed of everything that is in him, than any other human, noted at random—or is it simply, rather, that the unsurpassed strength of the race permits of the chopping into myriads of fine fragments without loss of race-quality? There are small strange animals, known to natural history, snakes or worms, I believe, who, when cut into pieces, wriggle away contentedly and live in the snippet as completely as in the whole. So the denizens of the New York Ghetto, heaped as thick as the splinters on the table of a glass-blower, had each, like the fine glass particle, his or her individual share of the whole hard glitter of Israel" [*The American Scene,* 100]) as "a productive openness . . . marked by a brooding ambivalence about the 'intensity' of the Jew's 'aspect' and 'race-quality'" (Blair, 178) is to sidestep James's own connections with what Blair herself rightly terms the "culture of racist gentility" (Blair, 161). The point is not to focus intellectual energy on indicting James, but simply to be frank about the political configurations he—or any other writer—participates in. Nor do I wish to single out Blair's fine study, for this kind of rhetorical hesitation is the rule rather than the exception in scholarly treatments of the author. Further references to this study will appear in the text.

8. For two compelling studies of Ruiz de Burton's significance to the Recovery Project and the questions her work raises about interpretation and pedagogy, see John M. González, "Romancing Hegemony: Constructing Racialized

Citizenship in María Amparo Ruiz de Burton's *The Squatter and the Don*"; and Manuel M. Martín Rodríguez, "Textual and Land Reclamations: The Critical Reception of Early Chicana/o Literature," both in Erlinda Gonzales-Berry and Chuck Tatum, eds., *Recovering the U.S. Hispanic Literary Heritage, Vol. II.* (Houston: Arte Público Press, 1996).

9. In fact, as José Aranda points out, Ruiz de Burton's narratives are produced within the context of wars both in the U.S. and Mexico: "Ruiz de Burton . . . would endure the consequences of the following wars: the Texas war of independence (1836), the Mexican American War (1846–1848), the U.S. Civil War (1861–1865), and the French occupation of Mexico (1864–1867)" in "María Amparo Ruiz de Burton," in Sharon Harris, ed., *Dictionary of Literary Biography,* (New York: Gale Publications, 1999), 4. Further references to this essay will appear in the text. While I am interested here in the literary relationships between the Civil War and the U.S.-Mexican War in my consideration of the regional inflections of U.S. identity, Aranda's fuller contextualization situates Ruiz de Burton on the dividing line between two American nations in provocative ways.

10. This phrase and those of the previous sentence are James's own, as cited on the back cover of the 1978 Penguin Modern Classics edition of *The Bostonians.*

11. Besides Blair's book, see, among others, Jonathan Friedman's "The Poetics of Cultural Decline: Degeneration, Assimilation, and Henry James's *The Golden Bowl,*" in *American Literary History* 7 (Fall 1995), 3: 477–99; and Ross Posnock's "The Politics of Nonidentity: A Genealogy," in Donald Pease, ed., *National Identities and Post-Americanist Narratives* (Durham: Duke University Press, 1994).

12. It is worth noting how the icons for peace and power her name encodes develop this critique of feminine will as a contradiction in terms: what she *should* be (a dove/olive branch) is pitted against what she *wishes* to be (a ruler).

13. While her figure dates to the Civil War, however, his own "peculiar views" (185) push him even farther into the past.

14. *The Bostonians* includes everyone within the scope of its satire, but the mixture of affection and disdain with which James treats most of the characters does not preclude nostalgia. In fact, this admixture of irony and wistfulness characterizes his canon as a whole. The mere fact that he continues to focus on the representation of Americans (whether transplanted to the European scene or on home ground) demonstrates this nostalgia. Nevertheless, there are moments where James fails to sustain irony in this text, and I have suggested that it is precisely at these moments that Ransom is conflated with black Americans. At such junctures, *The Bostonians,* tonally, sounds like portions of *The American Scene.* Despite the presumed shifts in self-identification over the 20-year gap between the novel and the travel memoir, James's position on "gross aliens" in the United States—as distinct from his own civil foreignness in England—is constant.

15. James writes to Wharton in February 1905 of Vanderbilt's Asheville, North Carolina, estate: "one's sense of the extraordinary impenitent madness (of millions) which led to the erection in this vast niggery wilderness, of so gigantic and elaborate a monument to all that isn't socially possible there," as cited in Susan Luria, "The Architecture of Manners: Henry James, Edith Wharton, and the Mount," *American Quarterly* 49, no. 2 (June 1997), 298. The conflation of such racist language about the South with a classically northern template (the language of the Puritan errand invoked by "vast" and "wilderness"), suggests that James is parodying Vanderbilt's secular mission over and against the northern spiritual quest that forms the bedrock of ideas of the U.S. nation.

16. These processes of evasion and substitution are not idiosyncratic to James's method in *The Bostonians,* but form part of the writer's modus operandi, as Sara Blair points out. She suggests that his "master texts achieve their version of culture-building precisely by erasing their tracks; their strenuously subtle performances of Anglo-American 'character' and gentility assist in their own detachment from the historical conditions in and through which racial and national identities are historically being forged" (9).

17. As cited in Blair, 138. Blair's astute reading of *The Tragic Muse* suggests we read in Miriam's accents James's obliquely rendered attention to nation-building during an age of increasing immigration to the U.S. As an actress, "[h]er career will be not a job but . . . a 'mission' . . . to recover the '[p]urity' of English speech from contamination, from the 'vulgarity' and 'crudity' of 'abominable dialects' that threaten its historical integrity and its power to set a cultural 'standard'" (138).

18. Eric Lott's focus upon minstrelsy as a form of substitution resonates with my argument about Ransom's value as a euphemistic figure. "Cities experienced cultural blackening as a vast profusion of ambiguous signs," Lott suggests, "that like the minstrel mask itself, offered the experience of 'blackness' even as they absented it," in *Love and Theft: Blackface Minstrelsy and the American Working Class* (New York: Oxford University Press, 1993), 100. This curious way of "managing" interracial relations through intraracial performance is precisely what James does in *The Bostonians.* Further references to Lott's study will appear in the text.

19. This self-punishment of course operates on two levels, since the representation of Olive's homoeroticism as grotesque cannot help but reflect some form of self-disgust on the part of the more carefully controlled—displaced?—sexuality of the author himself.

20. See Lott: "The chiefly working-class orientation of cultural interchange in the North . . . was responsible . . . for installing this new entertainment in its northern class context and for the kinds of racial reference to be found there" (38).

21. María Amparo Ruiz de Burton, *The Squatter and the Don,* eds. Rosaura Sánchez and Beatrice Pita (1885; Houston: Arte Público Press, 1993), 69. Further references will appear in the text.

22. Owen Wister, *The Virginian* (1902; New York: Oxford University Press, 1998) 95. Succeeding references will appear in the text. In fact, James and Wister enjoyed a close personal and literary connection. Wister's mother remained one of James's closest friends, and Wister himself read several of his manuscripts to James. Wister read portions of the southern plantation fiction he published in 1906 as *Lady Baltimore* to James while the latter sojourned in Charleston and composed his own commentary on the postwar South that became, the year following Wister's novel, *The American Scene.* See Richard Shulman's introduction to the 1998 edition of *The Virginian* for further discussion of this relationship.

23. Richard White's suggestive comments on nineteenth-century perceptions of California testify to this sense of the state as vacant: "The U.S. was a young nation lacking both an ancient history and a cultural tradition rich in art, architecture, or literature. Americans looked to scenery as compensation for the cultural riches they lacked. They hoped nature at its most monumental would provide the inspiration, the sublimity, and the glimpse of timelessness that American culture had not yet achieved. It became a matter of national pride. . . . the result was an exercise in 'scenic nationalism'" (*"It's Your Misfortune and None of My Own": A New History of the American West* [Norman: University of Oklahoma Press, 1991], 410).

24. See also Richard Henry Dana's condescending *Two Years Before the Mast* (1840; New York: New American Library, 1964); and William H. Prescott's *History of the Conquest of Mexico* (1843; Chicago: University of Chicago Press, 1966); as well as the extensive histories of California by Hubert H. Bancroft. For more sustained attention to Anglo American representations of Californios, see Genaro Padilla's *My History, Not Yours: The Formation of Mexican American Autobiography* (Madison: University of Wisconsin, 1993) and Rosaura Sánchez's *Telling Identities: The Californio testimonios* (Minneapolis: University of Minnesota Press, 1995).

25. Without in any way dismissing the depth of Ruiz's relationship with Captain Burton, Aranda's politically contextualizing comments on this wartime marriage to Captain Burton are suggestive: "In light of the unlikelihood of the Mexican military coming to their rescue, Ruiz de Burton's family must have sought out, like other families, crucial relations with Anglo American officers" (draft of "Contradictory Impulses: María Amparo Ruiz de Burton, Resistance Theory, and the Politics of Chicana/o Studies"). See in addition Aranda's reading of family in Ruiz's work: "In the Spanish language, *familia,* family or *familiar,* as in what pertains to the family, conveys the understanding of not only an extended family, but also a network of in-laws, godparents, friends, neighbors, business associates, and even, at highly charged rhetorical moments, the nation" (draft of "Contradictory Impulses"). See also the published version of this essay in Cathy Davidson, ed., *American Literature* 70, no. 3 (September 1998): 551–79.

26. Steven Fink reminds me that there are major theological differences between the Presbyterian circles Ruiz de Burton invokes in her 1872 novel and the

Emersonian-Unitarian tenets James describes in *The Bostonians*. Notwithstanding their historical discreteness, Ruiz de Burton and James exploit these two theological circles toward the same literary end, to satirize the ways in which religious language speaks in the service of particular class interests.

27. Zane Grey, *Riders of the Purple Sage* (1912; New York: Viking Penguin, 1990), 47.

28. Sui Sin Far, "Leaves from the Mental Portfolio of an Eurasian" in Jeffery Paul Chan, Frank Chin, Lawson Fusao Inada, and Shawn Wong, eds., *The Big Aiiieeeee! An Anthology of Chinese American and Japanese American Literature* (New York: Meridian, 1991), 120.

29. House slaves often slept on the floor outside the bedrooms of their owners so that they could be called upon for service at any point during the night.

30. As noted by Rudolph M. Lapp in his classic study, *Blacks in Gold Rush California* (New Haven: Yale University Press, 1977), 220.

31. José Aranda clarifies the unforgiving political climate within which Ruiz de Burton positions herself as "a 'white' Mexican": "after the Treaty of Guadalupe Hidalgo . . . racist cultural practices in the United States soon found their way into laws that openly discriminated against people of Mexican descent, in employment, housing, the purchasing of property, and legal representation. To make matters worse, these racist practices conjoined with pre-existing racist practices in Mexican culture to encourage not only the internalization of new racist ideologies but also the creation of an additional social policing mechanism that exaggerated the already privileged status of 'whiteness' within Mexican American communities" (draft version of "Contradictory Impulses: María Amparo Ruiz de Burton, Resistance Theory, and the Politics of Chicana/o Studies").

32. Amelia María de la Luz Montes, "Rereading the Nation in Nineteenth-Century American Literature: The Life and Works of María Amparo Ruiz de Burton," Modern Language Association Conference, Toronto, Canada, December 28, 1997. In full, Montes's juxtaposition of writing contemporaries Child and Ruiz de Burton is framed as follows: "In *Hobomok*, Hobomok the Indian Chief marries the Puritan Mary Conant. However, Hobomok eventually dies and the product of the marriage, a little boy named Charles, is subsumed into an anglo environment where he eventually graduates from Cambridge 'and by degrees his Indian appellation was silently omitted' (150)."

33. See for instance Ruiz's ironic use of a military lexicon to deflate New England's celebratory rhetoric at the close of the Civil War: "Lavinia's heart pranced like a war-horse at the sound of martial music, making the chest of the maiden resound with its galloping. Her patriotic fire spread to the Misses Cackle, until nothing but making sacrifices for their country's cause would satisfy them . . . For weeks and weeks, the Misses Cackle and Lavinia canned beef-tea and made jellies and jams in the daytime, and lint and bandages and havelocks at night. They knitted a great number of stockings also. They made underclothes, and large, very large night-shirts; for these patriotic

ladies seemed to take measure by their enthusiasm, and very possibly imagined that the heroes for whom the shirts were made must all be as large in size as in deeds" (105).

The "separate spheres" Ruiz de Burton yokes together when she equates the religious conflicts between Lola and the Norval ladies with the military conquests the descendents of the "Pilgrim fathers" enjoy over those of Mexican ancestry thus undermine two sets of ideological borders at once. Such twin deconstructions are provocative because they suggest we reconsider the facility with which the sentimental novel, construed as a "feminine" literary form, is still assumed to be "political" only against its own generic grain.

34. Steven Fink suggests that the phrase "blue Presbyterians" may refer to the 1861 split between northern and southern Presbyterians over slavery. It is thus anachronistic in the time frame of the novel (Hackwell announces his affiliation in 1857). With it, however, Ruiz de Burton underscores the classed registers of abolitionist discourse: "as I intended to settle in New England, I knew there was no risk of my going too far as a Presbyterian. One can't be too blue in these regions, you know" (56), Hackwell counsels his friend Hammerhard. Like Mrs. Norval, Hackwell's espousal of the antislavery cause goes only skin deep, a hypocrisy that is unattractive enough in the doctor's social-climbing wife, but an ethical affront when it issues from the mouth of a divine. As well as indicting the class pretensions of a New England bourgeoisie that in this novel is more interested in liberating its white members from social oblivion than southern blacks from the bonds of slavery, the phrase resonates with other tropes for color and race. Lola is blackened as a Mojave captive, introduced through the displacement of the "red shawl" she hides behind when she arrives at the Boston home of Dr. Norval, and finally revealed as a blue-blood by Hackwell himself, whose rueful assessment of Lola's father's eyes ("Who ever heard of a blue-eyed Mexican?" he asks rhetorically) articulates Ruiz de Burton's critique of racist assumptions about Mexicanos. See chapter 3 in this volume for more sustained analysis.

35. It is useful to stress here that the focus is on culture; or rather, as Genaro Padilla points out, Mexican *cultural* authority is counterpoised against the *political* weight (literalized in the thumping foot of the president keeping time to the base drum of the band) of the United States. The latter, as Padilla argues, "is power, the other is the affectation of power in the refinement of reading and fine wine" (correspondence with the author, June 1996).

36. Letter to Mariano Vallejo, March 8, 1861, as cited in Amelia de la Luz Montes, "Es Necesario Mirar Bien: Nineteenth-Century Letter Making and Novel Writing in the Life of María Amparo Ruiz de Burton," in María Herrera-Sobek and Virginia Sánchez-Korrol, eds., *Recovering the U.S. Hispanic Literary Heritage, Vol. III* (Houston: Arte Público Press, 2000), 18.

37. For additional background on Ruiz de Burton's stay in the East, see Rosaura Sánchez and Beatrice Pita's comprehensive introduction to the republished edition of *Who Would Have Thought It?* (Houston: Arte Público Press,

1995); José F. Aranda Jr.'s essay "María Amparo Ruiz de Burton," in Harris, ed., *Dictionary of Literary Biography.* New York: Gale Publications, 1999; Amelia María de la Luz Montes's "María Amparo Ruize de Burton Negotiates American Literary Politics and Culture," in Joyce W. Warren and Margaret Dickie, eds., *Challenging Boundaries: Gender and Periodization* (Athens: University of Georgia Press, 2000); as well as her piece "Es Necesario Mirar Bien: Nineteenth-Century Letter Making and Novel Writing in the Life of María Amparo Ruiz de Burton," in Herrera-Sobek and Sánchez-Korrol, eds., *Recovering the U.S. Hispanic Literary Heritage.*

## Chapter 2

1. As cited by William Deverell in *Railroad Crossing: Californians and the Railroad, 1850–1910* (Berkeley: University of California Press, 1994), 9. Additional citations will appear in the text.

2. Genaro M. Padilla, *My History, Not Yours: The Formation of Mexican American Autobiography* (Madison: University of Wisconsin Press, 1993), 58. Further references to this book will be cited within the text.

3. María Amparo Ruiz de Burton, *The Squatter and the Don,* ed. Rosaura Sánchez and Beatrice Pita (1885; Houston: Arte Público Press, 1993). Thanks to the imperviousness of narrative iconography—consider the continued popularity of such representations of nineteenth-century California history as the pony express (Wells Fargo gold cards), the mission bell (Taco Bell and fourth grade curricula in California), prospecting pans and picks (the Gold Rush exhibit produced in honor of the quincentennial)—such representations of western narrative remain surprisingly calcified to this day. Ivan Doig's 1987 novel of Montana, *Dancing at the Rascal Fair* (New York: Harper & Row) recycles pioneer tropes that have remained in the narrative vocabulary for over a century. A discussion of the effects of the Homestead Act includes Indians who "have had to give way ever since. . . . To the likes of us" [Anglo American settlers], but any recognition of conflict is defused by the following passage: "'So much land here, and . . . so empty. It's hard to think of men killing each other over it.' 'A great mighty struggle . . . with two casualties.' . . . 'What if we were the Indians and they were us? Who'd be joking then?' 'Anyway it wasn't the Battle of Culloden, now was it'" (169).

4. Surprisingly, despite his exhaustive survey of Anglo American literature, Cecil Robinson finds in *With the Ears of Strangers: The Mexican in American Literature* (Tucson: The University of Arizona Press, 1963) that "The defeat and dispossession of the dons, an episode that had much of poignancy in it, was a tale that remained, except for a limited treatment of it by a few writers, untold at the time that it was happening" (154). Further references will be cited within the text.

My own research seeks to demonstrate that, on the contrary, beginning as early as three decades after the conquest, Anglo American writers were relentlessly engaged in reworking the story of this dispossession. As, even more explicitly, were Mexicano writers: this essay builds on the work of many other scholars of nineteenth-century Mexican American literature, whose archival research has uncovered a wealth of material treating the repercussions of conquest. For writing on California in particular, see, among others, Antonia I. Castañeda, "The Political Economy of Nineteenth Century Stereotypes of Californianas" in Adelaida R. Del Castillo, ed., *Between Borders: Essays on Mexicana/Chicana History* (Encino, California: Floricanto Press, 1990); Douglas Monroy, "They Didn't Call Them 'Padre' for Nothing: Patriarchy in Hispanic California" in *Between Borders* and *Thrown Among Strangers: The Making of Mexican Culture in Frontier California* (Berkeley: University of California Press, 1990); Lisbeth Haas, *Conquests and Historical Identities in California, 1769–1936* (Berkeley, University of California Press, 1995); Genaro M. Padilla, *My History, Not Yours: The Formation of Mexican American Autobiography*, and Rosaura Sánchez, *Telling Identities: The Californio testimonios* (Minneapolis: University of Minnesota Press, 1995). Since this chapter was initially drafted, scholars such as Jesse Alemán, José Aranda, and Amelia de la Luz Montes have begun examining her canon in ways that will reshape our thinking about Ruiz de Burton's relation to nineteenth-century American literature as a whole. See in particular Alemán's "Novelizing National Discources: History, Romance, and Law in María Amparo Ruiz de Burton's *The Squatter and the Don*," in *Recovering the U.S. Hispanic Literary Heritage. Vol. III*. Edited by María Herrera-Sobek and Virginia Sánchez-Korrol. Houston: Arte Publico Press, 2000, which also historicizes her romance over and against Helen Hunt Jackson's *Ramona*.

5. "monuments . . . , " Elizabeth Hughes, *The California of the Padres; or, Footprints of Ancient Communism* (San Francisco: I. N. Choynski, 1875), 2; "crumbling into ruin," Helen Hunt Jackson, *Ramona* (1884; New York: Signet Classic, 1988), 35; " . . . long procession . . ." Hughes 2. Further references to both books will appear in the text.

   From the mid-1850s through the turn of the century, the *Overland Monthly* enjoyed a particularly authoritative status as the voice of the literary Anglo American West. See Cecil Robinson's *With the Ears of Stranger* and this description: "The *Overland Monthly*, which was to be Western America's answer to the *Atlantic Monthly* and which had pretensions to being a formulator of opinion in the West, carried a number of stories and articles on Mexico, most of them uncomplimentary" (73).

6. Sandra Gunning, *Race, Rape, and Lynching: The Red Record of American Literature 1890–1912* (New York: Oxford University Press, 1996). Further references will appear in the text.

7. Kevin Starr notes in *Material Dreams: Southern California Through the 1920s* (New York: Oxford University Press, 1990) that D.W. Griffith, producer of Thomas Dixon's *The Birth of a Nation*, was also the first film producer to "graft the film industry . . . onto Southern California root stock" when he

took his "troupe of Biograph players out to Mission San Gabriel to film the story of Ramona" (115). In fact, Wister's own contribution to plantation fiction was informed by his complex biographical legacy: his grandfather Pierce Butler was responsible for incorporating the Fugitive Slave Law into the Constitution, a law Wister's grandmother, the English actress Fanny Kemble, vociferously objected to. Wister read portions of *Lady Baltimore* to Henry James in Charleston the year before it was published, while the latter was drafting his own *The American Scene.*

8. Haas, *Conquests,* 126. Haas suggests that as "told by Californios and Indians in an era when American ethnic consciousness was strong, it represented an appropriation of mission history to contest unfavorable attitudes toward "Mexicans" (91). My own sense is less of contestation than of continuation; instead of the mission as witness of a deteriorating civilization, it is the site for continued worship. Rather than stand as aestheticized secular monument, I would argue, it is valued for its uninterrupted function as spiritual site. Nonetheless, Haas's provocative thesis begs further attention.

9. Josephine Clifford McCrackin, "La Graciosa," *Overland Tales* (San Francisco: A. L. Bancroft and Co., 1877), 33. Further citations to this story will appear in the text.

10. Charles Stuart, *Casa Grande: A California Pastoral* (New York: Henry Holt, 1906) 1. Stuart sustains this emphasis on the antiquity of Mexican California throughout the novel, but the chronological imperative of the following passage, which occurs near the close of the narrative, is particularly striking: " . . . the way had been full of charm, and as he approached Casa Grande, in the falling shadows, it seemed like riding to the land of knights-errant. . . . A spear and a sword, a coat-of-mail and a prancing steed—and smouldering fancies could easily be glowing realities" (239–40).

11. McCrackin, *Overland Tales,* 54. Further references to this story will appear in the text.

12. Gertrude Atherton, *Los Cerritos: A Romance of the Modern Time* (1890; Ridgewood, New Jersey: The Gregg Press, 1968).

13. Josiah Royce, *The Feud of Oakfield Creek: A Novel of California Life* (1887; New York: Johnson Reprint Corporation, 1970), 72; Frances Fuller Victor, "El Tesoro," in *The New Penelope and Other Stories and Poems* (San Francisco: A. L. Bancroft and Co., 1877), 247.

14. Gertrude Atherton, "The Ears of Twenty Americans," *The Splendid Idle Forties: Stories of Old California* (New York: Macmillan, 1902), 72. Further references will appear in the text.

15. See chapter 4 for a discussion of the ways in which the California romance provides domestic resolutions for imperial conflicts.

16. Antonio María Osio, *The History of Alta California: A Memoir of Mexican California,* trans., ed., and annotated by Rose Marie Beebe and Robert M. Senkewicz (Madison: University of Wisconsin Press, 1996), 209. Further references will be cited within the text.

17. Gertrude Atherton, *Before the Gringo Came* (1893; New York: Frederick A. Stokes Company, 1915). Further citations will appear in the text.

18. Atherton's racial genealogy anticipates the Darwinian "social work" Willa Cather's southwestern novels perform. See the next chapter for an extended discussion of this issue.

19. Gertrude Atherton, *The Californians* (1898; Ridgewood, NJ: The Gregg Press, 1968). Further references will appear in the text.

20. Compare Atherton's fiction with Osio's memoir, where "the stars and stripes . . . alleged to be the symbol of liberty" are "a lie," the flag belonging "to an oppressor who displayed arrogance against the weak" (209).

21. It is worth noting that this kind of euphemism is not restricted to fiction. In *California's Daughter: Gertrude Atherton and Her Times,* Emily Wortis Leider points out that the country estate Atherton and her husband shared, originally part of the Las Pulgas land grant, was "once owned by Louis [sic] Argüello, first Mexican governor of California" [(Stanford, CA: Stanford University Press, 1991), 40]. In her own history of the state, Atherton—perhaps out of guilt at this land transfer?—singles out Argüello ("my friend Luis") as "far more active and enterprising than most of his countrymen; he belongs to that small band of exceptions in the history of Old California that deserved to have been planted on one of the higher terraces of civilization. He thought for himself; was never dissipated until misfortune and bitterness overwhelmed him, and was devoted to the military service" (*California; An Intimate History.* 2nd ed. [1914; New York: Blue Ribbon Books, Inc., 1936], 62). Further references will be cited within the text. The writer's appropriation of Argüello ("my friend Luis"), whom she defines as the best of "Old California" at the expense of the Californios more generally, reiterates textually the appropriation of the Spanish land grant known today as Atherton, California.

22. "A Provincial Capital of Mexico," *The Century Magazine* 23: 3 (January 1882), 322.

23. As with Atherton, this rehearsal of intermarriage in California prior to 1846 identifies the subjected as the desiring agent of her own subjection: "It is remarkable how many of the daughters of the best families of the old Californian towns married Americans and Englishmen of standing. . . . The grace, beauty, and modesty of the women of the time were the admiration of every visitor. The freedom from care, the outdoor life and constant exercise, and the perfect climate of California had re-created the Andalusian type of loveliness" (Charles Howard Shin, "Pioneer Spanish Families in California, With Special Reference to the Vallejos," *The Century Magazine* 41:3 [January 1891], 382).

24. The assumption that Anglo cultural practices are preferred here is a peculiarly anachronistic form of wish-fulfillment, since it anticipates social conflicts that will not fully emerge until the decades following the Treaty of Guadalupe-Hidalgo rather than in the period preceding the war. In both nineteenth- and twentieth-century histories, (as well as in María Amparo

Ruiz de Burton's account of mixed marriages in *The Squatter and the Don*),
Anglo traders and businessmen do not hasten the cultural assimilation of the
Californios; they retard it, marrying "local girls" in order to "receive land
grants, and merge into the California upper class." David J. Weber, ed. *Foreigners in their Native Land: Historical Roots of the Mexican Americans* (Albuquerque: University of New Mexico Press, 1973), 57. See also Richard
White, who in *"It's Your Misfortune and None of My Own": A New History of
the American West* (Norman, Oklahoma: University of Oklahoma Press,
1991) describes marriages with Mexican women as providing traders "with
access to land grants and trade connections" (47). Further references to
White's study will appear in the text.

25. Pauline Hopkins, *Hagar's Daughter: A Story of Southern Caste Prejudice* in
*The Magazine Novels of Pauline Hopkins* (New York: Oxford University
Press, 1988), 80. *Hagar's Daughter* was originally published in serial form in
1901–02 in *The Colored American Magazine*. Further references will be cited
in the text.

26. The former scene is worth citing in full, to demonstrate the zeal with which
Atherton makes over maternal authority in the image of the Father: ("'God!
God! Mother of God! My son says this to me!' She caught him by the shoul-
der again and almost hurled him from the room. She took a greenhide reata
from the table and brought it down upon his back with long sweeps of her
powerful arm, but not another word came from her rigid lips. The boy quiv-
ered with the shame and pain, but made no resistance—for he was a Californian, and she was his mother" (169).

27. Interestingly, it is not only women writers who use "homely" metaphors to
euphemize conquest by domesticating it. As late as the 1930s, Charles Dobie
sentimentalized the U.S.-Mexican War in tones so determinedly cheery as to
sound Dickensian: "Twenty one guns boomed for the Portsmouth. Every-
body gave three rousing cheers and Yerba Buena became American soil for
all time with no greater casualty than a window pane or two shattered by the
vehemence of a presidential salute. . . . But Yerba Buena was having too
good a time to be seriously upset by alarms real or imaginary. It was busy,
too. . . . inspecting the calico sheets at the new hostelry and the moss from
Hawaii which stuffed the mattresses. It was getting ready to chuck the chin
of the hotel's Mormon waitress, Lucy Nutting, and it was speculating who
the lucky man would be to win its buxom housekeeper and widow, Mrs.
Mercy Larrimore" (*San Francisco: A Pageant* [New York: D. Appleton-Century Co., 1933], 100–101). Even the posters in the offices of contemporary
travel agencies could not make imperial appropriation sound more inviting.
I am indebted to Genaro Padilla for calling my attention to this book.

28. Amy Kaplan, "'Left Alone with America': The Absence of Empire in the
Study of American Culture," in Amy Kaplan and Donald E. Pease, eds., *Cultures of U.S. Imperialism* (Durham, NC: Duke University Press, 1993), 16.

29. Frank Norris, *The Octopus* (1901; New York: Penguin Books, 1986), 61.
Further citations will appear in the text.

30. This description of rancho life is from the back cover of the 1980 Signet Classic edition.

31. Helen Hunt Jackson, *A Century of Dishonor: A Sketch of the United States Government's Dealings With Some of the Indian Tribes* (Boston: Roberts Brothers, 1889). The citations are from the back cover of the Signet edition of Jackson's *Ramona*.

32. Ruiz de Burton's—prescient—championing of California wine could almost be a direct refutation of this churlish passage from Richard Henry Dana's *Two Years Before the Mast and Twenty-four Years After,* cited by Haas in *Conquests:* "Dana argued . . . [the Californios] 'are an idle, thriftless people, and can make nothing for themselves. The country abounds in grapes, yet they buy, at a great price, bad wines made in Boston and brought round by us'" (51).

33. Amy Kaplan, "Nation, Region, and Empire," in Emory Elliott, ed., *The Columbia History of the American Novel* (New York: Columbia University Press, 1991), 245.

34. Thanks to Sandra Gunning for pointing out that the Civil War is ignored in this account of "change."

35. Francisco Ramírez, celebrated young editor of Los Angeles's *El Clamor Público,* often called attention to the failure of federal policy to accord with regional practice. "No tenemos todos los mismos derechos igueales [sic] a la protección de las leyes" [Don't we have equal rights under the law?] he asks rhetorically in one edition, only to answer negatively in another: "No se les [Mexicanos en Alta California] administra justicia, no se les repeta a su propiedad, no se les deja libertad en el ejercicio de su industra [sic] . . . un ataque flagrante a los principios del derecho de gentes, una triste contradicción con los principios de que hace alarde el gobierno americano [They do not administer justice to us, they do not respect our property, they do not permit us freedom in the exercise of our industry . . . a flagrant attack on the principles of peoples' rights, a sad contradiction with the principles that the American government boasts of] "Americanos! Californios!," *El Clamor Público,* February 21, 1857; "Los Mexicanos en la Alta California," *El Clamor Público,* August 1, 1855, but scores of essays in newspapers throughout the country lament the separate and unequal treatment accorded the Mexicanos made U.S. citizens in 1848.

36. See, for instance, the following description of "American law" as unjust but incontrovertible: "The doctor said the land did not belong to Ysidro at all, but to the U.S. Government; and that he had paid the money for it to the agents in Los Angeles, and there would very soon come papers from Washington, to show that it was his. Father Gaspara had gone with Ysidro to a lawyer in San Diego, and had shown to this lawyer Ysidro's paper,—the old one from the Mexican Governor of California . . . but the lawyer had only laughed at Father Gaspara for believing that such a paper as that was good for anything. He said that was all very well when the country belonged to Mexico, but it was no good now; that the Americans owned it now; and

everything was done by the American law now, not by the Mexican law anymore" (257).

37. I am indebted to Sandra Gunning for her help with this argument.

38. "Niñita," (anonymous) *The Century Magazine* 23 (April 1882), 934. Although I do not have the space to gloss it here, this story of a nameless young Mexicana who falls in love with and is finally jilted by the Anglo railroad official sent to purchase her father's land deserves fuller attention as a refiguration of land politics, cultural conflict, and the corporate interests that underlie them.

39. "A Provincial Capital of Mexico," *The Century Magazine* 23:3 (January, 1882): 324.

40. Frances E. W. Harper, *Iola Leroy* (1892; Boston: Beacon Press, 1987) 130. Further references will appear in the text.

41. Lorna Dee Cervantes, "Poema para los Californios Muertos," *Emplumada* (Pittsburgh: University of Pittsburgh Press, 1981), 43.

42. In their excellent introduction, Rosaura Sánchez and Beatrice Pita also insist on the narrative's "historicity": "*The Squatter and the Don,* like all romances, textualizes a quest which necessarily involves conflict and resolution, given here as the trials and tribulations standing in the way of the felicitous union of a romantic couple. Because the novel is also marked by its historicity, however, the quest is not merely for the love of a maiden, but also for land and justice. The narrative thus follows two tracks, one historical and one romantic, with the latter serving to frame the reconstruction of a critical period in the history of the Southwest" (5). I am indebted to their analysis, but my own reading subordinates the romantic plot to the historical agenda of the narrative, which I see as its major formal component and ideological work. I would not characterize the text, as do Sánchez and Pita, as "two-tracked" or bifurcated in structure.

43. Consider for instance the words of Francisco Ramírez, the celebrated young editor of Los Angeles's *El Clamor Público,* who likewise faults a legal system pretending impartiality when he insists: " . . . creo que su [los senadores de Sonoma y Sacramento] objeto es protejer [sic] a los pobladores de *mala fé*. Cualquier hombre imparcial que examine la ley mirará que proteje [sic] al esquatter, y que por bien ó mal despoja al dueño del terrano de sus justos derechos" [I think that their (the senators of Sonoma and Sacramento) objective is to project the colonizers of bad faith. Any impartial man who examines the law will see that it protects the squatter, and that for good or ill it despoils the landowner of his just rights], *El Clamor Público,* April 26, 1850.

44. Note how openly critical of the "Americanos" are writers of the Spanish language press, and how consistently papers like San Francisco's *La República* define Mexican and American as oppositional terms, identifying the Californios as a subject Mexican colony rather than a hyphenated (i.e., Mexican-American) community. In this letter from Tehachape, one F. Elias writes the editor: "recibió una carta de Colima, Mexico, de un amigo de el [el Senor W.

Kuetz]. . . . y dicen que los Mexicanos tratan al extrangero [sic] y en particular al alemán con mas respeto y consideración que los Americanos" [he received a letter from Colima, Mexico, from a friend of his . . . and they said
that Mexicans treat the foreigner and in particular the German with more
respect and consideration than do the Americans] "Carta de Tejachipe," *La
República,* August 5, 1882. Another writer, reporting on a theatrical event,
makes this swipe at the "American" press: "La prensa americana, que raras
veces hace un cumplimiento a nuestra colonia, confiesa la mencionada fes-
tividad es la mejor que aquí se ha visto entre la raza española" [The American press, which on few occasions pays our colony a compliment, admitted
that the mentioned festivity is the best that has been seen here among the
Spanish race.] *La República,* August 5, 1882.

45. Counterpointing the Don's indictment is the equally clear acknowledgement, via the squatters, of the racism underlying federal legal policy: "'Those
greasers ain't half crushed yet. We have to tame them like they do their mus-
tangs, or shoot them, as we shoot their cattle,' said Mathews. 'Oh, no. No
such violent means are necessary. All we have to do is to take their lands, and
finish their cattle,' said Hughes, sneeringly'" (73).

46. See, for instance, the analysis of an 1872 law, p. 80: "In the very first section it recited, that 'every owner *or occupant* of land, whether it is enclosed
or not,' could take up cattle found in said land, etc., etc. It was not stated
to be necessary that the *occupant* should have a good title. All that was required seemed to be that he should *claim to be an occupant* of land, no
matter who was the owner"; or the gloss of "settle" as framed by Congress,
p. 88.

The tone and diction of the book's critique of the justice system refigures
the language of Ruiz's own legal communications—perhaps providing her
with the consolations of an interpretive authority denied her in court. The
bitter outrage with which Don Mariano chastises Leland Stanford refigures
a letter Ruiz wrote to President Benito Juárez on behalf of her own land:
" . . . the said Judge of the Frontier refused to make the survey as he was in-
structed to do. . . . As I could not appear in person the complaint of the
Judge, I had to name a proxy to represent me, and the Judge forced him to
pay the sum of $190. . . . This being an extortion as arbitrary as it is shame-
ful in the authority charged with the administration of justice, I beg you
will deign to order that Judge Chacón . . . to avoid the repetition of a dis-
obedience which has caused me so much expense and loss and injury, I beg
also that you may explain to the Judge with all clearness the way in which
he shall run the lines" ("Title of Property to the Ensenada de Todos Santos
in Lower California granted to Don José Manuel Ruiz by the King of Spain
in 1804," Ruiz de Burton papers, Bancroft Library, University of California, Berkeley), 13–14.

47. Thanks to Sandra Gunning for this astute suggestion.

48. Osio's parody of Anglo American military heroism reads with as much relish
today as when it was first penned. This language seems to me characteristic

of the (once) landed Californios who identified themselves as gente de razón (gentlemen).

49. Thomas A. Janvier, "Pancha: A Story of Monterey," *The Century Magazine* 28 (September 1884), 657; "Niñita," 932.

50. See the study of Mariano Vallejo's public writing and personal correspondence in Genaro M. Padilla's *My History, Not Yours* for a more sustained theory of political rhetoric in post-1848 California.

51. The translation is mine, but I am indebted to Amelia de la Luz Montes for generously sharing this letter with me, a part of her ongoing project to recover the correspondence between Ruiz de Burton and Vallejo currently archived at the Huntington Library.

52. For another example of this kind of cultural pathology, consider this conflation of La Llorona and La Malinche: "There is a tradition that the ghost of Cortez's Indian mistress, the gentle Doña Marina, walks where the shadows are deepest in the cypress avenues. . . . What a company they would be . . . many times greater than the daily assemblage of the living on the Alameda—if all the restless and disappointed men and women who have inhabited Chapultepec in the past should gather like the twilight shadows in its melancholy walks, and look at each other as they passed, with dumb, wistful, reproachful, or threatening, or despairing eyes!" ("A Diligence Journey in Mexico," *The Century Magazine* 1 [November 1881], 2).

53. José Saldívar, *Border Matters: Remapping American Cultural Studies* (Berkeley: University of California Press, 1997), 181.

54. It is worth noting here the service Ruiz de Burton provides to southern California history, echoed by Richard White a century later: "By 1880 about 805 of the Hispanics in Santa Barbara were unskilled workers, and many of them lacked employment for at least part of the year. Only 11% of workers with non-Spanish surnames held such jobs" (323).

55. That the popularity of the historical romance for turn-of-the-century California moved men as well as women to exploit it alters neither the humble status of this form nor its feminine signature, as the dismissive comments of critics writing as late as the 1960s indicate. Cecil Robinson cites writer Harvey Fergusson as grumbling that "what ailed 'the huge and infantile body of our conventional Western romance, from Beadle's dime novels on down' was the result of its having been 'sired by Sir Walter Scott and dammed by the Genteel Tradition'" (151). Charles Stuart's *Casa Grande: A California Pastoral* (New York: Henry Holt, 1906) is subtitled "A California Pastoral," not "A California Romance," a choice of terms that is probably dictated by concern that the former appellation would ally the book with feminine sentimentality. Or consider the anxious insistence of Josiah Royce's editor in his introduction to *The Feud of Oakfield Creek*, who distinguishes this fiction by insisting it must be read not merely as "local-color" (feminine/regionalist) fiction, but also within the (masculine/ national) tradition of realism: "In writing the history of California," he claims, Royce "carefully stripped the

romantic element from adventurers such as John Charles Fremont, from the early mining camps, and from the San Francisco vigilantes. In his novel there is a notable absence of the sentimentality that dominates Helen Hunt Jackson's *Ramona*" (xx-xxi).

Women, too, were not impervious to the critical pressure brought to bear upon the sentimental. McCrackin's essay "A Bit of 'Early California'" tries to dispel this label by suggesting "That many strange and wonderful things happened in early times in California, is so trite a saying that I hardly dare repeat it. As my story, however, is neither harrowing nor sentimental, I hope I may venture to bring it before the reader" (274).

56. With his business partners, known as the "Big Four" (Sacramento merchants Collis P. Huntington, Mark Hopkins, and Charles Crocker), Leland Stanford made his fortune by investing $60,000 in the Central Pacific Railroad Company and then voting himself and his associates "construction contracts that paid them $90 million for work that cost them only $32.2 million." (See White, 249).

57. Well past the turn of the century, loss and deprivation are rendered epic in narrative. The plough "magnified across the distance by the horizontal light" of the setting sun in *My Ántonia,* for instance, becomes a synecdoche for the heroic stature of Ántonia in Willa Cather's 1918 novel (Boston: Houghton Mifflin, 1977). This passage is probably the most frequently cited in the novel: "Presently we saw a curious thing: There were no clouds, the sun was going down in a limpid, gold-washed sky. Just as the lower edge of the red disk rested on the high fields against the horizon, a great black figure suddenly appeared on the face of the sun. . . . On some upland farm, a plough had been left standing in the field. The sun was sinking just behind it. Magnified across the distance by the horizontal light, it stood out against the sun, was exactly contained within the circle of the disk; the handles, the tongue, the share—black against the molten red. There it was, heroic in size, a picture writing on the sun" (245). Or see, in Owen Wister's romantic western *The Virginian,* a tribute to the lost cowboy who "rides" eternally "in his historic yesterday" (6).

58. Ruiz de Burton is not alone in exploiting this kind of aesthetic commentary; Gertrude Atherton, for instance, celebrates the literary "picturesque" in "The Ears of Twenty Americans" when she insists: "Nor could anything be more picturesque than this scattered little town . . . its quaint church surrounded by the ruins of the old presidio; its beautiful, strangely dressed women and men who make this corner of the earth resemble the pages of some romantic old picture-book" (73). What is distinctive about Ruiz de Burton's own self-reflexiveness is that its ironical edge functions to question rather than confirm the virtues of the romance.

Since this chapter was originally drafted, José Saldívar has also called attention to this self-conscious play on genre by asserting in *Border Matters* that "Ruiz de Burton subtly reminds her readers that she is perfectly self-reflexive about her genre" (174).

## Chapter 3

1. All citations from *Who Would Have Thought It?* in this chapter are taken from the original 1872 edition of the novel (eds. Rosaura Sánchez and Beatrice Pita [Houston: Arte Público Press, 1996]). They will be referenced in the text.

2. In her discussion of Thomas Dixon, in whose narratives "the endangered white nation" is "refigured as the white home," Sandra Gunning demonstrates that this insistence on linking (congressional) House with private home is not restricted to women writers. As she explains in *Race, Rape, and Lynching: The Red Record of American Literature 1890–1912*, "Dixon's warning of a general black economic invasion is expressed in terms of domesticity and reproduction." In a speech on Booker T. Washington, Dixon complains that "'this . . . race will allow the Negro to master his industrial system, take the bread from his mouth, crowd him to the wall and place a mortgage on his house'" (New York: Oxford University Press, 1996), 32.

3. "Gringos y Greasers," *La Gaceta,* September 27, 1879.

4. Thanks to Amelia María de la Luz Montes, from whose forthcoming introduction to the letters of María Amparo Ruiz de Burton this letter dated February 15, 1869, is taken.

5. See for instance this anecdote on the "Origen de la palabra 'Gringo'" reprinted in *La Gaceta* from the Mexican newspaper *La Revista del Norte de Matamoros:* "con todo el respeto a nuestros vecinos del otro lado, sometemos [el siguiente] al juicio de algunos amigos. . . . ¿Pues qué te dijeron?–Me dijeron *green go.*—¿Y qué es eso?–Sepas Judas.–Pues déjalo, el lo será, o tal vez quizo decir, como entre nosotros, no hay pan, muchachito, véte." [with due respect to our neighbors on the other side, we submit the following for judgement to some friends. . . . Then what did you call them?—I called them green go. And what is this? To be a Judas. Then leave it alone, whatever will happen, or perhaps I want to say, between us, there's no bread, boy, go away.]

6. The phrase is Richard White's in *"It's Your Misfortune and None of My Own": A New History of the American West* (Norman: University of Oklahoma Press, 1991). In full, White describes this pragmatic Protestantism as follows: "This attitude that churches signified civility, permanence, and a belief in progress . . . became what California Methodists by the 1870s approvingly called 'business Christianity.' Its equivalents could be found in the common desire of western town boosters, Christian and non-Christian alike, to encourage church buildings as a sign of town stability and prosperity. . . . Indeed, so ecumenical could be the appeal of a Protestant church as a sign of . . . urban health that Jewish merchants in many western towns often contributed to Protestant church building funds" (309–10). As a kind of spiritual vocabulary for Manifest Destiny, this "business Christianity" would no doubt have been familiar to Californiana Ruiz de Burton, writing in the 1870s and 1880s.

7. Passages like this one may also implicitly chide imperial "reformers" who exploit the language of service to justify their own "well-meaning" encroachments, given the inevitable association of nurses with the figure of Florence Nightingale in the Crimea.

8. See for instance the following passage: "Lavinia's prayers were always extemporaneous and multifarious, shaped by passing incidents,—for Lavvy had the faith in prayer of a strict Roman Catholic" (163).

9. Pauline Hopkins, "Talma Gordon," republished in Paula L. Woods, ed., *Spooks, Spies, and Private Eyes: Black Mystery, Crime, and Suspense Fiction of the 20th Century* (New York: Doubleday, 1995), 6. In her 1892 volume of essays, *A Voice from the South,* Anna Julia Cooper lampoons both southern aristocrats and northern bluebloods with similar vitriol: "If your own father was a pirate, a robber, a murderer, his hands are dyed in red blood, and you don't say very much about it. But if your great great great grandfather's grandfather stole and pillaged and slew, and you can prove it, your blood has become blue and you are at great pains to establish the relationship. So the South had neither silver nor gold, but she had blood; and she paraded it with so much gusto that the substantial little Puritan maidens of the North, who had been making bread and canning currants and not thinking of blood the least bit, began to hunt up the records of the Mayflower to see if some of the passengers thereon could not claim the honor of having been one of William the Conqueror's brigands, when he killed the last of the Saxon Kings and, red-handed, stole his crown and his lands ("Woman vs. the Indian" in *A Voice from the South* [1892; New York: Oxford University Press, 1988], 103–4).

10. Given its representation in the California newspapers, Popocatapetl was a particularly pregnant metaphor with which to undermine raced conceptions of feminine sexuality because it resonated with discourses of commerce and imperialism as well. See this note in *El Clamor Público,* titled, portentously, "Riqueza Durmiente": Los papeles de México anuncian que el volcán de Popocatapetl está cubierto por la parte interior de una capa sólida de azufre puro de uno hasta diez pies de profundidad. El comercio de azufre y ácido sulfúrico en los Estados Unidos, sola producirá treinta millones de pesos anualmente." October 18, 1856. ["Sleeping Riches": The Mexican papers announced that the Popocatapetl volcano is covered on the inside with a solid pure sulfur cap of one to ten feet in depth. The marketing of sulfur and sulfuric acid in the United States amounts to 30 million dollars annually.] Appropriately enough for Mrs. Norval, whose guilty conscience and immoral behavior are personified by Ruiz de Burton as a series of "imps," the "slumbering" giant conceals an explosive substance (sulfur) that will be a boon for Mexico's balance of trade with the United States. Just so the metaphorical "conflagration" of the New England matron allows the Californiana writer to redress a representational imbalance.

11. This passage not only maintains the bird metaphor but plays upon its colloquial expression, that of a chatterer.

12. At greater length this passage reads as follows: "Bella es la muger [sic] en su infancia, porque es la imagen de un ángel que sonríe a la tierra, porque forma el encanto del hogar doméstico . . . bella y querida como hija, interesante como esposa y como hermana, de valor inmenso como amiga, hay tadavía [sic] un estado en que a su belleza añade la santidad de su carácter, en que es casi una imagen viva de la inmensa Providencia; ese estado es el de la maternidad. . . . La muger ama a su hijo desde el momento en que lo concibe, lo lleva un su seno, y desde entonces lo sacrifica su tranquilidad y sus placeres. . . . la muger sacrifica su vida a la familia. . . . Para una madre consiste la felicidad en la dicha de sus hijos. . . . Una madre en fin es el único ser en la tierra que ama desinteresadamente." [Beautiful is the woman as an infant, because she is the image of an angel who smiles on the earth, because she is the charm of the hearth . . . beautiful and dear as a child, interesting as spouse and as sister, of immense value as a friend, there is yet a state in which her beauty adds to the sanctity of her character, in which she is almost a living image of Providence in its immensity; this state is that of maternity. . . . The woman loves her child from the moment in which she conceives him, brings him to the breast, and from then on sacrifices for him her peace and her pleasures. . . . The woman sacrifices her life for her family. . . . For a mother, happiness consists of the happiness of her children. . . . A mother finally is the only being on the earth who loves unselfishly.]

13. Note the following rather disingenuous tribute to "mugeres" [sic] called "¡Pobres Hombres! . . . ¿Será Verdad?—mugeres" [Poor Men. . . . Could it be true?—women] part of which I excerpt here: "Es la muger invariable,/ Sumisa, fiel, cariñosa,/ Compasiva, generosa,/ Hospitalaria y amable. El hombre, egoísta, variable/ Y altivo con su poder,/ Sin llegar conocer/ Que teniendo cualquier nombre,/ Entre todos, no hay un hombre/ Que merezca una muger" [The woman is constant,/ Submissive, loyal, loving,/Compassionate, generous,/Hospitable and kind. The man, egoistical, moody/And haughty with his power,/ Without knowing him/ Whatever name he has,/ Between us, there is no man/ Who deserves a woman] (*El Clamor Público,* August 2, 1856).

14. Thanks to Amelia María de la Luz Montes for her generosity in sharing this letter with me.

15. Letter to George Davidson, December 4, 1875, Ruiz de Burton papers, Bancroft Library, University of California at Berkeley.

16. I am indebted to Vicki Ruiz for bringing this quotation to my attention; it is cited from the first chapter draft of *From Out of the Shadows: Mexican Women in Twentieth-Century America* (New York: Oxford University Press, 1998).

17. Since Lavinia (in her role as repressed spinster if not as competent nurse) is as much condescended to as lauded by Ruiz de Burton, it is possible to distance this ordering of labor and leisure from authorial vantage point. Ruiz de Burton's own class standing as the descendent and legatee of several very prominent Californio families, her insistently hierarchical portrait of "Spanish Californians" as the true "natives" of the state in *The Squatter and the*

*Don,* and her self positioning in her personal correspondence all militate against this reading, however. Besides her historical romance, see the following defensive representation in this letter to George Davidson: " . . . for six weeks after coming here I did not even have a cook! I had to be nurse night and day, and cook every thing else besides! and finances! Oh! the sick finances! how they did sicken me! They aren't any healthier, but now at least I have a cook, a Chinaman, a 'celestial' truly, for he is heavenly to me doing the cooking in this hot weather. So, though my hands are brown yet, and rough, I don't have to get up at 6 AM to cook breakfast after being up all night taking care of my sick darling . . ." (July 26, 1880).

18. Hine, *Black Women in White: Racial Conflict and Cooperation in the Nursing Profession, 1890–1950* (Bloomington: Indiana University Press, 1989) is citing historian Janet Wilson James here (xviii). If American nurses prior to the advent of professionalization in the 1870s were stigmatized as "immoral and sexually promiscuous" (Hine, 49), Anne McClintock notes that British women who transgressed the Victorian boundary between private and public, labor and leisure, paid and unpaid work became increasingly stigmatized as specimens of racial regression" (*Imperial Leather: Race, Gender and Sexuality in the Colonial Contest* [New York: Routledge, 1995], 42). Further references to Hine and McClintock will appear in the text.

19. Gertrude Atherton, *Senator North* (New York: Grosset and Dunlap, 1900), 356.

20. Susan Shelby Magoffin, *Down the Santa Fe Trail and into Mexico: The Diary of Susan Shelby Magoffin, 1846–1847,* ed. Stella M. Drumm (1926; Lincoln: University of Nebraska Press, 1982). Vicki Ruiz also cites this passage. Magoffin's other mention of Mexicanas is noteworthy: "I did think the Mexicans were as void of refinement, judgement etc. as the dumb animals till I heard one of them say '*bonita muchacha!*' And now I have reason and certainly a good one for changing my opinion; they are certainly a very *quick and intelligent people*" (98). So vanity erases, momentarily, the racial hierarchy! Such openly dismissive and derogatory representation remained the rule for decades. Genaro Padilla calls attention to this letter from Sir James Douglas, quoted by Hubert Howe Bancroft in his 1888 *California Pastoral:* "The ladies in California are not in general very refined or delicate in their conversation . . . indulging in broad remarks which would make modest women blush. It is also said that many, even of the respectable classes, prostitute their wives for hire; that is they wink at the familiarity of a wealthy neighbor who pays handsomely for his entertainment" (115–6).

21. *El Clamor Público,* April 26, 1856. This expression of betrayal was not infrequent in Californio writings of the period. See for instance, Antonio María Osio's *The History of Alta California: A Memoir of Mexican California,* where the Vallejo family are described as follows: "They operated with incredible and praiseworthy energy, but because they were Californios, they did not even receive the thanks that they deserved, for no

hijo del país was recognized by the Mexican government during its difficult periods" (44). Similarly, he makes this comment on the Californios
more generally: "They knew very well that the Spanish kings had been
keenly bent on the conquest of Baja California ever since they became
aware of its existence. . . . However, from then on the Mexican government declared itself California's stepfather and denied it protection as if
it were a bastard child" (80).

22. Letter of September 14, 1869 as cited in José F. Aranda, Jr., draft version of
"Contradictory Impulses: María Amparo Ruiz de Burton, Resistance Theory
and the Politics of Chicana/o Studies" published in Cathy Davidson, ed.,
*American Literature* 70, no. 3 (September 1998).

23. Her own satire of American barbarism mirrors Henry James's derisive portraiture in *The American Scene*. See for instance, the following passage: "The
interference of the monumental spittoons, that of the immense amount of
vulgar, of barbaric, decoration, that of the terrible artistic tributes from, and
scarce less to, the different States—the unassorted marble mannikins in particular, each a portrayal by one of the commonwealths of her highest worthy, which make the great Rotunda, the intended Valhalla, resemble a
stonecutter's collection of priced sorts and sizes" (1907; Middlesex, England:
Penguin Modern Classics, 1994), 265–66.

24. Patriotic verses, together with sentimental lyrics, comprised the vast majority of literary contributions to the Spanish language press, both midcentury
and toward the close of the nineteenth century. In tone and language, the
following introduction to an "Oda Patriótica" published in *El Nuevo Mundo*
on June 28, 1864, is characteristic of such literature, which insists on Mexican identity for citizens of post-1848 Alta California: "Los mejicanos resi-
dentes en San Francisco celebraron el glorioso aniversario del triunfo
alcanzado sobre los franceses por el ejército mejicano a los órdenes del in-
trépido general Zaragoza, el 5 de Mayo de 1862." [The Mexicanos living in
San Francisco celebrated the glorious anniversary of the triumph necessi-
tated over the French by the Mexican army at the orders of the intrepid General Zaragoza, the 5th of May 1862.] As late as the turn of the century,
Mexican Americans writing for the newspapers often situated themselves as
Mexican enclaves ["colonias"] in a foreign land.

25. On the subject of protesting U.S. mistreatment of Mexicanos, see also John
González, who convincingly argues of Ruiz de Burton's 1885 novel that "what
the novel can provide is an articulation of collective protest, which, even if
clearly class-based and coded for a Californio elite, nonetheless figures a later,
greater oppositional collectivity. . . . The utopian allegory functioning beyond
the known narrow interests of class, such that a small number of nineteenth-
century elite Californios can represent, or at least prefigure, a twentieth-century Chicano working-class" ("Romancing Hegemony: Constructing
Racialized Citizenship in María Amparo Ruiz de Burton's *The Squatter and the
Don*," in Erlinda Gonzales-Berry and Chuck Tatum, eds., *Recovering the U.S.
Hispanic Literary Heritage, Vol. II* [Houston: Arte Público Press, 1996], 26–7).

26. Ruiz de Burton's celebration of the "leading men" of Mexican politics and letters responds as well to contemporary Anglo American representations that orientalized Mexico and romanticized it as a kind of American Egypt. Nine years after *Who Would Have Thought It?*, for instance, *The Century Magazine*, 23:1 (November 1881) featured a travel piece that beckoned Anglo tourists to a Mexico that would become familiar to early twentieth-century readers of Lummis, Austin, and Lawrence. In "A Diligence Journey in Mexico," as in scores of other essays, Mexico is a somnolent lotusland complete with "an interior full of indefinite promise" and "strange figures . . . who had come over the mountains on their sandal-shod feet from a country of which travelers said 'There is nothing stranger out of Egypt'" (1). As with ethnographic representation more generally, Mexico is an anachronism, titillating "modern" visitors with its "moving pictures out of another century; the silence of the streets, the air of suspended activity" (321). What follows is a particularly stunning example of this exoticizing, enfeebling language: "The houses repose . . . with a dull, slumbrous dignity which ignores the pathetic look of social decadence general discomfort creeping over them. . . . The gardens look weedy and wild; the strong sunlight spares no detail of decrepit woodwork, or faded paint, broken tile, or stain of leaking spout meandering down the stuccoed wall with a grotesque suggestion of unwiped tears on unwashed cheeks" (1–2). Further citations to this essay will appear in the text. See chapter 2 for a more sustained discussion of such representation.

## Chapter 4

1. Gertrude Atherton, *Senator North* (New York: Grosset & Dunlap, 1900), 28. Further references to this novel will appear in the text.
2. Pauline Hopkins, *Hagar's Daughter: A Story of Southern Caste Prejudice* in *The Magazine Novels of Pauline Hopkins* (New York: Oxford University Press, 1988), 80. *Hagar's Daughter* was originally published in serial form in 1901–02 in *The Colored American Magazine*. Further references will be cited in the text.
3. Charles D. Stuart, *Casa Grande: A California Pastoral* (New York: Henry Holt and Company, 1906), 272.
4. That such violence in Hopkins coincides with imperialism abroad has been persuasively demonstrated by scholars including Kevin Gaines and Amy Kaplan. See for instance, Kaplan's incisive gloss of Roosevelt's *The Rough Riders* in "Black and Blue on San Juan Hill," ("Roosevelt's confrontation with the black troops reestablishes the reassuring order of the domestic color line in a foreign terrain. . . . Their presence raises the white fear of armed insurrection and of national self representation," [222]); and Kevin Gaines's richly contextualized appraisal of Hopkins's work in "Black Americans' Racial Uplift Ideology as 'Civilizing Mission': Pauline E. Hopkins on Race and Imperialism," ("The war in the Philippines, and in Cuba before

it, coincided with a wave of antiblack violence throughout the South, fu-
eled by the racist rhetoric of imperialists and white supremacists in Congress," [441]); both in Amy Kaplan and Donald E. Pease, eds., *Cultures of
United States Imperialism* (Durham: Duke University Press, 1993). I wish to
consider relations between region, nation, and empire by considering its
national coordinates. Both Kaplan and Gaines, however, articulate the intersections between international and domestic conflict very persuasively.

5. Pauline Hopkins, "Talma Gordon" in Paula L Woods, ed., *Spooks, Spies,
and Private Eyes: Black Mystery, Crime, and Suspense Fiction of the 20th Century* (1900; New York: Doubleday, 1995), 4. Further citations will appear
in the text.

6. In his recent literary history of California, *Five Fires: Race, Catastrophe, and
the Shaping of California* (New York: Addison-Wesley, 1997), David Wyatt
frames the gender of genre in a similar way, reading Bret Harte's hypermas-
culine story "The Luck of Roaring Camp" in relation both to Louise
Clappe's letters from California, published as *The Shirley Letters,* 1854–55,
and to sentimentality itself: "Harte's Gold Rush stories get at a profoundly
disturbing truth: that the 'sentimental,' a category traditionally associated
with women, actually flourishes in their absence" (77).

7. Because substantial treatment of the tragic mulatta in turn-of-the-century
African American narrative has been available for some time in the critical
literature, I am not rehearsing the literary configurations of this icon here.
My own readings depend largely upon Barbara Christian's pioneering *Black
Feminist Criticism: Perspectives on Black Women Writers* (New York: Perga-
mon Press, 1985); and Hazel Carby's *Reconstructing Womanhood: The Emer-
gence of the Afro-American Woman Novelist* (New York: Oxford University
Press, 1987).

8. Carby, *Reconstructing Womanhood,* 141–42. Additional references will appear in the text.

9. Richard Yarborough, Introduction to Pauline Hopkins, *Contending Forces*
(1900; New York: Oxford University Press, 1988), xxxiv. Yarborough's very
useful essay provides a cogent appraisal of Hopkins's politically ambivalent
representations of race.

10. Sui Sin Far, "Leaves From the Mental Portfolio of an Eurasian" in Jeffery
Paul Chan, Frank Chin, Lawson Fusao Inada, and Shawn Wong, eds., *The
Big Aiiieeeee! An Anthology of Chinese American and Japanese American Liter-
ature* (New York: Meridian, 1991), 113.

11. The abolitionist invokes color to locate the two women at different ends of
the sliding scale of moral values, but Hopkins ultimately makes this distinction specious by assigning the women the same decorative function; jewels
and flowers are not, after all, very far apart. If they are assigned opposite
charges, the writer describes their temperaments using the same iconography. Sumner mistakes Jewel, the "Western girl" (210), for a "white angel,"
but like Aurelia, she has "fire and life, and a little diablerie" (114). A hunter,
Jewel uses the "jewelled toy" her father makes her a gift of with "deadly ef-

fect" (210–11). Aurelia, likewise, is a "tiger" who, when provoked, "sees the hunter approaching" (237) and "[stands] to her guns with the determination to face the worst that fate might have in store for her" (238). The parallel appears to confirm physiology ("black blood," that is), but ultimately, the insistence on their twin natures as "hunters" points to regional acculturation.

12. *The Bostonians* chastises Basil Ransom by describing his "interior" as a "low-ceilinged basement, under the conduct of a couple of shuffling negresses, who mingled in the conversation and indulged in low, mysterious chuckles when it took a facetious turn" (161).

13. Betty's ostensibly visceral "disgust" for the "despised . . . unspeakably inferior race" similarly depends for its existence upon the transgression of class distinctions. Like Sally, she condemns Harriet for occupying too high a social niche: "To her, the entire race were . . . entitled to all kindness so long as they kept their place, but to be stepped on the moment they presumed. She recoiled . . . from this girl with the hidden drop of black in her body" (79–80).

14. Kevin Starr, *Material Dreams: Southern California Through the 1920s* (New York: Oxford University Press, 1990), 254–55.

15. Ivan Doig, *Dancing at the Rascal Fair* (New York: Harper & Row, 1987) 12.

16. At more length, this passage reads as follows: "There can be no doubt of this:—All America is divided into two classes,—the quality and the equality. . . . It was through the Declaration of Independence that we Americans acknowledged the *eternal inequality* of man. For by it we abolished a cut-and-dried aristocracy. . . . Therefore, we decreed that every man should thenceforth have equal liberty to find his own level. By this very decree we acknowledged and gave freedom to true aristocracy" (101). As Robert Shulman deftly argues in his introduction to the novel, the Virginian, "A simple 'son of the soil,' turns out to be a vernacular patrician gentleman. The East-West conflict disguises underlying gender and class issues. . . . Through the Virginian, Wister succeeds in establishing the victory of masculine and élitist values" (xxv).

17. Evelyn A. Schlatter, "Drag's a Life: Women, Gender, and Cross-Dressing in the Nineteenth-Century West," in Elizabeth Jameson and Susan Armitage, eds., *Writing the Range: Race, Class, and Culture in the Women's West* (Norman: University of Oklahoma Press, 1997), 343.

18. Sandra Gunning, *Race, Rape, and Lynching: The Red Record of American Literature 1890–1912* (York: Oxford University Press, 1996), 101. Further citations will appear in the text.

19. Thanks to Genaro Padilla, who called my attention to this minstrel figure.

20. See Sandra Gunning's astute discussion of Hopkins's classed representation in *Race, Rape, and Lynching*, pp. 96–107; and Kevin Gaines's essay in *Cultures of United States Imperialism*: "Hopkins's ambivalent discussion of racial ideologies of the period illustrates the dilemma of black writers torn between the desperate aspiration for the status of respectability, a strategy which tacitly endorsed prevailing assumptions of racial and social hierarchy, and the

struggle to articulate an autonomous and oppositional racial group consciousness. Hopkins's genteel discourse on race was limited in its attempt to refute crudely irrational racist ideologies" (449–50).

21. See also Ellis Enson's calm assertion of the inevitability of race mixing: "Amalgamation has taken place; it will continue, and no finite power can stop it" (270).

22. When she reexamines the moral shortcomings of abolitionist New England, Hopkins participates in one of the ongoing discussions of nineteenth-century African American literature. See for instance Harriet Wilson's conflation of regional values in *Our Nig* (a text whose proprietary address makes the phrase "free black" a contradiction in terms) as well as Harriet Jacobs's ironized representation of Northern mistresses in *Incidents in the Life of a Slave Girl, Written by Herself* (1861; Cambridge: Harvard University Press, 1987).

23. Jane Tompkins's *West of Everything: The Inner Life of Westerns* (New York: Oxford University Press, 1992) provides a case in point. One of the few contemporary book-length studies to focus upon literature about the western United States, it conflates the cultural topography of the West with the (Anglo) cowboy western. My interest here is in nuancing this monochromatic and single-sex critical portrait by reminding readers that eastern popular literature such as Beadle's dime novels series and Hollywood films dramatizing it half a century later are not the only source of western representations. Blake Allmendinger's more recent *Ten Most Wanted: The New Western Literature* (New York: Routledge, 1998) provides a significant exception to this generalization. Allmendinger's study opens up the terrain of western literature in rich and productive ways. Interestingly, however, his title parodies this overreliance on the western.

24. In fact, in *Reconstructing Womanhood,* Carby herself depends upon precisely the same language of spirited femininity I am relying upon here ("spark," "spitfire," etc.) to argue on behalf of the strong-mindedness of another heroine, Frances Harper's Iola Leroy: "Physically, Iola met the requirements of acceptable standards of womanhood. She was beautiful, fair, and virtuous yet not compliant or passive; her spark of defiance Harper often accented in terms such as 'spitfire'" (74).

25. Here I am juxtaposing Harriet Jacobs' personal narrative, *Incidents in the Life of a Slave Girl,* published nine years before the Civil War, with Hopkins's fictionalized account of the postwar period, because both texts figure space as a trope for agency. Just as the costs of Jacobs's control over her master are literalized in the cramped confines of her attic hiding place, so the limits of Jewel's own escape through the tunnels of the plantation house are metaphorically rendered by their narrow "aperture" (215). Jacobs, *Incidents in the Life of a Slave Girl.*

26. This working-class figure flouts both gender and geography during her successful capture of the women taken prisoner, just as the red-nosed Lavinia, sweet but vulgar, succeeds in extricating her brother from his captivity in a

southern prison. Both novelists cannot risk besmirching the good names of their aristocratic heroines, so contain their transgressive behavior, displacing this rebelliousness onto working-class women whose station leaves them less vulnerable to critique.

27. In full, Hopkins's introduction to this character reads: "an elderly man of dark complexion, in stylish street costume, but with a decidedly Western air, came down the capitol steps. . . . 'That is Senator Bowen, his wife and daughter. He is the new millionaire senator from California'" (76).

28. The language of expansion is marked throughout her canon. See in particular "Talma Gordon" and *Of One Blood*.

29. Equally conventional is the sexual battleground *Senator North* depicts. Like Hopkins, Atherton genders the political life of the Capitol from the outset of her novel. The text opens with Betty's flippantly racist announcement that she plans to do something "even worse" than enter into a mixed marriage: she is "going in for politics" (6). Like Hopkins, who as I have suggested in the previous section is interested in exploring more flexible public roles for "ladies," Atherton flirts with ideas of feminine agency, only to sacrifice independent action to a class-inflected notion of ladylike pressure.

30. Henry James, *The Bostonians* (1886; Middlesex, England: Penguin Modern Classics, 1978), 6.

31. See chapter 1 for a more sustained argument about James's racial figures in *The Bostonians*.

32. Thanks to Amelia de la Luz Montes for sharing her typescript of this letter with me.

## Chapter 5

1. Willa Cather, *The Song of the Lark* (1915; Boston: Houghton Mifflin Company, 1965), 408. Further references will be cited within the text.

2. Willa Cather, *The Professor's House* (1925; New York: Vintage Classics, 1973), 78. Further references to this novel will appear in the text.

3. As cited from the close of *The American Scene* in Sara Blair, *Henry James and the Writing of Race and Nation* (Cambridge: Cambridge University Press, 1996), 208. Further references will appear in the text.

4. This passage from *The Song of the Lark* reads as follows: "The first message that ever crossed the river was, 'Westward the course of Empire takes its way' . . . Thea remembered that message *when she sighted down the wagon-tracks* toward the blue mountains. She told herself she would never, never forget it. The spirit of human courage seemed to live up there with the eagles. For long after, when she was moved by a Fourth-of-July oration, or a band, or a circus parade, she was apt to remember that windy ridge" (69, emphasis added). This recollection solders nationalism with empire (imperialism invokes a train of patriotic associations that includes the Fourth of July, bands, and circus parades). By choosing to describe Thea's survey of the

panorama using the expression "sighted down," Cather also, though more obliquely, underscores the violence attendant upon both. History is apprehended through a gun barrel.

5. This particular citation describes Padre Martínez of *Death Comes for the Archbishop*; (1927; New York: Vintage Classics, 1990) 140, but, as I will show in the next section, such naturalistic representation runs throughout her work. Further citations to this book will appear in the text.

6. Zane Grey, *Riders of the Purple Sage* (1912; New York: Penguin Books, 1990). Further references will be cited in the text.

7. Frederick Turner's essay implicitly highlights literary regionalism as a cultural commodity crucial in contemporary equations of topographical character and nationalism. He asserts in particular that *Death Comes for the Archbishop* is not "there on the gift shop's racks [at Santa Fé's La Fonda hotel] as a touch of local color: the book is bought and read by a great many of those smart-looking strangers who throng through the lobby. The clerk at the shop's desk said it was 'probably our number one seller,' an observation echoed down San Francisco Street by the staff at Los Llanos Bookstore and at Collected Works" ["Willa Cather's New Mexico," *New Mexico Magazine* (March 1986), 33].

8. New Mexico, for instance, became a state in 1912.

9. Loretta Wasserman, "Cather's Semitism," in Susan J. Rosowski, ed., *Cather Studies* vol. 2. (Lincoln: University of Nebraska Press, 1993), 7. Further references will be cited within the text. Our readings are distinct, but if she arrives at a different conclusion about what she calls "Cather's Semitism," Wasserman raises important questions about the way Cather, and other modernists, use the figure of the Jew to further their arguments about American culture.

10. See the close of chapter 16. Significant here is not so much the inflection Cather gives to Louie's apprehension of the slight as the fact that she works hard to call the reader's attention to it. The distinction between Louie's self-making and the authority of others to define him underscores the racial hierarchy of the novel's social life.

11. Joaquin Miller, "Jewess," in *The Century Magazine* 24:2 (175). Additional citations will appear in the text.

12. See for instance Stevenson's long short story "The Silverado Squatters" serialized in *The Century Magazine* (November-December 1883). This piece is notable for the sustained way in which Stevenson absents everyone but Jews from the story. The latter, however, are "good-natured" (32), remarkable for "geniality" and "vagueness" (34), as well as a proven irresponsibil[ity], like children" (34). Such imagery is of course standard in contemporary Anglo American literature for both Mexicans and Native Americans, and appears to position Jews as a substitute for the former, who are displaced from the narrative with a parenthetical ("Our driver gave me a lecture by the way on Californian trees: a thing I was much in need of, having fallen among painters who knew the name of nothing, and Mexicans who knew the name

of nothing in English") and the latter, who haunt the story as a ghostly presence: "Here, doubtless, came the Indians of yore to paint their faces for the war-path, and cinnebar, if I remember rightly, was one of the few articles of Indian commerce. Now, Sam had it in his undisturbed possession, to pound down and . . . paint his rude designs with" (29).

13. In "Ranch and Mission Days," Guadalupe Vallejo invokes Jews as quintessential "foreigners" who visit the Missions: " . . . at the Mission San José, about 1820 . . . a man came to the village for food and shelter, which were gladly given. But the next day it was whispered that he was a Jew, and the poor Indians, who had been told that the Jews had crucified Christ, ran to their huts and hid. Even the Spanish children, and many of the grown people, were frightened. Only the missionary father had ever before seen a Jew, and when he found that it was impossible to check the excitement he sent two soldiers to ride with the man a portion of the way to Santa Clara" (189).

14. Contemporary studies on Jews in the West echo rather than deny their nineteenth-century literary appearances, however. See, among others; Henry J. Tobias's *A History of the Jews in New Mexico* (Albuquerque: University of New Mexico Press, 1990); Moses Rischin and John Livingston, eds., *Jews of the American West* (Detroit: Wayne State University Press, 1991); Harriet and Fred Rochlin, eds., *Pioneer Jews: A New Life in the Far West* (Boston: Houghton Mifflin, 1984); and Kenneth L. Kann's *Comrades and Chicken Ranchers: The Story of a California Jewish Community* (Ithaca: Cornell University Press, 1993).

15. "A Diligence Journey in Mexico," *The Century Magazine* 23: 1 (1).

16. The same strategy mitigates political rancor with respect to Californio-Anglo land conflicts; see, for instance, the focus on Eulalia Pérez's advanced age in various American accounts of her life in Santa Barbara prior to the conquest.

17. Genaro Padilla, *My History, Not Yours: The Formation of Mexican American Autobiography* (Madison: University of Wisconsin Press, 1993), 210. Chapter 6 provides a brilliant analysis of this discursive context and its relation to Hispano textual production.

18. Helen Hunt Jackson, "The Present Condition of the Mission Indians in Southern California," *The Century Magazine* 26: 4 (August 1883), 526. Additional citations will appear in the text.

19. Carolyn Porter, "What We Know that We Don't Know: Remapping American Literary Studies," *American Literary History* 6, no. 3 (Fall 1994), 519.

20. Paul Gilroy, *The Black Atlantic: Modernity and Double Consciousness* (Cambridge: Harvard University Press, 1993), 9.

21. Ivan Doig, *Dancing at the Rascal Fair* (New York: Harper & Row, 1987), 55.

22. Walter Benn Michaels, "The Vanishing American," *American Literary History* 2, no. 2 (Summer 1990), 238. Additional references to this essay will be cited in the text.

23. See Eve Kosofsky Sedgwick, "Across Gender, Across Sexuality: Willa Cather and Others," *South Atlantic Quarterly* 88, no. 1 (Winter 1989); and Judith

Butler, "'Dangerous Crossing': Willa Cather's Masculine Names" in *Bodies That Matter: On the Discursive Limits of "Sex"* (New York: Routledge, 1993). Further references to these essays will be cited in the text.

24. Willa Cather, *Death Comes for the Archbishop*. Further citations will appear in the text.

25. Cather's novelization of Padre Martínez is dismissive, obscuring his significance as a historical figure. Martínez's resistance to the Americanization of the liturgy in the period following the U.S.-Mexican War earned him excommunication by Archbishop Lamy. This revision is characteristic of Cather, one she most fully sustains in *Sapphira and the Slave Girl,* her midcentury glance backward at the peculiar institution, a story that, as Toni Morrison notes in *Playing in the Dark: Whiteness and the Literary Imagination,* "was published in 1940, but has the shape and feel of a tale written or experienced much earlier" (New York: Vintage Books, 1992). See Morrison's "Black Matters," and her discussion of Cather's text as illuminating what she frames as the textual "sycophancy of white identity" (19).

26. In *West of Everything: The Inner Life of Westerns* (New York: Oxford University Press, 1992), Jane Tompkins unconsciously affirms this tenet when she notes both the absence of "real" Indians in the western, and the presence of "real" horses. Compare, for instance, the following passage about the representation of Native Americans: " . . . to the surprise of some, including myself, Indians will not figure significantly in this book . . . I expected to see a great many Indians . . . But the Indians I expected did not appear. The ones I saw functioned as props, bits of local color, textural effects. As people they had no existence. Quite often they filled the role of villains, predictably, driving the engine of the plot, threatening the wagon train, the stagecoach, the cavalry detachment. . . . But there were no Indian characters, no individuals with a personal history and a point of view" (7–8); with this comment on the significance of horses in the western: "Horses, in Westerns, are precisely what meets the eye; that is, physically, visually, they are right there in front of you, but no one seems to notice them in the sense of paying them any attention. Because of this strange invisibility they are the place where everything in the genre is hidden. Besides doing all the work in a literal sense, getting the characters from place to place, pulling wagons, plowing fields, and such, they do double, triple, quadruple work in a symbolic sense. The more you look at them, the more indispensable they seem" (90). Substitute the word "Indian" every time you read the word "horse," and the "symbolic work" race plays in the western becomes far less "invisible," I would argue.

27. As cited in Frederick Turner, "Willa Cather's New Mexico," 37.

28. Genaro Padilla cites "D. H. Lawrence's 'pine tree' Apaches and Cather's Ácoma 'crustaceans in their armour'" as instances of this (*My History, Not Yours,* 210).

29. Frank Dobie, *San Francisco: A Pageant* (New York: D. Appleton-Century Company, 1933), 24–5.

30. Willa Cather, "Scandal" (162–3) and "The Diamond Mine" (107) in *Collected Stories* (New York: Vintage, 1992). Further references will be cited in the text. Granted, this is a step up from Henry James's smug ethnography in *The American Scene,* in which ghetto tenements are not only described as "human squirrels and monkeys" residing in "some great zoological garden" but also as "small strange animals . . . snakes or worms . . . who, when cut into pieces, wriggle away contentedly and live in the snippet as completely as in the whole" (102, 100).

31. John R. Commons, *Races and Immigrants in America* (New York, 1900).

32. Besides Stein, who is rumored to be having an affair with an "American" opera singer he and his wife are cultivating, see also the "The Old Beauty," which narrates an attempted rape by an "immigrant" coded Jewish "who has made a lot of money" and who "does not belong" (359), as well as the intimations of sexual intimacy between Miletus Poppas and Cressida Garnett in "The Diamond Mine." Finally, of course, there is Louie Marsellus, whose "eyes were vividly blue, like hot sapphires" and about whom "There was nothing Semitic about his countenance except his nose—that took the lead. It was not at all an unpleasing feature, but it grew out of his face with masterful strength, well-rooted, like a vigorous oak-tree growing out of a hillside" (43).

33. Or *her:* as Eric Peterson reminds me, Mrs. Nathanmeyer's "aggressive, knowing posture towards Thea aligns her with this coercive sexuality" (correspondence with the author).

34. The railroad proves a compelling metaphor for nationalism because it encodes both the effort of "bind[ing] states" (William Deverell suggests in *Railroad Crossing* [Berkeley: University of California Press, 1994] that "[m]any looked to it as an iron thread with which to stitch up the wound of disunion" [12]) and the violence that undergirds this effort. Train accidents were frequent and, as Deverell notes, "horrific. . . . Railroad work crippled countless thousands. Shop or yard foremen in the nineteenth-century were said to be able to judge a job applicant's experience by the number of fingers he was missing" (3). Sara Blair, too, comments on the hazards of railroad work for porters, mostly black Americans, noting that "[w]hen Pullman porter Theodore Selden later died in a wreck, authorities were able to identify his disfigured body only by his Dartmouth Phi Beta Kappa key" (*Henry James and the Writing of Race and Nation,* 205). In this sense, the railroad, as literary figure, furthers the cultural work of empire.

35. This affinity is simultaneously censured by the provincial (Thea's brother Gunner is disgusted with her own racial insouciance, saying of Mexican Johnny "'Well, I think that's a dirty Mexican way to keep house; so there!'" [61] and condoned by the educated ("Thea often thought that the nicest thing about Ray was his love for Mexico and the Mexicans, who had been kind to him when he drifted, a homeless boy, over the border" [64]). Thus Cather distinguishes her own treatment as hostile to vulgar racism like Gunner's, without, in fact, revising the kind of picture Gunner presents. It is not

so much the representation of a racial other the narrative works to eluci-date—hence Cather's raced naming of Johnny, left without a surname—as the comportment of "Americans" toward this object.

36. Flint's *Francis Berrian* was published serially in 1825–6, and is cited here from Henry Nash Smith's *Virgin Land: The American West as Symbol and Myth* (1970; Cambridge: Harvard University Press, 1950), 220.

37. The sentence, in full, reads as follows: "Cultural purity thus emerges as an ideal of miraculous preservation, like the Cliff City; a high-tech racial purity that can survive the cruel hurts that flesh is heir to and even transform those hurts into the technology of survival: becoming extinct, the Indians become the 'first Americans,' the 'forefathers' of Tom Outland" (235).

38. Correspondence with the author.

39. See also Fred's patronizing comment in *The Song of the Lark* when he ob-serves "a big black French baritone who was eating anchovies by their tails at one of the tables below. . . . 'Do you know, Mr. Ottenburg,' he said deeply, 'These people all look happier to me than our Western people do. Is it sim-ply good manners on their part, or do they get more out of life?'" (455). This is one of those timeless comments that does so much cultural work, as reso-nant with the "happy darkies" of slavery as with contemporary reformula-tions of "these people" (consider McDonald's "Eddy" ads, which foreground Jewish usury [double the product/getting something for nothing], or Taco Bell's Chihuahua ads, which parodically dismiss anxieties about immigration from Mexico by shrinking Mexican "interlopers" to the size of this smallest of dogs, trying to find a way into the "American" household.

Eric Peterson notes this spelling out of the culinary metaphor in Cather's essay "On Shadows on the Rock": "And really, a new society begins with the salad dressing more than with the destruction of Indian villages" (corre-spondence with the author).

Zane Grey's Bern Venters uses the same numerical figure ("a thousand years and more," 151) in his own discussion of native ruins in *Riders of the Purple Sage*. The resonances with Cather's novel are striking. Here again, shards of Indian pots indicate both the presence of lost tribes and their demise at the hands of a more warlike people: "Maybe we're higher in the scale of human beings—in intelligence" Venters muses, but insists that the cliff dwellers "fought their enemies and made their homes high out of reach" in order to protect their "homes, food, children" and "wives" (152).

40. See the close of Michaels's piece on *The Professor's House*: " . . . the essence of culture is that it cannot be reduced to either the social or the biological; cul-ture's project . . . is to reconcile them. And such a project is as available to Jews about whom there is "nothing Semitic" (43) but their noses as it is to Tom Outland who doesn't exactly look Indian. If, then, *The Professor's House* provides a model of cultural Americanism, it does so only by providing a model of culture that can by no means be limited to native Americans" (238).

41. Here I am refusing the consolations of Cather's own class-contingent distinction between a kind of vulgar commodity exchange (the kind practiced by Roddy, who Tom Outland critiques for selling the "pots and pans that belonged to my poor grandmothers" [*PH*, 243]) and a more cultured fetishism, the "sensitive" engagement practiced in *The Song of the Lark* by Thea and Otto (recall that the latter owns Panther Canon) and in *The Professor's House* by Tom (forms of domestic imperialism that leave such "pots and pans" physically intact but that exploit their supposed crudity in order to articulate a more refined Euro-American art).

42. "The Best Years," *Collected Stories*, 383.

43. Cather typically exploits gendered difference as a metaphor for distinguishing artistic "mastery" ("what was to come" when "civilization proper began when man mastered metals") from "the beginnings." The insistently feminine character of the remains Cather's artist-figures find in *The Song of the Lark* and *The Professor's House* is characteristic of her canon. Significantly, "the clan feeling" Cather frames as antithetical to the demands of high art that exalt "the individual" over the community is itself defined as feminine in "The Best Years." If to be an artist like Thea is to be self-focused to the point of selfishness, to be connected to others is in this story framed as a maternal, sisterly impulse that kills the consciousness of being alive that is the genesis of artistic expression. "The boys were much the dearest things in the world to her. . . . The feeling of being at home was complete, absolute: it made her sleepy. And that feeling was not so much the sense of being protected by her father and mother as of being with, and being one with, her brothers. It was the clan feeling, which meant life or death for the blood, not for the individual" (383). No wonder, given such self-estranging feminine figures, that "fetters" resonate so strongly, not only for Thea, or for Tom, but for Cather as a woman writer herself.

44. The citation is from Toni Morrison's *Beloved*. The gerund deftly encodes the long-standing effects of imperial violence. In the very effort of refusing the violent past through the effort of "beating it back," the characters rearticulate it through (self) battery. The same residues of empire, I want to argue in this chapter, are implicitly witnessed in Cather's work as well, where guilt and complicity, if not recognized overtly, continue to make themselves felt.

45. "The Enchanted Bluff," *Collected Stories*, 412. Further references will be cited within the text.

46. Amy Kaplan, "Nation, Region, and Empire," in Emory Elliot, ed., *Columbia History of the American Novel* (New York: Columbia University Press, 1991), 255. Further references to this essay will appear in the text.

47. See, for instance, contemporary Laguna writer Leslie Marmon Silko's refiguring of Ácoma—and the Enchanted Mesa—in *Storyteller* (New York: Arcade, 1981). If you go to Ácoma today, you can see its near neighbor, the Enchanted Mesa, and listen to stories about this place as you look at the pitched whorls and curves of its beautiful stone face.

48. I wish to stress here that the story of the Enchanted Bluff is central to the Cather canon, not only thematically/ideologically, by virtue of the number of times its author refigures its geography across her novels, but structurally as well. As retold in *The Professor's House*, "Tom Outland's Story" comprises the central book of three. Cather herself called attention to this story when she indicated that she wished it to be excerpted and published separately in her posthumous *Collected Stories*.

49. Cather frequently uses Aztec "savagery" to invoke passion. For instance, the southwestern story Don Hedger tells Eden Bower in "Coming Aphrodite!" is an explicitly erotic narrative that makes up the structural center of the story and culminates in Hedgers and Bowers becoming lovers.

50. Like the arrested plan to climb the Enchanted Bluff, this desire goes unrealized. The archbishop articulates his loneliness but in so doing gives up his friend: "I sent for you because I felt the need of your companionship. I used my authority as a Bishop to gratify my personal wish. That was selfish, if you will, but surely natural enough. We are countrymen, and are bound by early memories" (D, 251). And note the way their parting is framed, when Father Latour insists his friend take both mules: "' . . . if you take Contento, I will ask you to take Angelica as well. They have a great affection for each other; why separate them indefinitely? One could not explain to them. They have worked long together.' Father Vaillant made no reply. He stood looking intently at the pages of his letter. The Bishop saw a drop of water splash down upon the violet script and spread. He turned quickly away and went out through the arched doorway" (252–3).

51. A contemporary version of this play with a racialized "primitive" that simultaneously reaffirms sexual and racial identity can be seen in the annual "Burning Man" festival in the Black Rock Desert. Cather's "Boy's Life," that is, is simply one variant of a long-standing imperial performance that continues in the southwestern desert.

52. Charles Stuart, *Casa Grande: A California Pastoral* (New York: Henry Holt, 1906), 44–45.

53. See also Stuart's unabashed and sweeping expression of this difference in power here: "However much the man that was hesitating might despise the Mexican race and all spirits kindred to it, he realised with almost savage resentment that in Manuel, who now served cheerfully, although he once had been served, there was no faltering in duty" (44–5). What is most striking here, I think, is the alacrity with which such markers of difference get elided: the imperial "spirit" harbors an "almost savage resentment."

 It is worth underscoring here the affinity between the turn-of-the-century sentimental novel and Cather's own twentieth-century domestic fictions, given the vigorous insistence with which she, as a modernist, is generally located in opposition to the nostalgic formations characteristic of the pastoral.

54. Silver in Cather indicates exoticism. See for instance this description of silver work in *Death Comes for the Archbishop*, which neatly conflates orientalism and the raced Southwest: "The Spaniards handed on their skill to the

Mexicans, and the Mexicans have taught the Navajos to work silver; but it all came from the Moors" (45). Given the looseness of Cather's ethnographic geography, I think it is fair here to suggest that "the Moors" encode Jewish difference as well.

55. Cather uses a similar language to describe Henry's low social status and his position as (feminized) cook and housekeeper as she uses to figure Mexicans in *Death Comes for the Archbishop*. Like the Archbishop's flock, consistently demeaned as "simple almost to childishness" (85), "children who played with their religion" (211), who are "boyish" in their "simplicity" (61), Henry, according to his employer Tom, "was such a polite, mannerly old boy; simple and kind as a child" (117).

56. Given the associations of the Jewish "foreigner" with banking *and* tribalism throughout Cather's canon (recall the banker of "Scandal" and the Nathan-meyers of *The Song of the Lark,* for instance), Louie's position here as exchange agent between the "primitive" Southwest and the "modern" U.S., as aesthetically sophisticated as Europe, is particularly resonant.

57. Anne McClintock, *Imperial Leather: Race, Gender and Sexuality in the Colonial Contest* (New York: Routledge, 1995), 40. Further references will appear in the text.

58. Gertrude Atherton, *The Splendid Idle Forties: Stories of Old California* (New York: Macmillan, 1902), 260–61.

59. Because it has already been argued convincingly by both Eve Sedgwick and Judith Butler, I will not rehearse this reading of homoerotic desire here. See the essays already cited for sustained glosses.

60. On the subject of Mother Eve, see Father Duchene, who tells Tom "Perhaps her husband thought it worth while to return unannounced from the farms some night, and found her in improper company. The young man may have escaped. In primitive society the husband is allowed to punish an unfaithful wife with death" (223). On the subject of Tom's relationship with Professor St. Peter, see the latter's recollection: "Lillian had been fiercely jealous of Tom Outland. As he left the house, he was reflecting that people who are intensely in love when they marry, and who go on being in love, always meet with something which suddenly or gradually makes a difference. Sometimes it is the children, or the grubbiness of being poor, sometimes a second infatuation. In their own case it had been, curiously enough, his pupil, Tom Outland" (49). Compare this marital difficulty with Tom's "happiness unalloyed" on the mesa, linked with Blake and Henry, his "happy family."

61. Butler, 162. Butler suggests that "though there are clearly good historical reasons for keeping 'race' and 'sexuality' and 'sexual difference' as separate analytic spheres, there are also quite pressing and significant historical reasons for asking how and where we might read not only their convergence, but the sites at which the one cannot be constituted save through the other" (168). Regardless of such "historical reasons" (left unspecified in Butler's argument), I fail to see why we as critics would ever want to distinguish race, sexuality, and sexual difference as "separate analytic spheres." Like the practice

of literary periodization, this kind of intellectual compartmentalizing does not seem to me to lend itself to producing the richest readings. Rather than see them as distinct lines of inquiry that only "converge" at specific "sites," I would argue that such interpretive systems are contingent, inextricable, and always constituted through each other.

62. Here I wish to position my own reading at a distance from Sedgwick and Butler. I would argue that if these critics ignore the racial mechanics that drive her experiments with sexual identity, they overstate the extent to which Cather allows herself, finally, to endorse the homoerotic desires she gives voice to. Cather seems to me not only circumspect but also often proscriptive of such extra-institutional sexual affiliations. In early stories and late novels, sexual transgressors are often punished, killing themselves intentionally (Paul in "Paul's Case") or by accident: in *The Song of the Lark,* for instance, Ray is cut up by the railroad, and in *The Professor's House,* Tom succumbs to war, Henry to snakebite, and Blake to oblivion. Desire, in Cather, is most deeply felt when it is arrested by youth or otherwise contained, and although this kind of closure is hardly unique, it is nevertheless sanctioned by her in such a way as to make any wholehearted celebration of her depictions of queer desire difficult to endorse.

63. Butler, 19.

64. In full, this passage from Cather's "The Best Years" recirculates Norris's language in *The Octopus,* his "cyclopean" "monster . . . with its single eye . . . red, shooting from horizon to horizon" (51) the obvious precedent for Cather's own "dragon": "It was a fine sight on winter nights. Sometimes the great locomotive used to sweep in armoured in ice and snow, breathing fire like a dragon, its great *red eye shooting* a blinding beam along white roadbed and shining wet rails. When it stopped, it panted like a great beast. After it was watered by the big hose from the overhead tank, it seemed to draw long deep breaths, ready to charge afresh over the great Western land. Yes, they were grand old warriors, those towering locomotives of other days. They seemed to mean power, conquest, triumph" (382, emphasis added). Such literary recycling blurs critical boundaries between "Realism," "Naturalism," and "Modernism" in suggestive ways.

   Compare the trapping of movement registered by the fly in amber with the cross-racial, cross-gender "trespass" confirmed three decades later by Tennessee Williams in *Suddenly, Last Summer* where "Pablo," hydra-headed in deference to growing first-world fears about third-world birth rates, hysterically tears civilization to pieces.

65. A country whose very people, as the example of Pablo reminds us, blend into the sand in the manner of an Egyptian sphinx.

### Epilogue

1. This is not surprising if we consider that in the interval between the two novels, the U.S. finally granted citizenship to native peoples. I would argue

that the question of who is "native" to America becomes more vexed in literature produced after this federal act.

2. See Richard Slotkin, *Regeneration Through Violence: The Mythology of the American Frontier, 1600–1860* (1975; Tulsa: University of Oklahoma Press, forthcoming 2000).

3. Carl Gutiérrez-Jones, "Haunting Presences and the New Western History: Reading Repetition, Negotiating Trauma" in Forrest G. Robinson, ed., *The New Western History: The Territory Ahead* (Tucson: The University of Arizona Press, 1997) 142.

4. The phrase "empire of geography" is from *Dancing at the Rascal Fair,* Ivan Doig's novel of pioneer Montana (New York: Harper & Row, 1987). The complete phrase reads "the empire of geography the forest ranger had delineated to us was stunning" (239); the other citations are drawn from Lopez's own "The American Geographies," *About This Life: Journeys on the Threshold of Memory* (New York: Vintage, 1998) 132. Further references to Doig's novel will appear in the text.

5. Fray Angelico Chavez, *The Short Stories of Fray Angelico Chavez,* ed. Genaro M. Padilla (Albuquerque: University of New Mexico Press, 1987) 5.

# Works Cited

Alemán, Jesse. "Novelizing National Discourses: History, Romance, and Law in *The Squatter and the Don.*" In *Recovering the U.S. Hispanic Literary Heritage. Vol. III.* Edited by María Herrera-Sobek and Virginia Sánchez-Korrol. Houston: Arte Público Press, 2000.

Allmendinger, Blake. *Ten Most Wanted: The New Western Literature.* New York: Routledge, 1998.

Arac, Jonathan. "Nationalism, Hypercanonization, and Huckleberry Finn." In *National Identities and Post-Americanist Narratives.* Edited by Donald Pease. Durham: Duke University Press, 1994.

Aranda, José F., Jr. "Contradictory Impulses: María Amparo Ruiz de Burton, Resistance Theory, and the Politics of Chicana/o Studies." Edited by Cathy Davidson. In *American Literature* 70, no. 3 (September 1998): 551–79.

———. "María Amparo Ruiz de Burton." In *American Women Prose Writers, 1870–1920.* Edited by Sharon Harris. *Dictionary of Literary Biography.* New York: Gale Publications, 1999.

Atherton, Gertrude. *Before the Gringo Came.* 1893. New York: Frederick A. Stokes Co., 1915.

———. *California: An Intimate History.* 2nd. ed. 1914. New York: Blue Ribbon Books, Inc., 1936.

———. *Los Cerritos: A Romance of the Modern Time.* 1890. Ridgewood, New Jersey: The Gregg Press, 1968.

———. *Senator North.* New York: Grosset and Dunlap, 1900.

———. *The Splendid Idle Forties: Stories of Old California.* New York: Macmillan, 1902.

Austin, Mary. *Western Trails: A Collection of Short Stories by Mary Austin.* Edited by Melody Graulich. Reno: University of Nevada Press, 1987.

Blair, Sara. *Henry James and the Writing of Race and Nation.* New York: Cambridge University Press, 1996.

Butler, Judith. *Bodies That Matter: On the Discursive Limits of "Sex."* New York: Routledge, 1993.

Carby, Hazel V. *Reconstructing Womanhood: The Emergence of the Afro-American Woman Novelist.* New York: Oxford University Press, 1987.

Castañeda, Antonia I. "The Political Economy of Nineteenth Century Stereotypes of Californianas." In *Between Borders: Essays On Mexicana/Chicana History.* Edited by Adelaida R. Del Castillo. Encino, California: Floricanto Press, 1990.

Cather, Willa. *My Ántonia*. 1918. Boston: Houghton Mifflin, 1977.

———. *Collected Stories*. New York: Vintage Classics, 1992.

———. *Death Comes for the Archbishop*. 1927. New York: Vintage Classics, 1990.

———. *The Professor's House*. 1925. New York: Vintage Classics, 1973.

———. *Sapphira and the Slave Girl*. 1940. New York: Vintage Books, 1975.

———. *The Song of the Lark*. 1915. Boston: Houghton Mifflin Company, 1965.

Cervantes, Lorna Dee. *Emplumada*. Pittsburgh: University of Pittsburgh Press, 1981.

Chavez, Fray Angelico. *The Short Stories of Fray Angelico Chavez*. Edited by Genaro M. Padilla. Albuquerque: University of New Mexico Press, 1987.

Cooper, Anna Julia. *A Voice from the South*. 1892. New York: Oxford University Press, 1988.

Dainotto, Roberto Maria. "'All the Regions Do Smilingly Revolt': The Literature of Place and Region." *Critical Inquiry* 22 (Spring 1996): 486–505.

Dana, Richard Henry. *Two Years Before the Mast*. 1840. New York: New American Library, 1964.

Deverell, William. *Railroad Crossing: Californians and the Railroad, 1850–1910*. Berkeley: University of California Press, 1994.

"A Diligence Journey in Mexico." *The Century Magazine* 23, no. 1 (November 1881): 1–14.

Dippie, Brian W. "American Wests: Historiographical Perspectives." In *Trails: Toward a New Western History*. Edited by Patricia Limerick, Clyde Milner II and Charles E. Rankin. Lawrence: University Press of Kansas, 1991.

Dirlik, Arif, "The Global and the Local." In *Global/Local: Cultural Production and the Transnational Imaginary*. Edited by Rob Wilson and Wimal Dissanayake. Durham: Duke University Press, 1996.

Dobie, Frank. *San Francisco: A Pageant*. New York: D. Appleton-Century Company, 1933.

Doig, Ivan. *Dancing at the Rascal Fair*. New York: Harper & Row, 1987.

Egli, Ida Rae. *No Rooms of Their Own: Women Writers of Early California*. 2nd ed. Berkeley: Heyday Books, 1997.

Elias, F., "Carta de Tejachipe." *La República*. August 5,1882.

Fisher, Philip, ed. *The New American Studies: Essays from Representations*. Berkeley: University of California Press, 1991.

Far, Sui Sin. "Leaves From the Mental Portfolio of an Eurasian." In *The Big Aiiieeeee! An Anthology of Chinese American and Japanese American Literature*. Edited by Jeffery Paul Chan, Frank Chin, Lawson Fusao Inada, and Shawn Wong. New York: Meridian, 1991.

Friedman, Jonathan. "The Poetics of Cultural Decline: Degeneration, Assimilation, and Henry James's *The Golden Bowl*." *American Literary History* 7 (Fall 1995): 477–99.

Gaines, Kevin. "Black Americans' Racial Uplift Ideology as 'Civilizing Mission': Pauline E. Hopkins on Race and Imperialism." In *Cultures of United States Imperialism*. Edited by Amy Kaplan and Donald E. Pease. Durham: Duke University Press, 1993.

Gilroy, Paul. *The Black Atlantic: Modernity and Double Consciousness*. Cambridge: Harvard University Press, 1993.

Goldman, Anne. "'I Think Our Romance is Spoiled,' or Crossing Genres: California History in Helen Hunt Jackson's *Ramona* and María Amparo Ruiz de Burton's *The Squatter and the Don*. In *Over the Edge: Remapping the American West*. Edited by Valerie Matsumoto and Blake Allmendinger. Berkeley: University of California Press, 1998.

——. "'Who Ever heard of a Blue-Eyed Mexican?' Satire and Sentimentality in María Amparo Ruiz de Burton's *Who Would Have Thought It?*" In *Recovering the U.S.-Hispanic Literary Heritage, Vol. II*. Edited by Erlinda Gonzales-Berry and Chuck Tatum. Houston: Arte Público Press, 1996.

González, John. "Romancing Hegemony: Constructing Racialized Citizenship in María Amparo Ruiz de Burton's *The Squatter and the Don*." In *Recovering the U.S. Hispanic Literary Heritage. Vol. II*. Edited by Erlinda Gonzales-Berry and Chuck Tatum. Houston: Arte Público Press, 1996.

Grey, Zane. *Riders of the Purple Sage*. 1912. New York: Penguin, 1990.

"Gringos y Greasers." *La Gaceta*. September 27, 1879.

Gunning, Sandra. *Race, Rape, and Lynching: The Red Record of American Literature 1890–1912*. New York: Oxford University Press, 1996.

Gutiérrez-Jones, Carl. "Haunting Presences and the New Western History: Reading Repetition, Negotiating Trauma. In *The New Western History: The Territory Ahead*. Edited by Forrest G. Robinson. Tucson: The University of Arizona Press, 1997.

Haas, Lisbeth. *Conquests and Historical Identities in California, 1769–1936*. Berkeley: University of California Press, 1995.

Harper, Frances E. W. *Iola Leroy*. 1892. Boston: Beacon Press, 1987.

Hine, Darlene Clark. *Black Women in White: Racial Conflict and Cooperation in the Nursing Profession, 1890–1950*. Bloomington: Indiana University Press, 1989.

Hopkins, Pauline. *Hagar's Daughter: A Story of Southern Caste Prejudice*. In *The Magazine Novels of Pauline Hopkins*. 1901–2. New York: Oxford University Press, 1988.

——. *Of One Blood, Or, the Hidden Self*. In *The Magazine Novels of Pauline Hopkins*. 1902–3. New York: Oxford University Press, 1988.

——. "Talma Gordon." In *Spooks, Spies, and Private Eyes: Black Mystery, Crime, and Suspense Fiction of the 20th Century*. Edited by Paula L. Woods New York: Doubleday, 1995.

Hughes, Elizabeth. *The California of the Padres; or, Footprints of Ancient Communism*. San Francisco: I. N. Choynski, 1875.

Jackson, Helen Hunt. *A Century of Dishonor: A Sketch of the United States Government's Dealings With Some of the Indian Tribes*. Boston: Roberts Brothers, 1889.

——. "The Present Condition of the Mission Indians in Southern California." *The Century Magazine* 26, no. 4 (August 1883): 511–29.

——. *Ramona*. 1884. New York: Signet Classics, 1988.

Jacobs, Harriet. *Incidents in the Life of a Slave Girl, Written by Herself*. Edited by Jean Fagan Yellin. 1861. Cambridge: Harvard University Press, 1987.

James, Henry. *The American Scene*. 1907. Middlesex, England: Penguin Modern Classics, 1994.

——. *The Bostonians.* 1886. Middlesex, England: Penguin Modern Classics, 1978.

——. *Hawthorne.* London and New York: Macmillan and Co., 1887.

Janvier, Thomas A. "Pancha: A Story of Monterey." *The Century Magazine* 27, no. 5 (September 1884): 655–68.

Kann, Kenneth L. *Comrades and Chicken Ranchers: The Story of a California Jewish Community.* Ithaca: Cornell University Press, 1993.

Kaplan, Amy. "Black and Blue on San Juan Hill." In *Cultures of United States Imperialism.* Edited by Amy Kaplan and Donald E. Pease. Durham: Duke University Press, 1993.

——. "Nation, Region, and Empire." In *Columbia History of the American Novel.* Edited by Emory Elliott. New York: Columbia University Press, 1991.

Kaplan, Amy and Donald Pease, eds., *Cultures of United States Imperialism.* Durham: Duke University Press, 1993.

Kaplan, Caren. *Questions of Travel: Postmodern Discourses of Displacement.* Durham: Duke University Press, 1996.

Lapp, Rudolph M. *Blacks in Gold Rush California.* New Haven: Yale University Press, 1977.

Leider, Emily Wortis. *California's Daughter: Gertrude Atherton and Her Times.* Stanford: Stanford University Press, 1991.

Limerick, Patricia. *The Legacy of Conquest: The Unbroken Past of the American West.* New York: W.W. Norton, 1987.

Lopez, Barry. *About This Life: Journeys on the Threshold of Memory.* New York: Vintage Books, 1998.

Lott, Eric. *Love and Theft: Blackface Minstrelsy and the American Working Class.* New York: Oxford University Press, 1993.

Luria, Susan. "The Architecture of Manners: Henry James, Edith Wharton, and the Mount." *American Quarterly* 49, no. 2 (June 1997): 298–327.

Magoffin, Susan Shelby. *Down the Santa Fe Trail and into Mexico: The Diary of Susan Shelby Magoffin, 1846–1847.* Edited by Stella M. Drumm. 1926. Lincoln: University of Nebraska Press, 1982.

McCarthy, Cormac. *Blood Meridian, or The Evening Redness in the West.* 1985; New York: Vintage International, 1992.

McClintock, Anne. *Imperial Leather: Race, Gender and Sexuality in the Colonial Contest.* New York: Routledge, 1995.

McCrackin, Josephine Clifford. *Overland Tales.* San Francisco: A. L. Bancroft and Co., 1877.

Mena, María Cristina. *The Short Stories of María Cristina Mena.* Edited by Amy Dougherty. Houston: Arte Público Press, 1998.

Michaels, Walter Benn. "The Vanishing American." *American Literary History* 2, no. 2 (Summer 1990): 220–41.

Miller, Joaquin. "Jewess." In *The Century Magazine* 24, no. 2 (June 1882) 175.

Miyoshi, Masao. "A Borderless World? From Colonialism to Transnationalism and the Decline of the Nation-State." In *Global/Local: Cultural Production and the Transnational Imaginary.* Edited by Rob Wilson and Wimal Dissanayake. Durham: Duke University Press, 1996.

Monroy, Douglas. "They Didn't Call Them 'Padre' for Nothing: Patriarchy in Hispanic California." In *Between Borders: Essays on Mexicana/Chicana History.* Edited by Adelaida R. Del Castillo. Encino, California: Floricanto Press, 1990.

Montes, Amelia María de la Luz. "Es Necesario Mirar Bien: Nineteenth-Century Letter Making and Novel Writing in the Life of María Amparo Ruiz de Burton." In *Recovering the U.S. Hispanic Literary Heritage. Vol. III.* Edited by María Herrera-Sobek and Virginia Sánchez-Korrol. Houston: Arte Público Press, 2000.

———. "María Amparo Ruiz de Burton Negotiates American Literary Politics and Culture." In *Challenging Boundaries: Gender and Periodization.* Edited by Joyce W. Warren and Margaret Dickie. Athens: University of Georgia Press, 2000.

———. "Rereading the Nation in Nineteenth-Century American Literature: The Life and Works of María Amparo Ruiz de Burton." Modern Language Association Conference, San Francisco, 1997.

Morrison, Toni. *Beloved.* New York: Alfred A. Knopf, 1987.

———. *Playing in the Dark: Whiteness and the Literary Imagination.* New York: Vintage Books, 1992.

Nakamura, Lisa. "Race." In *Unspun: Key Terms for the World Wide Web and Culture.* Edited by Thomas Swiss. New York: New York University Press, forthcoming 2000.

"Niñita." *The Century Magazine* 23 (April 1882): 932–39.

Norris, Frank. *The Octopus: A Story of California.* 1901. New York: Viking Penguin, 1986.

"Oda Patriótica." *El Nuevo Mundo.* June 28, 1864.

Osio, Antonio María. *The History of Alta California: A Memoir of Mexican California.* Translated, edited, and annotated by Rose Marie Beebe and Robert M. Senkewicz. Madison: University of Wisconsin Press, 1996.

Padilla, Genaro M. *My History, Not Yours: The Formation of Mexican American Autobiography.* Madison: University of Wisconsin Press, 1993.

Paredes, Américo. *"With His Pistol in His Hand": A Border Ballad and Its Hero.* Austin: University of Texas Press, 1958.

Pease, Donald. "National Identities, Postmodern Artifacts, and Postnational Identities." In *National Identities and Post-Americanist Narratives.* Edited by Donald Pease Durham: Duke University Press, 1994.

"Pobres Hombres! . . . Será Verdad?" *El Clamor Público.* August 2, 1856.

Polan, Dana. "Globalism's Localisms." In *Global/Local: Cultural Production and the Transnational Imaginary.* Edited by Rob Wilson and Wimal Dissanayake. Durham: Duke University Press, 1996.

Porter, Carolyn. "What We Know that We Don't Know: Remapping American Literary Studies." *American Literary History* 6, no. 3 (Fall 1994): 467–526.

Posnock, Ross. "The Politics of Nonidentity: A Genealogy." In *National Identities and Post-Americanist Narratives.* Edited by Donald Pease. Durham: Duke University Press, 1994.

Prescott, William H. *History of the Conquest of Mexico.* 1843. Chicago: University of Chicago Press, 1966.

"A Provincial Capital of Mexico." *The Century Magazine* 23, no. 3 (January 1882): 321–33.

Ramírez, Francisco. "Americanos! Californios!" *El Clamor Público*. February 21,1857.

———. "Los Mexicanos en la Alta California." *El Clamor Público*. August 1,1855.

"Riqueza Durmiente." *El Clamor Público*. October 18, 1856.

Rischin, Moses and John Livinston, eds., *Jews of the American West*. Detroit: Wayne State University Press, 1991.

Robinson, Cecil. *With the Ears of Strangers: The Mexican in American Literature*. Tucson: University of Arizona Press, 1963.

Robinson, Forrest G. "Clio Bereft of Calliope: Literature and the New Western History." In *The New Western History: The Territory Ahead*. Edited by Forrest G. Robinson. Tucson: The University of Arizona Press, 1997.

Robinson, Forrest, G., ed. *The New Western History: The Territory Ahead*. Tucson: The University of Arizona Press, 1997.

Rochlin, Harriet and Fred, eds., *Pioneer Jews: A New Life in the Far West*. Boston: Houghton Mifflin, 1984.

Rogin, Michael. *Blackface, White Noise: Jewish Immigrants in the Hollywood Melting Pot*. Berkeley: University of California Press, 1996.

Royce, Josiah. *The Feud of Oakfield Creek: A Novel of California Life*. 1887. New York: Johnson Reprint Corporation, 1970.

Ruiz, Vicki. *From Out of the Shadows*. New York: Oxford University Press, 1998.

Ruiz de Burton, María Amparo. Letter to George Davidson. December 4, 1875. George Davidson papers, Bancroft Library, University of California, Berkeley.

———. *The Squatter and the Don*. Edited by Rosaura Sánchez and Beatrice Pita. 1885. Houston: Arte Público Press, 1992.

———. *Who Would Have Thought It?* Edited by Rosaura Sánchez and Beatrice Pita. 1872. Houston: Arte Público Press, 1996.

Saldívar, José David. *Border Matters: Remapping American Cultural Studies*. Berkeley: University of California Press, 1997.

———. *The Dialectics of Our America: Genealogy, Cultural Critique, and Literary History.*Durham: Duke University Press, 1991.

Sánchez, Rosaura. *Telling Identities: The Californio testimonios*. Minneapolis: University of Minnesota Press, 1995.

Schlatter, Evelyn A. "Drag's a Life: Women, Gender, and Cross-Dressing in the Nineteenth-Century West." In *Writing the Range: Race, Class, and Culture in the Women's West*. Edited by Elizabeth Jameson and Susan Armitage. Norman: University of Oklahoma Press, 1997.

Sedgwick, Eve Kosofsky. "Across Gender, Across Sexuality: Willa Cather and Others." *South Atlantic Quarterly* 88, no. 1 (Winter 1989): 53–72.

Shin, Charles Howard. "Pioneer Spanish Families in California, With Special Reference to the Vallejos." *The Century Magazine* 41, no. 3 (January 1891): 377–89.

Silko, Leslie Marmon. *Storyteller*. New York: Arcade Publishing, 1981.

Slotkin, Richard. *Regeneration through Violence: The Mythology of the American Frontier, 1600–1860*. 1975. Tulsa: University of Oklahoma Press, forthcoming 2000.

Smith, Anna Deavere. "The Shades of Loss." Berkeley Repertory Theatre stagebill for the production of Twilight: LA, 1992. Directed by Sharon Ott. Marines Memorial Theatre, January 26 – March16, 1996.

Smith, Henry Nash. *Virgin Land*. Cambridge: Harvard University Press, 1950.

Starr, Kevin. *Material Dreams: Southern California Through the 1920s*. New York: Oxford University Press, 1990.

Stegner, Wallace. *Angle of Repose*. New York: Penguin, 1971.

——. *Crossing to Safety*. New York: Penguin, 1987.

Steinbeck, John. *Cannery Row*. 1945. New York: Penguin, 1994.

Stevenson, Robert Louis. "The Silverado Squatters: Sketches from a California Mountain." Serialized in *The Century Magazine* 27, no.1 (November 1883): 26–39 and *The Century Magazine* 27, no. 2 (December 1883): 182–193.

Stuart, Charles. *Casa Grande: A California Pastoral*. New York: Henry Holt, 1906.

"Title of Property to the Ensenada de Todos Santos in Lower California Granted to Don José Manuel Ruiz by the King of Spain in 1804." María Amparo Ruiz de Burton papers, Bancroft Library, University of California, Berkeley.

Tatum, Steven. "The Problem of the 'Popular' in the New Western History." In *The New Western History: The Territory Ahead*. Edited by Forrest G. Robinson. Tucson: The University of New Mexico Press, 1997.

Tobias, Henry J. *A History of the Jews in New Mexico*. Albuquerque: University of New Mexico Press, 1990.

Tompkins, Jane. *West of Everything: The Inner Life of Westerns*. New York: Oxford University Press, 1992.

Turner, Frederick. "Willa Cather's New Mexico." *New Mexico Magazine* (March 1986): 32–39.

Vallejo, Guadalupe. "Ranch and Mission Days in Alta California." *The Century Magazine* 41, no. 2 (December 1890): 183–192.

Victor, Frances Fuller. *The New Penelope and Other Stories and Poems*. San Francisco: A. L. Bancroft and Co., 1877.

Wald, Priscilla. *Constituting Americans: Cultural Anxiety and Narrative Form*. Durham: Duke University Press, 1995.

Wasserman, Loretta. "Cather's Semitism." In *Cather Studies*. Vol II. Edited by Susan J. Rosowksi. Lincoln: University of Nebraska Press, 1993.

Weber, David J., ed., *Foreigners in their Native Land: Historical Roots of the Mexican Americans*. Albuquerque: University of New Mexico Press, 1973.

White, Richard. *"It's Your Misfortune and None of My Own": A New History of the American West*. Norman: University of Oklahoma Press, 1991.

Williams, Tennessee. *Garden District: Two Plays; Something Spoken and Suddenly, Last Summer*. London: Secker and Warbury, 1959.

Wilson, Harriet E. *Our Nig; or, Sketches from the Life of a Free Black, In A Two-Story White House, North. Showing That Slavery's Shadows Fall Even There*. 1859. New York: Vintage Books, 1983.

Wilson, Rob and Wimal Dissanayake. "Introduction: Tracking the Global/Local." In *Global/Local: Cultural Production and the Transnational Imaginary*. Edited by Rob Wilson and Wimal Dissanayake. Durham: Duke University Press, 1996.

Wister, Owen. *The Virginian*. 1902. New York: Oxford University Press, 1988.

Wyatt, David. *Five Fires: Race, Catastrophe, and the Shaping of California*. New York: Addison-Wesley, 1997.

Yadav, Alok. "Nationalism and Contemporaneity: Political Economy of a Discourse." *Cultural Critique* 26 (Winter 1993–94): 191–229.

Yarborough, Richard. Introduction. *Contending Forces: A Romance Illustrative of Negro Life North and South*. By Pauline Hopkins. 1900. New York: Oxford University Press, 1988.

# Index